D1645154

# Dancing Machines

# Dancing Machines

CHOREOGRAPHIES OF THE AGE OF
MECHANICAL REPRODUCTION

FELICIA MCCARREN

*Stanford University Press*
*Stanford, California*
*2003*

Stanford University Press
Stanford, California

© 2003 by the Board of Trustees of the
Leland Stanford Junior University.
All rights reserved.

Printed in the United States of America,
on acid-free, archival-quality paper.

Library of Congress Cataloging-in-Publication Data

McCarren, Felicia M.
  Dancing machines : choreographies of the age of
mechanical reproduction / Felicia McCarren.
      p.   cm.
  Includes bibliographical references (p. ) and index.
  ISBN 0-8047-3988-9 (cloth : alk. paper) —
ISBN 0-8047-3997-8 (pbk. : alk. paper)
    1. Modern dance.   2. Mechanization in dance.
3. Machinery.   I. Title.
GV1783 .M25   2003
792.8—dc21                              2002015661

Original Printing 2003
Last figure below indicates year of this printing:
12   11   10   09   08   07   06   05   04   03

Typeset by Heather Boone in 10/14 Sabon.

# Contents

# Acknowledgments

For invitations to teach or speak about my work, I am grateful to Jean-Michel Rabaté, Peggy Phelan, Barbara Browning, Ruth Tsoffar, Constance Sherak, Pamela Cheek, and Cristina Caprioli. Thanks also to the colleagues and students who have made the lonely work of scholarship rewarding, and to the camaraderie of friends and neighbors during the writing and rewriting of this book in New York, New Orleans, and Paris. All of those thanked in my first book should consider themselves thanked again here, but in particular I thank Michel Serres, Tomiko Yoda, Hasok Chang, and Felipe Smith, and, for their comments on the manuscript, Michèle Pridmore-Brown, Ramsay Burt, and Nell Andrew. This project could not have come to fruition without the support of Helen Tartar at Stanford University Press, Hope Glidden, chair of the department of French and Italian at Tulane University, Teresa S. Soufas, dean of the Tulane Faculty of the Liberal Arts and Sciences, and Valerie Greenberg, former dean of Newcomb College.

This volume is dedicated to the women who gave me their keys during the years of nomadism: Claire, Cheryl, Pam, Maddi, Connie, Ruth, Mimi, and Jef; and to my beloved nomads, Ali and Adil.

# Dancing Machines

# Introduction

Asserting the importance of dance—particularly ballet—in the United States in 1972, George Balanchine complained that "Europeans think we only make machines and automobiles."[1] Because Balanchine's dances for Bertolt Brecht's 1933 *ballet chanté*, *The Seven Deadly Sins*, had staged exactly that idea—an American dancer must herself become a dancing (and money-making) machine in order for her greedy family to fully realize their capitalist dreams—the statement signals the choreographer's shift of perspective along with his citizenship. Beyond the supposed incompatibility between technological superiority and high culture that Balanchine is trying to refute, the remark also serves as a reminder of an age in which dance vied with automobiles and machines for global attention, and rivaled them in importance. Balanchine's easy slide from ballet to machines reads as a vestige of the thinking of the early-twentieth-century European avant-garde that is the subject of this book.

Balanchine's statement also reveals a continuum in the thinking that has connected dancers to technology across the century and around the globe. The July 2000 *Stagebill* for dance events at the Lincoln Center Festival in New York City featured an advertisement by a "Lead Sponsor," an automobile manufacturer, under the caption "the relentless pursuit of perfection" and above a sales pitch proclaiming the "extraordinary performances" of their cars, with two mechanical models of dancers in ballet costumes and poses, with ball bearings and other movable machine parts connecting their molded limbs. The advertisement reenacts links between dancers and sports cars made almost a century earlier by F. T. E. Marinetti's techno-fantasy Futurist choreographies and reminds us that the image of the dancing machine is two-sided: on the one hand, dancers embody the natural force that technology harnesses; on the other, the dancing body represents the structure that captures and translates that force. This double resonance of machines—active and passive, natural and artificial—resounds in words such as "motor" on the one hand and "mechanization" on the other.

Modernity rides the rails of two different kinds of movement: the *shock* that Walter Benjamin identified in nineteenth-century responses such as Poe's and Baudelaire's to mechanization, and the *smoothness* that machines have promised if not always produced. In the literature, paintings, and press of nineteenth-century Paris, the creature most often compared with the ballerina was the racehorse; like racehorses, ballerinas were animal machines—fleet, swift, smooth. In the twentieth century, dancers became auto-mobiles: driven, motorized, mechanized. In the transition to a highly technologized world, dancers continued to be compared with finely tuned machines. Isadora Duncan, whose carriage was unhorsed and drawn by German students after an early triumph, an honor that had been conferred on nineteenth-century divas, became a twentieth-century icon, one of the first who moved with and died in the automobile. Half a century later, Mikhail Baryshnikov, after immigrating to the United States in the mid-1970s from the Kirov Ballet, described learning how to dance like a "sports car" in Twyla Tharp's *Push Comes to Shove*.

The automobile that is imagined dancing and the dancer imagining himself as an automobile represent the hybrid beings that this book refers to as "dancing machines." Although they suggest that there has been little progress in the public image of dancers, these examples reveal that what has changed is the importance of dance in a culture that has ceded its place to technology. Instead of driving dancers in homage to their art, today's dance public, attending the kind of dance events staged at Lincoln Center, is prompted to imagine dancers as instruments of luxury, the next best thing to a Lexus.

What is a dancing machine? The Jackson Five's 1960s hit, which my title will recall to most American readers of a certain age, suggests two interlocked and inverse images: a stylized robotics and an unstoppable energy. In fact, this book argues, earlier versions of this two-edged image can be found in Europe a half century earlier, in the importation of American ideas, in the art of Americans in exile there, and in dance forms that both incorporated and resisted American, African, and Asian influences. The "dancing machine" elaborated in the first decades of the twentieth century engages two very different kinds of energy, or styles of dance: the first, dancing that looks mechanical, like machines; and the second, dancing that works like a machine, producing the image of a force of nature, a superhuman functioning.

This book will disappoint readers who come to it looking for a catalogue of the first image only: the many forms of machine dancing that flourished across the twentieth century and that played with mechanics, from constructivism to contemporary performance art, from the cakewalk to hip-hop. Many of the key figures and texts from this already well-documented history, including theories of acting and emotion, and mechanical performances, including puppetry and pantomime, cabaret and cinema, are only briefly mentioned here. Instead, this history is complicated by the inclusion of models of the second kind of energy produced by a "dancing machine": an indefatigable *perpetuum mobile*, a dancing that emulates machine logic rather than machinelike movement. Under this heading, readers familiar with dance history will find in these pages modern dancers they would never have associated with machines. Thus, even dancing inspired by images from ancient or so-called primitive art—for example, that of Isadora Duncan or Josephine Baker—engaged with contemporary thought about machines in ways that they might have denied, even while their performances responded to the culture of the machine.

The dancing machines considered in this book represent a range of responses to machine culture, starting with real dancers whose discipline in performance serves to illustrate, metaphorically, the work of the motor or the mechanics of the automaton. Dancers' training makes their bodies extra-human, capable of physical feats beyond the range of normal human movement. Like athletes, dancers push physical limits but also style the body itself by developing certain muscle groups rather than others to create a particular look or line. And like athletes, dancers are often read as moving unconsciously, or naturally, with a kind of animal speed or grace—as if their movement were driven by instinct. Their use of movement for expression connects dancers to the realms of the pre-linguistic or pre-technological, the animal or the "primitive" that is the obverse, but not the opposite, of the machine. Dancers have represented both the capabilities of a highly mechanized body and the pre-technological body whose powerful naturalness is imitated by machinery.

After 1900, a new hybrid of the dancing machine developed in theater, poetry, technology, and industry—in the machine dances of the new ballet companies, the mechanical ballets of avant-garde cinema, the real and imagined motorization of dancers and carriages, the jolting puppetry of the assembly line, the marionette-like or military cadence of the chorus line. Along with recent critical reevaluations of the early-twentieth-century avant-garde, this book attempts to reconcile two narratives of the development of new dance forms in the late nineteenth and early twentieth centuries. One narrative—applied especially to American modern dance— has held to the modernist rhetoric and reception of dance as natural, unconnected to the theories and practices of the machine age and the so-called machine ballets of the historical European avant-garde. Yet although there was a strong current of resistance, especially in American modern dance of the 1930s, to machine and cinema culture, and this resistance has been one of the enduring images of modern dance, it is possible to see, before this, dance helping to shape the very machine culture to which it would eventually cede its central place, pushed onto the "entertainment" side of a Taylorist-Fordist work-entertainment divide.[2] Although some modern dance responded to machine culture in parodic critique or aesthetic detachment, the freedom of movement that dance represents (with or against machines)—its very energy and "naturalness"—was co-opted by machine theory and constructed by mass media and markets. The rhetoric of the machine elaborated the ease, or freedom, that dancing manifested.

More than a paradox, the dancing machine is a vestige of the era of dance's centrality and a sign of its co-optation, an image of the tyranny of industry disguised by technophilia. *Dancing Machines* goes back to the waning moments of concert dance's cultural centrality in Europe to explore how industrial, mechanized modernity created the fantasy of the dancing machine, even while sidelining dancing as diversion.

Although recent work on the European avant-garde movements of the early twentieth century has focused increasing attention on the political consequences of their technological fantasies, the grave realizations of science fiction in war and other technologies, a history of dance that moves into this territory may seem to readers to miss much of what is beautiful and liberating in modern dance. But the pleasure taken in the traces that remain of this dancing—texts, pictures, films—needs to be understood in the context of the production of these dances within and against the artistic, social, and scientific thinking of its historical context.

Modern dance promoted the idea that the body can move in new ways and speak new languages that are no longer submitted to a system of interpretation in which movements, I have argued, were pathologized. Modern dance in line with Isadora Duncan announced itself as liberatory and humanistic, suggesting that it staged a certain freedom of expression and mobility of identity, a redefinition of bodily subjectivity. Yet twentieth-century dance—especially African American dance—was often pathologized by mainstream white culture, even though it staged bodies liberated not only by changing cultural and interpretive codes but also by technologies freeing us into speed and space. As Hillel Schwartz has argued in the case of torque, technological developments were paralleled in dance techniques.[3] At the same time, modern dances—with a critical distance—has represented our enslavement to technologies, our imprisonment within bodies whose capacities are limited, the mechanization of bodily will, the burden of the malfunctioning machine, the madness of technophilia.

Although cultural changes surrounding its creation in part released dance from its long-standing interpretive association with illnesses mental and physical, in the twentieth century the interpretive grid not of medicine but of modern industry pushed dance toward the margins even as the form maintained great popularity. Because dance performance is physical labor, it glorifies the human body's capacities even as it belittles industry's manpower. Arguably important to a cultural reconception of gesture and rhythm in labor, dance offers ways of thinking both about the movement possible with machines and about machines moving themselves. Yet dance would nevertheless be sidelined in the modernity produced by movement physiology, work science, and scientific management.

My earlier study of dance's pathologization in the context of the rise of scientific medicine centered on excessivity, the excess of gesture that is symptom. *Dancing Machines* treats "economy of gesture": scientific management's minimum gesture; industry's disciplined, fragmented, interrupted gesture; cinema's serial gesture; techno-theory's coded, cosmic, gesture. The story here is not one of healthy, expressive movement being pathologized but the reverse, as dysfunctional movements (the shock, the tic) are registered under the rubric of ultimate productivity. The discourse of efficiency in work production might be read along with the study of effort in work such as that of Rudolf von Laban on transforming energy into effort. Instead, in chapter 5, for example, I focus on texts that treat dance in hauntingly Tayloresque terms of efficiency and productivity even while theorizing dance's poetic antiproductivity.

This book attempts to take the choreographies of the machine age on their own terms while also exploring their historical contexts, to consider not only choreographic intentions but also choreographic effects: dance as a nexus of ideas, inspiring and inspired. This work depends on the assumption of a cultural sphere much broader than one defined by dance alone, and when using the term "choreography" I am referring to the writing of dance as well as its dancing, to its imagination in many media as well as its real reception. Rather than surveying the dance of the period, I follow a network of exchanges between historical dance performances, modernist texts of all kinds, and technological thinking and practice from the late nineteenth century through the first three decades of the twentieth, to consider encounters between dancers, artists, photographers, filmmakers, writers, and physiologists as representative of a larger culture of movement and movement analysis.

In these pages, canonical figures from what is now called high modernism—figures whom we would not normally associate with dance, such as Ezra Pound or Gertrude Stein—turn out not only to be seeing but also thinking about dance, and even, surprisingly, rethinking their own work in terms of dance. And writers who seem to have little in common—for example, William Butler Yeats and Siegfried Kracauer—turn out to be thinking about dance in similar ways. Very different kinds of dancing—such as Isadora Duncan's and Josephine Baker's—are co-opted by modernism and sometimes described in strangely similar terms. Yet dancers get written out of the cultural history they themselves were writing, and that was written around them, in part because they are not principally writers. This book tries to integrate the wide range of "texts" they left with the broader textual heritage of writing about them.

Although the writers and dancers considered here are canonical—the ones whom historical accounts and images of the period have preserved—bringing them into dialogue means reconsidering their mutual influences and giving to dance a greater place in the mix. To look only at the stage would mean missing much of dance's inner qualities, qualities that often are the most influential on thinking in other domains. A little poem by Pound, as insignificant as the suicidal dancer it describes, can become part of the magisterial oeuvre of literary history; the dancer remains obscure. My aim here is to reintroduce, into the texts of modernism, the living presence of dancers or, as Ramsay Burt has written, "bring dancing bodies back into the discussion"—of twentieth-century intellectual and cultural history both inspired by and inspiring dance. By reconsidering modernism's focus on the dancers of its time, this book addresses what Amy Koritz has called the "intellectual and institutional marginalization of dance" while exploring the greater trend toward sidelining of dance in an increasingly technologized culture.[4]

While trying to gauge dance's progressive marginalization in the twentieth century (dance is no longer front-page news as it was in nineteenth-century Paris), I am simultaneously inserting dance into its deserved place in the history of ideas, taking dance on its own terms, as an art form expressive of cultural concerns and inventiveness on a grand scale, even while not considering it only as "grand" or "great" art produced by gifted geniuses. Attempting to understand both what is fascinating in dance and what culture projects onto it, this book assigns to dance a more important place in mainstream European modernisms and machine culture than it is usually given, and considers modernism-in-the-making as well as its masterful performances.

A third machine, whose significance for the understanding of twentieth-century dance is here reconsidered, is embedded in the image of the dancing machine: the motion picture camera that captures and diffuses choreography while remaining outside it. If my title reminds readers of Motown, my subtitle points earlier, to Walter Benjamin's 1936 essay "The Work of Art in the Age of Mechanical Reproduction." The chapters of this book take as their terrain the years between the imagining of the cinematograph and Benjamin's landmark essay focusing on its effects, attempting to locate the image of a dancing machine around the invention of a mechanical reproducibility that changed perception and gesture, the aura and status of the work of art, driven by "the desire of contemporary masses to bring things 'closer' spatially and humanly."[5]

With the patenting of mechanical reproducibility in the movie camera in 1895, several different kinds of concert dancing also take recognizable shape. This book begins slightly earlier, proposing an exploration of modern dance forms in the context of the developing practices of "mechanical reproduction" not simply because they have, ultimately, won out, but also because the very conception of modern dance's "liveness" and presence was constructed in the face of the mechanization of bodies in industry and the invention of recording devices that widened its audiences.

Not a history of dance and film, nor of dance on film, this is a history of the modernist idea of economies of gesture taking shape across domains surrounding dance: derived from physiology; applied in work science or scientific management's economy of effort; imaged via photography or chronophotography; expressed in poetics through the pictogram, code, or seriality; expressed in painting as abstraction, fragmentation, or fusion of forms.

Although the camera would take over and make mechanical many of choreography's experimental discoveries, it would keep a certain kind of dance before the public, manipulated and eventually marginalized. Much of the concert dance of the 1920s and 1930s in Europe has working-class, labor ambitions, yet ultimately the machine that would bring dance to the masses—showing them what they would no longer have gone to see live on stage, assuring dance a wider audience and longer life—is also the machine that would kill it.

# 1.
## Economies of Gesture

MECHANICS, THERMODYNAMICS, CINEMATICS

Our age of high tech is haunted by the persistence of an image from the last century: the dancing machine, paradox of the ease of mechanization and its tortures, image of fusion and fragmentation, of diversion and work. The dancing machine represents both an idealization of the body's performative prowess and a critique of its mechanization, the coordinated precision of rhythmic ensembles and the fragmented but functional isolated gesture of industrial production. It poses the questions of workers' enslavement to technology, or the autonomy and freedom of movement it can bring. In science, art, and industry, on stage and screen, the dancing machine manifests a critique of mechanization or its idealization, the staccato movement of bodies with machines or the stylization of their hybrid potential.

Dance—and especially modern dance—is usually the site for discussion of the "aura" that, as Walter Benjamin famously argued, withers in the age of mechanical reproduction. From what sources, then, comes this image of the dancing machine that dominated early-twentieth-century avant-garde art and choreography, cinema, design, and industry? Its persistence and its triumphs suggest that it is more than a nightmare of modernity. The twentieth century's precision chorus line, cinematic *ballets mécaniques*, or machine ballets are anticipated in many earlier dance forms, even in the tulle-skirted corps de ballet of the romantic ballet. In Baudelaire's image of the sylph sliding away backstage, Benjamin finds an emblem of "aura" vanishing into modernity. There is already a haunting premonition of the culture of mechanical reproduction in the army of sylphs the ballet supplies to back her up. In spite of her aura of ephemerality, the romantic ballerina is the harbinger of a culture of mechanical reproduction that will crush her.

From the period of what has come to be called modernism, this book gathers material across a spectrum of arts and industry: the instant photograph serialized in chronophotography or projected in cinema; the condensed ideogram or vortex of modernist poetics, described by Pound as a dance; the prose of iteration with slight variation, used to describe dances and described by Stein as cinematic; the mixing of technological reality and fantasy in concert dance for which Apollinaire used the term "surreal"; the fragmentation of the object in painting and film in what Léger called mechanical "equivalences"; the minimum gesture of Taylorist work-science; the rhythm of this choreographed labor, cubist abstraction, and cinematic projection; the anatomic anonymity of the assembly line and the chorus drill, the erasure or stereotyping of identity in the automata of machine ballets; the "hieroglyphs" of cinema, Asian, or African dance; the Brechtian *gestus*; the "resonance" of the photographic or the cinematographic image. *Dancing Machines* provides a ground for asking what connects these forms across many domains: the possibility of the freezing or fragmentation of the image in instantaneity or time-motion studies; the possibility of its condensation—photographic, mechanical, or theatrical—in gesture, in pictographic ideogram or prose; the possibility of its projection—in rhythmic seriality, in chorus line or cinema; and the "best speed" for choreographed labor or cinematic projection.

What connects these forms, from work-science to dance, is a common culture, from physiological movement studies to cinema, and a common idea—economy of gesture. Across these forms, modernist economy of gesture takes two quite different shapes: one is a minimum effort, gauged to fit the machine; the other, a mechanical that is cosmic rather than comical, an *oikos* or system expansive rather than reductive. Explorations of the different forms that economy of gesture takes in modernism reveal that it is not only a movement quality connected to machines but also a way of perceiving movement produced by machines.

Born from physiology, imaged via chronophotography and elaborated in cinematography, the minimum gesture developed in nineteenth-century work-science became central to the aesthetics of a range of avant-garde modernisms. Representing efficiency and minimum effort in the realm of physiology, representing the speed or rhythm of modernity in poetics, photography, or performance, economy of gesture can be understood as fragmented or condensed, reductive or repetitive, partial or essential. In choreographies of the machine age, the minimum gesture can signal the mechanical operation of the monster machine that drives it, the automatic gesture that flips the switch on. It can also embody the cosmic energy of that machine condensed into a single body, the "human motor" powering the universe with a single pair of arms and legs. This second form of machine implies a very different meaning of "economy" of gesture: not minimized movement but movement defining and powering the universe.

Two different economies of gesture, identifiable in the art and thought of modernism, are generated from two historical models of the machine. Economy of gesture has one source in mechanics, the gesture that hides the work or agency behind it. It has a second source in thermodynamics and the redefinition of labor around it. Whereas medicine and work-science contain or reduce the gesture to the minimum, isolating the smallest muscle first in the service of ergonomic safety but eventually for maximum productivity, such gesture takes on a poetic, pictographic, or even spiritual cast in some modernist writing and dancing. This book charts two simultaneous histories: one recounting the stripping down of gesture and bodies to machine aesthetics and the minimum gesture, from Mareyism to Taylorism; the other recounting the fleshing out of machines with bodies, reconnecting technology to its mythic, ritual, or religious functions. Dancing, in modernism, lends itself to both stories and both movement styles, one explanation of why it remains a persistent image for machines despite its obvious humanity.

MECHANICS: THE HUMAN MACHINE

Michel Serres has historicized these two conceptions of machines—the automaton and the motor—and their relations both to bodies and to the cosmos by locating them in the context of the sciences of the eighteenth and nineteenth centuries. Automata were imagined functioning in a Newtonian universe of multiple and disparate motivating forces, controlled by a force outside them, and functioning at external demand.[1]

The science and fiction linking dancers and machines are as old and varied as these conceptions of machines themselves. In scientific traditions, in the literary imagination, and in stage representations, our technologies have often been anthropomorphized by dancers who appear to be simultaneously superhuman in their feats of flexibility and endurance, and subhuman in their wordless physicality. Between machines' not-quite-human functioning and humans' not-quite-machine-like performance, choreographers, philosophers, writers, filmmakers, and artists have situated dancers.

Twentieth-century machine ballets followed a theater tradition in which dancers performed contemporary conceptions of machinery and thus commented on them: from baroque ballets staging Cartesian thinking about mind and body, body and cosmos, through the nineteenth-century ballets staging automata, either machines that emulated humans—such as the life-size doll Coppélia—or humans transformed into machines—such as the Nutcracker.[2] In these and other ballets, a central figure is the magician or man of science who drives the story: the wily craftsman who cobbles together Coppélia, or the mysterious Drosselmeyer who somehow controls the Nutcracker's transformation, or the maestro of Petrouchka who pulls the puppet's strings.

One type of "human machine," the automaton or robot, has often been imagined as a mechanized mover, a dancer. Writing about Babbage's Difference Engine—a calculator now seen as an early ancestor of the computer, designed in the 1820s, built in part in the 1830s and 1840s, and reconstructed in the 1990s—Jenny Uglow describes it as slipping "from the realm of engineering and calculation into the numbered rhythms of dance, the abstraction of mobile sculpture."[3] But Babbage's machine is not only describable, metaphorically, as a dancer; his machine was inspired by automata with an even closer connection to dancers.

Babbage's greatest interest was in re-creating the human mind in a machine, and for this project he drew inspiration from the contemporary performance art of automata. In "Babbage's Dancer and the Impresarios of Mechanism," Simon Schaffer analyzes the "neat connection between passion, exoticism, mechanism and money" in the London showrooms in which mechanized automata were displayed.[4] Often created for the European courts or for aficionados in Asian markets (East India Company's China trade), some of these machines figured "Oriental" types such as the famous chess-playing Automatic Turk (built for Maria Teresa at the end of the 1760s by Wolfgang Von Kempelen), and often they figured dancers, for example, an automatic rope dancer displayed in 1818 London, whose movements were described on the exhibition poster as "scarcely to be distinguished from those of a living performer; it sits perfectly free on the rope, and moves with the utmost correctness without any apparent Machinery."[5]

One such figure, designed by John Merlin, was viewed by a young Babbage in Merlin's London Mechanical Museum around 1800; Babbage described her as "an admirable *danseuse*. . . . The lady attitudinized in a most fascinating manner. Her eyes were full of imagination, and irresistible."[6] Schaffer connects this twelve-inch-tall silver dancer, eventually owned by Babbage, to his great calculating Difference Engine, next to which she was displayed at his home. Although Babbage "worked hard to make, then exploit this distinction between catchpenny and serious machines,"[7] he had a dress made for the dancer and continued to be fascinated by the human-imitative potential for automata. In particular, he imagined a games machine that he would dress up as well and use to fund his project for an Analytical Engine, an *intelligent* machine. What made machines intelligent was that "they could foresee, they could remember, and they could switch their behaviour in ways which seemed random but were really determined."[8] This invention was a hybrid creature, embodying the seduction of a dancer and the determination of a machine.

For Schaffer, "Babbage's dancer was never just a gaudy trick. She was rather an alluring emblem of the aestheticized gaze of the impresarios of intelligence."[9] Although the automata were seductive performers, Schaffer argues that their role in the upheavals of the machine age was significant: "theatrical automata really had inspired the Industrial Revolution."[10]

> The tale of the automata and their impresarios confirms that the places whence machines come, where machines are put on show and the places within machine systems where intelligence is supposed to reside raised, and still raise, delicate political and philosophical issues. Most of these problems hinge on the problem of work and its visibility. . . . This is the point of the tale of the Dancer and the Difference Engine. The intelligence attributed to machines hinges on the *cultural invisibility* of the human skills which accompany them.[11]

Schaffer continues: "If such machines look intelligent because we do not concentrate on where their work is done, then we need to think harder about the work which produces values and who performs it."[12] In the case of "intelligent machines," much of the intelligence resides in the operators and operation of the machine—the specific tasks we ask it to do.[13]

In Shaffer's reading of Babbage, the automaton, representing concealed labor and mechanical determination in the shape of aesthetic seduction, challenged the definition and valuation of labor in anticipation of the Industrial Revolution and reflected a disappearing culture, as Georges Vigarello has pointed out in regard to the sixteenth and seventeenth centuries, that was marked by limited gestures rather than motor effects or energies ("effets moteurs et energetiques").[14] The example of Babbage's Difference Engine reveals that dancers were understood as central to a machine logic and aesthetic well before the twentieth century. Aspects of the automaton's hidden mechanics and its Orientalized or exoticized character are also found in twentieth-century examples considered in this book. Characterized by hidden workings, such mechanical movement—jerky or smooth—provides an apt figure for dancing that conceals its mastery.

In a second conception of the machine important for this dance history, the "human motor" focuses on machines' manifest rather than concealed mechanics, and on expenditure of energy rather than external control. Whereas the automata hides its work and agency in an exercise of inanimate animation, the human motor openly exhibits both, manifesting a different facet of the energy available to industry and a different form of economy of gesture.

## THERMODYNAMICS: THE HUMAN MOTOR

Although ballets such as *Coppélia* and *The Nutcracker* staged the link between dancing and the automaton, it is also evident in what might be called the science fiction texts of Villiers de L'Isle-Adam's *Future Eve* and F. T. E. Marinetti's Futurism, which are considered in following chapters. Against this misogynist image of the female dancer as a kind of robot, linked to disease or destruction, Isadora Duncan announced her own modern "dancer of the future" in the terms of thermodynamics.

In the course of the nineteenth century, machines were reconceived as motor forces linked to thermodynamics and ruled by internal, dynamic principles.[15] Whereas the mechanical automata gave a face to the problems of human agency, the power of mind over body, concealed work, and the mystery of the "automatic," the motor concretized the problem of perpetual movement. The concept of the motor has a rich history of associations: first, as the prime motor (or mover) of Aristotelian metaphysics and subsequent medieval cosmologies, or its substitute—the agent or force producing mechanical motion. As a term in anatomy, the muscle or nerve that promotes movement, "motor" has another history, registered, among others, by Descartes in his physiological treatise *Sur l'homme*, which interprets the physiology of matter in motion.[16] The use of the term for a host of machines, ultimately including the motorcar, the self-propelling "auto-mobile," follows after these philosophical and physiological acceptations. Already in the use of the word "motor" across these domains, to describe the movement of things and people, cosmos and limbs, can be seen the interlocking conceptions of human and machine; its continued use in medicine (motor reflexes, motor nerves) marks the extended analogies between machine and human movement.

Taking his title from a 1914 treatise on human mechanics by Jules Amar, Anson Rabinbach in *The Human Motor* traces turn-of-the-century work-science to the nineteenth-century thermodynamic conception of "kraft" or universal energy, as applied to humans and their labor in the work of Helmholtz and Marx.[17] After Descartes's and La Mettrie's treatises on the human machine, scientific materialism produced a different idea of the relation between the human and the mechanical, imagining the body as working machine. Rabinbach summarizes: the automaton, ruled by external force, followed a biomechanical model; the *perpetuum mobile* was imagined as a human motor in which the life force is linked to the force of nature.

Following from the laws of thermodynamics—the conservation of energy (credited to Helmholtz, 1847), and the inevitable dissipation of force and loss of heat characterized by entropy (credited to Clausius, 1850s)—the motor was conceived as harnessing natural force and was understood both in nonhuman (artificial—or natural) and human terms. Eventually, the body too would be imagined as a machine and analogized as a motor also harnessing such force and using it in labor. Significantly, Helmholtz applied the character of an energy-converting machine to the body, rather than reducing the human to the machine; in Rabinbach's summary, "the metaphor of the machine rather than the machine itself—the automata—is anthropomorphized."[18]

Drawing on the French engineering tradition that referred to *travail* or *puissance du travail* (work power) as a measure for the energy yield of machines in the 1830s, Helmholtz used the term *Arbeitskraft* to describe work identical to expenditure of force: the body is a thermodynamic machine, and work could be the product of man, nature, or the machine.[19]

Amar's *Le Moteur humain et les bases scientifiques du travail professionel* suggests the confusion of human and machine in work-science, elaborating parallels between human and machine that proceed from mechanics of the *machine humaine* to the interaction of bone and muscle with metal.[20] In a preface to the second edition (1923), Henri Le Chatelier says Amar applies "mécanique rationelle" to "human limbs, that is to say, to the different mechanical parts of the machine."[21] On the other hand, Le Chatelier relates that workers are aghast when treated like machines, for example, in experiments with chronometrage.[22] But he also acknowledges that machines have often been treated better and that it is impossible to refuse humans the care that the steam engine has long received.[23]

The worker may be viewed as superior to the machine in some cases but always risks losing humanity in the comparison. In a passage at the end of *Le Moteur humain* on the subject of production, Amar details the superiority of humans to machines made possible by a longer work life, greater flexibility, and adaptability. The upkeep of the human machine must be "the constant preoccupation of industry leaders, officers in charge of troops, colonials exploiting the considerable energy of thousands of indigenous laborers, of all those who pursue the valorization of human work in the best possible conditions. Because the upkeep of the living machine is not less delicate than that of everyday motors."[24]

For Le Chatelier, Amar's work addresses two reciprocal problems: how to maintain a level of production while keeping fatigue at a minimum and how to maintain a stable level of fatigue while arriving at maximum production.[25] Amar's text describes an "art of work" that is "firmly established on scientific bases."[26] The opening page of *Le Moteur humain* is peppered with terms from mechanics that describe the range of scientific study of the art of moving: from *machine* to *mécanique*, from bodies in movement to *cinématique* ("science du mouvement") and *dynamique* ("science des forces"). The scientific goal is to "proportion work," ("proportionner le travail"); quoting from his 1910 work *Le Rendement de la machine humaine*, Amar notes that science helps humans economize effort, recharge, and adapt better than any machine.[27]

In Rabinbach's history, the metaphor of the human motor inspires in the European work-science of the late nineteenth and early twentieth centuries the development of techniques to harmonize the movements of the body with those of the industrial machine and then to measure the expenditure of mental and physical energy.[28] As the scientific term *puissance*—power or force (referred to, for example, in Sadi Carnot's 1824 *Reflections sur la puissance motrice du feu*)—becomes associated with the force or energy mobilized in labor power, it intersects with the term "performance," used in engineering and mechanics to describe technology. With a different resonance, and a different history, from *puissance*, the idea of "performance" as measurable productivity becomes important in European work-science late in the nineteenth century and in theories of productivism inspired by the application of thermodynamics to working bodies.

The redefinition of "performance" as productivity brought with it questions of rhythm and movement that would be studied by ergography and ergonomics, with an intense focus on the use of the muscles for the purpose of identifying a minimum gesture. Rabinbach sees the early practice of work-science as well-intentioned: for Emil Kraepelin, for example, "industrial work was based on adjusting minute physiological and psychic processes to the rhythms of the machine."[29] Kraepelin, working with Hugo Munsterberg, the pioneer of psychotechnics, in Berlin and at Harvard University,

> compared the "rhythmically structured" work of past epochs with the rigid economy of force imposed on the body by machinery. Influenced by Bucher's ethnological work on the rhythms of primitive work habits, they saw an intimate connection between the development of modern technology and the "unnatural" character of modern work processes. . . . Mechanized work, they observed, reduced physical effort to those muscles directly engaged in the actual process, eliminating all superfluous motion. Whereas the French physiologists tended to focus on single tasks such as vine cutting, hammering, or filing, Kraepelin was concerned with a uniquely physiological phenomenon, which he called "the principle of the smallest muscle."[30]

The principle of the smallest muscle would have tremendous resonance beyond physiology, and its exploration was far from an exercise in the scientific "impartiality" Amar invokes in his introduction. Alongside the abstraction of the effort of working bodies, the bodies themselves lose their identity in the work-science some have argued set out to help them. Although it would later be employed in the service of maximum productivity, this work-science, for Rabinbach, attempted to address the psychophysics of fatigue and muscle fatigue by understanding ways in which industrialization, requiring ever more precise tasks, demanded smaller movements. This displacement of work performance from muscles demanding greater expenditures of energy to those demanding less prompted ergonomists to create exercises to train muscles to more efficiently deploy the energy that machines required.[31]

Rabinbach summarizes: "Science constructed a model of work and the working body as pure performance, as an economy of energy, and even as a pathology of work."[32] These smaller gestures, at first elegantly designed as part of what Etienne-Jules Marey called "greater economy from training,"[33] would come to constitute the pathology of fragmented, repetitive work, as Taylorist Scientific Management, present in Europe before but more prevalent after the First World War, countered workers' resistance to machines and assured that maximum speed and productivity would not reduce the labor force in any sense.[34]

The redefinition and abstraction of labor in terms of energy, movement, muscle, and rhythm, in the application of thermodynamics to working bodies, reveals the profound sociocultural implications of work-science and suggests a common culture linking dance to the machine. Considering this history, Isabelle Stengers describes the age of the motor and the human motor in terms of the questions of reversibility and irreversibility central to thermodynamics and the broader reconceptions of force, and eventually human labor, organized around it. For Stengers, "the problem at the start of thermodynamics was to employ heat to make a motor work," but its starting point, Fourier's (mathematical) formulation of the law of heat diffusion, described "an irremediable waste," the spontaneous and irreversible diffusion of heat. The nineteenth-century imagination, "being at the same time haunted by the depletion of resources and carried away by the perspectives of revolution and progress, could not ignore reversibility."[35] These fears, as well as the "leveling of productive differences," determined the original interpretation of the second principle of thermodynamics: "Thermodynamics is thus set up in relation *with* irreversibility but also *against* it, seeking not to know it but to avoid it. And Clausius' entropy would first describe the perfectly controlled, totally reversible conversions of calorific and mechanical energies." But Stengers points out that "physics recognized that dynamics—which describes nature as obedient and controllable in its being—only corresponds to a particular case. In thermodynamics, the controllable character is not natural but the product of artifice; the tendency to escape from domination manifests the intrinsic activity of nature."[36]

Stengers points out the profound social and cultural consequences of the application of ideas from thermodynamics to questions of labor and laboring bodies: "The refusal to restrict thermodynamics to systems artificially cut off from the world was produced by the desire to approach a world peopled by beings capable of evolving and innovating, of beings whose behavior we cannot render foreseeable and controllable except through enslaving them."[37] Taking shape as the exploitation of labor, a control over workers reduced to automata, such "enslavement" follows work-science's focus on the most efficient gesture, and scientific management's institutionalization of such gestures, with enforced rhythms of production, creating harmful results. The minimum gesture, aestheticized in modernist media, is also the iterated gesture of the assembly line, generating a pathology of work and a resistance to machines that Taylorism would try to combat. The energy of laboring bodies, including those of colonized or immigrant populations, produced work appropriated by management. In both cases, in Rabinbach's words, "the human organism was considered a productive machine, stripped of all social and cultural relations and reduced to 'performance,' which could be measured in terms of energy and output."[38] Kraeplin's and Amar's work on effort and fatigue was resonant with cultural and ethnic implications—and explicit, negative stereotypes—of work practices of a subject pool, including, in Amar's case, North African workers.[39]

This stripping work down to the minimum gesture and pumping workers up to maximum productivity are represented in the dancing of the early twentieth century, taking shape as a minimalist machine aesthetic or a parody of mechanistic madness. The gesture reduced by work-science to the smallest muscle, the "best speed," the maximum efficiency, has tremendous resonance in the dance and theater of its time, in the cinema that arises contemporary with it, and in the poetry and pictures that encode it. At the same time, dancing staged resistance to such modernization, erasure, and exploitation of individual bodies and insisted on the reality of real bodies giving in to time, weight, and the loss of energy. The dancing of Isadora Duncan or Josephine Baker, studied here, suggests not the smallest gesture but the cosmic energy that Isadora called, in Helmoltzian terms, "motor power" or that Michel Leiris identified in Josephine Baker as an icon for an age in thrall to the machine. Yet even dancing like Duncan's— as André Levinson said—could show the ravages of time,[40] and Baker's eternally energetic stomping and swinging also marks the human limit, the irreversibility of time. A third kind of machine, the cinematograph, patented during the early years of "modern" dance, avoided by Isadora and courted by Josephine, would seem to return to dance its mechanical, time-transcending, perpetual movement while promising to safeguard the anti-mechanical naturalness of dancing like theirs.

## CINEMATICS

The revolution in dance that began at the end of the nineteenth century took place at a pivotal moment, between what Martin Jay has called different "scopic regimes."[41] Jonathan Crary identifies these as the classical order of knowledge in which vision ruled and "regimes of machine vision which take off in the 20th century."[42] Principal among the new machinic forms of vision was photography, moving from posed long exposures to the "instantaneity" made possible by developing processes that permitted sequential serial chronophotography and then cinematography. Far from a moment of clear division between an old regime and a new one, the moment of the invention of cinema, concurrent with the elaboration of new dance forms, manifests overlapping currents of thinking about movement and its representation in both live performance and recording technology. Dance's prominence in the culture of fin-de-siècle Paris, and its links to both artistic and scientific projects and pictures, tie it closely to early conceptions of cinema. In chapter 2 of this volume, I argue that, before furnishing for cinema visual images with ready-made audience interest and musical-gestural performance apt for the medium's early spectacular capacities, choreography played a role in the scientific-philosophic imagining of, and physiological inspiration for, cinema before its mechanical "invention."

Some of cinema's multiple inventors and early experimenters did not imagine it true to movement, and these scientists' and philosophers' hesitations about the camera's ability to render movement closely parallel some modern dancers' concerns about the technology. One of them, Etienne-Jules Marey, is often described as the most important of the inventors because of his efforts to trace serial movement—in particular, in sequential chronophotographs executed in time-motion studies of the analysis of movement.

In 1873, Marey noted in the opening lines of *La Machine animale* that differences between the human and the machine had been so reduced that the distinction between them required reconsideration.

> Living beings have been frequently and in every age compared to machines, but it is only in the present day that the bearing and the justice of this comparison are fully comprehensible.

No doubt, the physiologists of old discerned levers, pulleys, cordage, pumps, and valves in the animal organism, as in the machine. The working of all this machinery is called *Animal Mechanics* in a great number of standard treatises. But these passive organs have need of a motor; it is life, it was said, which set all these mechanisms going, and it was believed that thus there was authoritatively established an inviolable barrier between inanimate and animate machines.

In our time it is at least necessary to seek another basis for such distinctions, because modern engineers have created machines which are much more legitimately to be compared to animated motors; which, in fact, by means of the little combustible matter which they consume, supply the force requisite to animate a series of organs, and to make them execute the most diverse operations.[43]

Seeking to move beyond vitalist explanations that distinguished living beings from machines through the concept of "life," Marey, claims historian of science François Dagonet, should not be read as a reductivist. Rather, his view is typical of a passion for the study of movement and of a comparative method that he employed in his work across disciplines.

Dagonet argues that the spirit of a cultural machine that could bring the image to life was Marey's life's work. Marey's machines were created to unearth and record what could not be seen, and his trajectory led from recording inner movements, such as the heartbeat, to the neuromuscular, outward expression of movement in kinetic, cinematic, and gymnastic form. His many inventions aimed not only to trace movement's flow but also to decompose and analyze its workings in the human body.[44]

Marey's chronophotographs manifest elements from the photographic forms that preceded them while anticipating some elements particular to film. Taking pictures of movement that isolated moments and reconstituted them in sequence, Marey created images of "instantaneity" new to the photography of the end of century and aimed at a sequentiality that would reproduce movement in a way that photography had not yet done. One goal was to photograph, in movement, what the eye could not see. In attempting to capture the "imperceptible," Marey would use machines to supercede the capabilities of the retina, and ultimately he resisted cinematic projection as too visual.

Marey worked toward perfecting a motion picture camera that could give the eye the sensation of real movement by projecting his chronophotographic images in succession onto a screen. Although Marey himself, as he describes at the end of *Le Mouvement*, left resolution of the projection's final details to his assistant Georges Demeny—and ultimately released him from his job because Marey did not wish his camera to be exploited for commercial purposes—Marey's work is considered foundational for both the idea and the mechanics of the cinematograph.[45] Dagonet, however, notes Marey's dissatisfaction with, and ultimate disinterest in, the apparatus. For Marey, the point of scientific method was to *supplement* the body's senses and to correct them;[46] early cinema failed to render movement smoothly or uninterruptedly because it was too "optical" and illusionistic, not scientific. Dagonet writes: "in his view, we were too content with seeing, we had to go beyond this screen, escape the prison of the retina."[47]

Marey himself positioned his chronophotography between science and cinema: "I envisaged, for the purposes of physiology, a method: chronophotography. . . . The most ingenious and popular application of this method was the creation of the motion picture projector by the Lumières."[48] In *Picturing Time*, Marta Braun summarizes, "Marey's lifelong desire to make visible what the unaided senses could not perceive would effectively bar him from avenues of research whose end was duplicating sensory perception, no matter how aesthetically pleasing the result. Nevertheless, although Marey chose to ignore the replication of what the eye could see, others very quickly understood the commercial possibilities of cinematic illusion."[49]

Yet it was Marey's abandoned invention that linked physiology and work-science to cinema and choreographies of the age of mechanical reproduction, and Marey's images that bridge the gap from European Taylorism to modernist art. Dagonet sees Marey as much more than an experimenter-inventor:

> More than simply providing it with a set of instruments, Mareyism unveiled another universe that the culture industry was invited to take up. Why stop at academic immobility or even kinetic melody

when one could uncover a world of tensions, phases, and fluctuations? . . . The living world is filled with jolts, rustlings, rhythms and continual tremors. In bringing to light muscle stimulation or the forcing power of the cardiac pump ceaselessly beating, Mareyism offered a distinctly dynamic image of life.[50]

The time-motion studies were driven by what Dagonet has called Marey's "passion for the trace," a concern with catching life in its incessant movement. Before Marey invented and then abandoned the motion picture camera, his various recording machines had scripted continuous movement into graphic patterns. His telescriptors permitted the "teledetection" of organs' functioning without penetrating them—as opposed to pathology's penetration of the organs via the medical "gaze." He dismissed the role of the senses in observation: the observer would put away sight, touch, and hearing to invent processes of direct inscription, forcing a "direct writing" or graphing of life. The moving image would "surrender its rhythms and variations in the form of graphic lines."[51]

Marey's chronophotographs, sequences of pictures taken with his "fusil photographique" or camera-gun, are also studies in the economy of representation: the reduction of bodies in motion to geometric patterns of lines along an axis-line of time. In "La Méthode graphique" Marey writes: "All movement is the product of two factors: time and space; to know the movement of a body is to know the series of positions which it occupies in space during a series of successive instants."[52]

Dagonet also sees Marey producing idealized images of nature with his telescriptors and *fusil photographique*, "recordings without recourse to the human hand or eye" in which "Nature had to testify to itself."[53] In "La Méthode graphique," Marey explains that "the Graphic method also gives expression to the most fleeting and complex movements that no language could ever express." Defined in these terms—as beyond language, allowing nature to speak for itself, without mediation—Marey's images join a particular conception of photographs as idealized "acheiro-poetic" images and of photography as an art without art, an art not made by humans.[54] Marey's conception of a graphic recording as an a-technical image, exact and natural, directly etched by nature rather than by human artifice, continued a tradition of thinking about physiological instruments, and about the invention of photography as discussed by François Brunet.[55]

Conceived in such a way, these images stand at the far end of the spectrum from earlier photographs of dancers. Portrait photography, made popular by the cheaper production and industrial reproduction of images that replaced daguerreotype, reached its height with the photographic *carte-de-visite* in Paris at midcentury. Disderi's famous "portrait" of dancers' legs circulated as a showpiece of the Opera's attractions, fragmenting performers' bodies and juxtaposing them in photo-collage. Disderi's image represented—as well as promoted—the availability of dancers whose fetishized representations were put into circulation in the market for pictures and performers.

As opposed to this image of dancers, motion studies such as Marey's represented a different use of the camera before a moving subject and a different "mechanical reproduction." Capturing the body at close intervals, Marey's chronophotographs represent moments and indicate the body's movement across the space and in time. Still photographs meant to be viewed in sequence both break down the movement for purposes of physiological study and allow its visual reconstruction. Between Disderi's photo-collage "group portrait" and Marey's chronophotographs there is a world of difference: rather than posed dancers, the legs multiplied in Marey's images belong to walking experimental subjects. In chronophotographs of a white-uniformed man jumping from a standing-still position, taken around 1882, the legs flying through the air multiply in a haunting way and prefigure images from modernist art, Futurist movement studies, and Cubist fragmentation, as in Duchamp's *Nude Descending a Staircase*. Modern dance's approach to deconstructing and reconstructing movement, including pedestrian movement, would follow—and resemble—Marey's chronophotographs more than a half century later.

Although dance is an all-too-human art, it has also sometimes been legitimized by the discourse of the "natural" or "superhuman." It is impossible to describe dance in terms of the achiero-poetic, yet in both "machine" dancing and more "naturalistic" modern dance there are elements of this quality, of bodies expressing a superhuman control. Describing dancers' work as an artless art, an art that conceals its workings, is to imagine it in such terms. The dancing machine is a being animated by something other than human artifice.

Even while giving dance on film this supernatural aura of the "natural image," traced by rays of light rather than the human hand, the cinematograph was also creating a record of the presence of living bodies. In fact, in tandem with a rhetoric of the "tracing of nature," Marey's photographic images, developing from the same inspiration as his telescriptors, kept a grounded physical connection to the bodies of their subjects, tracing their movements. In this way his chronophotographs also manifest another element that Brunet has discussed in the history of the conception of photography: its "indexicality" or relation of contiguity with its subject.[56] In Brunet's application of C. S. Peirce's terms to photography (informed by Peirce's work with photographs as well as the semiotic theory usually applied to the cinematographic sign), photographs represent a special case of "indexical" icon.

For Peirce, the photographic image sometimes looks like what it is representing; it always has a physical and causal link to it independent of the question of resemblance (the subject of the photo was present to the camera at the time of the taking of the picture). Yet even when photographs such as instant ones "are in certain respects exactly like" the objects they represent, this resemblance, Peirce says, is due to the "physical connection" that characterizes the second class of sign, the index.[57] In Brunet's reading of Peirce, the photograph's resemblance to its object is rooted in a relation of causality—the indexical, physical connection between the camera and its subject.[58]

The legacy of an indexical status—a proximity or contingency to its subject that provides a resemblance beyond visual reproduction and thus an iconic status—further solidifies connections between Marey's physiology and the dancing machine. It is precisely this "physical connection" that makes the camera a dancing machine, not simply reproducing or representing dancing but registering its presence to the camera, its simultaneity with the filming, its contiguity to the space of the representation. Although the camera takes pictures and reconstructs dance images, it resembles dancing not only by creating mimetic representations of dancers dancing. Cinematic images of dance qualify not simply as icons that resemble their subject but also as indices—indexical images linked to their subject through physical proximity. As I argue in the following chapter, the cinematograph makes machinic a vision that choreography had previously provoked.

The filmic image projected at twenty-four frames per second creates the illusion of constant movement. Yet beyond the neurophysiology of the "persistence of vision" that makes it work, film also brings to the eye what it could not, or otherwise would not, see. The "unconscious" element of film's optics is articulated in Walter Benjamin's well-known essay "The Work of Art in the Age of Mechanical Reproduction," which argues that photography does not simply make visible what was previously unseen—even unseeable—but "reveals entirely new structural formations of the subject." Cinema is a phenomenon that "extends our comprehension of the necessities which rule our lives" and also "manages to assure us of an immense and unexpected field of action." Benjamin writes:

> Then came film and burst this prison-world asunder by the dynamite of the tenth of a second, so that now, in the midst of its far-flung ruins and debris, we calmly and adventurously go traveling. With the close-up, space expands; with slow motion, movement is extended. The enlargement of a snapshot does not simply render more precise what in any case was visible, though unclear: it reveals entirely new structural formations of the subject. So, too, slow motion not only presents familiar qualities of movement but reveals in them entirely unknown ones "which, far from looking like retarded rapid movements, give the effect of singularly gliding, floating, supernatural motions." Evidently a different nature speaks to the camera than opens to the naked eye—if only because an unconsciously penetrated space is substituted for a space consciously explored by man. Even if one has a general knowledge of the way people walk, one knows nothing of a person's posture during the fractional second of a stride.

Mechanically reproduced images such as the photograph allow the visualization of what had previously been on the margins of vision, as psychoanalysis facilitates the verbalization of repressed material. "The camera introduces us to unconscious optics as does psychoanalysis to unconscious impulses."[59]

Cinema does not simply record movement but shapes it into superhuman forms and qualities. In this way, perhaps, the camera does what dance—or to be more precise, a certain apprehension or reception of dance—had done previously: making liveness into an image, taking the spectator into a different experience of time or space, bringing to the eye what was previously imperceptible.

In one explanation sketched above, borrowed from the history of photography, the camera can show what the eye cannot see because it produces a "natural" image, a tracing made by light and not by hand. In another perspective, the camera can show what the eye cannot see because it gives expression to an optical "unconscious" to which it gives the spectator access. But even while offering to dance a machine-made record of its images, a mechanical reproduction, cinematography also prolonged the indexicality that characterized the medium of photography. The physical relation to the subject before the camera, the tracing of continuous movement, grounded the early cinema in bodies and their physiology, in representations that were graphings of movement as much as visual copies of movement.

For Dagonet, Marey's importance lies in the complex visualization realized by his recording machines:

> 1. No one was as successful at making visible what kept to the shadows. How were those dark areas to be lighted? The forces of life are hidden; by transposing them he brought them fully into the light. 2. From this, Marey would try to go further and track down the imperceptible, the fleeting, the tumultuous and the flashing. The extraordinary "image-maker" would demonstrate how one could tame what was elusive. 3. He would gradually point researchers toward a different understanding of the relations between science and art, between the real and figuration which he would liberate.[60]

It might be argued that Marey's work signaled a turn away from the tendency to view bodily performance in terms of symptomatology or pathology—a view I have discussed elsewhere and that is also evident in Villiers's famous pre-cinematic scene from *L'Eve future* considered in the next chapter. But as Dagonet concludes, neuromotor movement analysis ultimately served the ends of industrial capitalism by focusing on the questions of productivity and efficiency linked to regulation of workers, standardization of products, and ultimately, profit. Measurement of effort output, like that crucial to work-science and then Taylorism, was begun in Marey's laboratory in experiments by Charles Fremont.[61] Reduction to graphic image and to economy of gesture also has its social and cultural implications, especially when it helps to produce anonymity of workers reduced to automatic tasks, and stereotypes based on appearance generated by the practice or theory of photographic cliché. In Dagonet's summation, Marey was not a vitalist but a mechanist who ultimately subscribed to overmechanization and Taylorism.[62]

These twin aspects of Marey's legacy interact in the dancing explored in this book: the abstraction of "pure movement" and the negative social ramifications of Taylorism's reduction of anonymous workers to stereotyped gestures. The two domains of work-science and cinema, in spite of their French and European roots, develop after World War I an American flavor. Taylorism, like U.S. cinema, becomes one of the most significant American imports. The omnipresence of the two, and their interrelation, marks the choreographies of the 1920s and 1930s danced in France.

The minimum gesture that the machine age cultivates is figured, and in part produced, by a picture-making process—photographic instantaneity—born toward the end of the nineteenth century. The minimum gesture is also a response to it: inspired by time-motion studies of bodies, anticipated by choreography, and in turn inspiring choreography, the photographic isolation of the smallest gesture and its cinematic fusion become emblematic of what Marey called economy of gesture.

Yet the economical gesture, the gesture represented in the fractioned, fleeting moment, can resonate with *more* information. Benjamin's essay defining the age of mechanical reproduction remarks that behavior on film lends itself to analysis more readily than does painting or theater: it presents a more precise situation that is more easily isolated. Even "a muscle of a body" screened becomes "fascinating" for both its artistic value and its "value for science." This space that film opens up, with "the dynamite of the tenth of a second," allows us to see what our "prison-world" conceals from the naked eye: the posture of the "fractional second of a stride" far more precise and profound than the "general knowledge of the way people walk." For Benjamin, the "fractional second of a stride" is not a cliché or still image: the mechanization of the image that takes place in photography or film permits the dynamiting of the prison of our perception and allows the penetration into what Rosalind Krauss has analyzed as the "optical unconscious."[63]

Until recently, cinema and dance historians have mostly worked separately, for disciplinary reasons, on the overlap between dance and cinema at its inception. Now, however, it is impossible not to consider how popular forms of ballet or music-hall dancing changed simultaneously into modern dance and into the stuff of film, at first sharing an audience and later, with the elaboration of discourses about modern dance's naturalness and cinema's mechanization, diverging.[64] This book focuses on an era in which the kind of mechanization dancers had previously represented (as automats, robots, motors) became cinematic, identified with the photographic still and with chronophotographic seriality. Thus, although chapter 2 suggests dance's leading role, pre-cinema, in fictions of the body-machine, other chapters show dance companies and choreographers in thrall to cinema and its effects.

Rather than simply understanding cinema as a tool that helps us to read historical dance, this book views early cinema as anticipated by, developing with, and eventually—as mass media—eclipsing contemporary explorations in choreography. Dancing did what the camera would come to do; choreographers did what cinematographers would do. At the end of a short film by Bull in which he is shown receiving admirers after a lecture, the well-respected man of science, Marey himself, performs for the camera one last trick, kicking up his heels in imitation of a cancan dancer. Marey's gag, the gesture of an inventor taken aback before his own invention, signals the end of an era dominated by dance and the rise of a new choreographic form. One of the inventors of cinematography responds with a dismissive gesture to this invention, and with the same gesture science relegates dance definitively to the realm of entertainment.

CHOREOGRAPHICS

If, in the history recounted here, the "dancing machine" is imagined and invented by European sciences and becomes part of a European aesthetic, how does it become associated with America, and in particular with African Americans three or four decades later?

In 1936, the date of the documents that provide the closing frame to this book, the dancing machine was viewed by one American modernist as a distinctly European phenomenon, in spite of the reign of American management methods in European industry and the international draw of the American cinema. Inverting the usual view of America as a country technologically obsessed—the view expressed in many of these European machine ballets—and defining an "American" dance against that of the European avant-garde, Martha Graham would write:

> Let us consider for a moment the striking difference in the Continent's and our own reaction to an important factor in modern times—the machine. Talk to the Continental, talk to the American of the machines' part in the tempo of modern life. The reactions are unmistakably characteristic.
>
> To the European the machine is still a matter of wonder and excessive sentimentality. Some sort of machine dance is a staple of every European dance repertory. But to the American sentimentality for the machine is alien. The machine is a natural phenomenon of life.
>
> An American dance is not a series of steps. It is infinitely more. The characteristic time beat, a different speed, an accent, sharp, clear, staccato.[65]

In this commentary, Graham naturalizes machines as connected to "life" in their American context, and then produces a national definition of American dance that emphasizes the country's "freshness, its exuberance of youth and vigor, its contrasts of plenitude and barrenness." Graham's message to dancers is to "know your country" and to band together, to focus on the "fundamentals of which we are all a part," for example, this implicit understanding of—and lack of sentiment for—the machine.[66]

In this statement, Graham reproduces, in part, the rhetoric of Taylorism while seeming to ignore its trajectory from the United States to Europe in the wake of the First World War. She neglects to mention that America had represented technology and modernity, and a cinematic space, in many of the very machine ballets she refers to, which also often involved American, including African American, artists working in Europe.

Nearly forty years later, George Balanchine turned this statement on its head, in a remark, cited earlier, about the way the United States, now a technological superpower, needed to prove its superiority in the domain of dance. What happened in the United States in the years between Graham's statement and Balanchine's is beyond the scope of these pages and has been studied elsewhere.[67] This book attempts an explanation of the transatlantic nature of the dancing machine primarily from a French perspective, considering a continuing tradition of African American performers in France, which significantly inflected the art of all Americans in exile in Europe while being understood as connected to French colonial Africa. At the same time that the presence of African American performers is acknowledged, and in France appreciated, a certain masking or erasure of performers typifies the adoption of African American forms into European arts. The idea of a mechanized dancer's driving energy took shape in modernism as abstraction or fragmentation, but it can also be connected to questions of sex, color, and dancing styles in the history of dancing bodies. In the case studies considered in this book, dancers are often appreciated for their formal qualities—whether the dancer is Isadora Duncan, Michio Ito, or Josephine Baker—and are associated with the aesthetic code of an idealized "feminine" expressivity (in Duncan's case), or "Asian" ideogrammic condensation (in Ito's case), or "African" formal beauty (in Baker's case). But at the same time, these idealizations rely on essentializing stereotypes that are negative: excessively "feminine" sentimentality, "Asian" detachment, or "African" possession. Race, color, or sex remain foundational to the image of the "dancing machine," even as these qualities are erased or abstracted in modernist machine aesthetics and its choreographies.

In the examples considered in this book, the dancing machine becomes "raced," often through its erasure of individual dancers' identities. An Orientalist idealization of automata extended to Asian performers makes them anonymous in a similar way without, among the examples here, producing any star image to equal Josephine Baker's. Yet national, ethnic, and racial characteristics of dancers, when they are made visible or re-marked, tend to layer stereotypes. One of her films discussed in chapter 5, *Princesse Tam-Tam*, presents Baker as an Indian "Princess of Parador" and as a North African Bedouin. In chapter 3, Blaise Cendrars is cited as describing Swedish dancer Jean Börlin as "mulatto, Negro, Hawaiian and savage." And the "Asian" exoticness of the Ballets Russes, for example, is described by contemporary dance critic André Levinson as a kind of "savageness." Thus, both African- and Asian-inspired movements are received as mechanical or motorized, with a confusion of stereotypes of race and physical energies added onto essentialist discourses about dancers' qualities.

In Isadora Duncan's formulation, Americanness is simultaneously something underpinning her dance and something to be avoided, a frankness she espouses and a literality she eschews, by distinguishing her art as symbolic and European while linking African American dance forms to "the real thing." In Jean Cocteau's perspective, African American dancers transfer their energies to machines, and machines absorb and reproduce their rhythms. In ballets by Jean Börlin that stage African plastic arts or American urbanity, African American dance forms are implicit yet significantly absent. With the loss of individual identity in rhythmic ensembles, with color represented as mask or traditional blackface, widely admired African American performances often disappear in art that everywhere invokes them.

Another explanation for the eventual construction of the dancing machine as a raced image involves considering the presence of African performers before a French public in the context of colonial exhibitions and in photographic and cinematographic representations. Josephine Baker, for example, is alternately identified as African and American, her dancing connected to a utopian "primordial" energy imagined as old-world and a cultural electric charge associated with the American cinema. But her dancing on film must also be read in the context of the ethnographic and documentary-style recording of African dance forms and Africa it-self, contemporary with her stage and screen career.[68]

Such essentializing stereotypes of dancing and dancers, following from the artistic abstraction, scientific erasure, or industrial exploitation of bodies, facilitate their imagined linking of the mechanized and the primitive. Modernist fascination with the technological has been seen not simply as the opposite of but parallel to a fascination with the pre-technological "primitive" or "tribal."[69] Levinson writes in the same breath about precision chorus lines and "barbarism" in the first twenty years of the century. Contemporary with Isadora, Dalcroze, and German movement choruses, "numerous battalions of Anglo-Saxon 'girls'—thanks to their automatic discipline and their sports culture—come to oust the corps de ballet of the old days. Then in turn, their collective, uni-form, anonymous style finds itself threatened by the invasion of Afro-American exoticism. The triumph of jazz has as its corollary the success of Negro 'steps' that draw their joyous and sensual frenzy from the sources of primitive barbarity."[70] Isadora also falls under a more affec-tionate banner of "jeune barbare."[71] Levinson's work is marked by re-ductive remarks on national, racial, and ethnic stereotypes; dancing summarizes palpably and immediately "the state of a civilization or orig-inality of a race."[72] Bad dancers are described in terms of slavery and ap-ing; Swedes are by nature bad dancers.[73] The Ballets Russes is described as savage; the Ballets Suédois as *mécanique* in their slavish imitation of the Ballets Russes, in their Americanness, and even in the African-in-spired ballets.[74]

Although encoding abstractions, such simplifications of dancers' bod-ies, in stereotypes of body types and movements, are charged with socio-cultural and political implications. The dancing machine gets identified as American or Asian and is raced through the erasure of the individual identity of performers; the resulting abstractions, however, must be read in a historical context broader than their aesthetic one, in the context of the much-debated common ground of avant-garde and modernist art.

In *Dancing Modernism/Performing Politics*, Mark Franko has argued that "until recently, dance historians have been reluctant to reevaluate the modernist spirit of historical modern dance. Paradoxically, the modern-dance master narrative is so inherently, that is, so 'blindly' modernist that critical distancing from its tenets appears at first unconscionable, a betrayal of the art itself."[75] Franko's book reconsiders the "high art" of dance modernism—typified by the choreography of Isadora Duncan, Martha Graham, and Merce Cunningham—in the context of lesser-known dance contemporaries (or, in some instances, predecessors), exploring the sociopolitical and formal-aesthetic dimensions of what he terms the politics of dance's expressivity. For Franko,

> The most salient trait of the modernist narrative is its progress from expression as spontaneity to expression as semiological system to the marginalizing of expressive intent. The Duncan-Graham-Cunningham cycloid, in particular, proceeds through a narrowing range of options that refine away each immediate precursor's stakes. Modernist accounts of modern dance history thus perform the telos of aesthetic modernism itself: a continuous reduction to essentials culminating in irreducible "qualities." Recent re-evaluations of aesthetic modernism, notably in new art history, expose the modernist narrative's omission of politics, mass culture, and sexual difference.[76]

What Franko identifies as the "marginalizing of expressive intent" in modern dance performance and theory can be compared with a modernist aesthetic for abstraction, which I connect, in this book, to a machine aesthetic or the "mechanization" of dance and dancers. Taken to an extreme degree in the work of some modernist poets and artists, this mechanization represents one tendency to sever art from the bodies producing it; yet the very absence, abstraction, or erasure of those bodies permits an encoding that imitates dance's formal qualities and allows various modernist media to take on aspects of dance without dancers. It was such severing, Amy Koritz has argued, that permitted modern dance to achieve the status of aesthetic object in British modernism.[77]

Reflecting on historical narratives of the polarization of mass culture and high art in the twentieth century, and its impact on dance history, Carol Martin responds to Franko's thesis: "Modernism does not only indicate stylistic difference in performance, but historical and theoretical attitudes toward the categories of 'high' and 'low' art. As Andreas Huyssen has pointed out, modernism was defined by the mind-set of machine aesthetics and espousal of progress, as well as by critiques of standardization and alienation."[78] For Martin, the critical categories—generally applied to dance in debates about high and low culture—of "high v. low, art v. life, objective v. subjective, formalist v. utilitarian and/or political, modern v. postmodern" fail to translate the complexity of modern dance or contemporary critical thought about it.[79] Martin explains that, facing what Huyssen calls "the great divide," choreographers and dancers "feared the taint of popular culture as did most modern artists. Initially, both critics and choreographers were absorbed in establishing the legitimacy of corporeal expression. The similarity of their concerns generated a complicity in their approaches."[80]

One hypothesis resulting from cases studied in these pages is that competition with cinema led dance to define itself as something other than technological or mass art, thus denying its links to cinema while using the medium. The perfectly autonomous, self-creating, liberated body of the modern dancer is itself a technological fantasy; Isadora's dancer of the future—with the highest intelligence in the freest body—is not Villiers's "future Eve," but she is an alternate ideal to the automaton.

In *After the Great Divide*, Huyssen argues for a greater importance of popular culture, and the avant-garde's interest in it, in histories of modernism. In Huyssen's account, the "great divide" marks the moment, across the 1930s, when earlier avant-gardes with political force (such as Saint-Simonism) separated into art avant-gardes and political avant-gardes, for different reasons, in different countries.[81] Huyssen points out that this account of the avant-garde insists on the categorical distinction between high art and mass culture and that most discussions of this period valorize the former. His goal is to redress the imbalance: "both modernism and the avantgarde always defined their identity in relation to two cultural phenomena: traditional bourgeois high culture (especially the traditions of romantic idealism and of enlightened realism and representation), but also vernacular and popular culture as it was increasingly transformed into modern commercial mass culture."[82]

Huyssen differentiates the historical avant-garde both from late-nineteenth-century modernism and from the high modernism of the interwar years: "despite its ultimate and perhaps inevitable failure, the historical avantgarde aimed at developing an alternative relationship between high art and mass culture and thus should be distinguished from modernism, which for the most part insisted on the inherent hostility between high and low."[83]

Crucial to Huyssen's differentiation of the historical avant-garde from late-nineteenth-century modernism and the high modernism of the interwar years is the avant-garde's response to technology and to mass culture: "Technology emerges as a pivotal factor in the avantgarde's fight against an aestheticist modernism, in its focus on new modes of perception, and in its perhaps deluded dream of an avantgardist mass culture."[84] But the avant-gardes studied by Huyssen generated at least a double response, both embracing technology and fearing, in the context of war, its destructiveness. This critique, he notes, took representational form in the images of puppets and automata often found in the machine dances: "On a more traditional representational level, which was never entirely abandoned, the avantgarde's radical critique of the principles of bourgeois enlightenment and its glorification of progress and technology were manifested in scores of paintings, drawings, sculptures, and other art objects in which humans are presented as machines and automatons, puppets and mannequins, often faceless, with hollow heads, blind or staring into space."[85] Especially in the case of the Berlin Dada group, Huyssen remarks, these images do not represent an abstracted "human condition" but rather a critique of the invasion of capitalist technological instrumentality into life and body. Arguing for the political force of such images, Huyssen dissociates them from modernist formalist abstraction and reconnects them to a politically motivated avant-gardism.

When presented in Paris's best theaters, by the best ballet companies, however, the dancing of machines and automata, puppets and mannequins, would have to be understood not only as avant-gardist but also as commentary on the "human condition" pitched to their largely bourgeois audiences. The dancing machine as radical critique of work pathology and the dancing machine as utopic fantasy—American, cinematic, productive—are often hard to tell apart, and the "economic" gesture—pared down, essential, or generating a universe of its own—can serve radically different ends in industry and poetry, on stage and on screen.

When they are not putting a face or body onto machine aesthetics, modern dancers stage a resistance to modernity that has taken shape either as parody or critique of technology, or as a return to a more ritualistic, poetic conception of *technē*. Martin Heidegger's "The Question concerning Technology" proposes, through the etymology of *technē* and its connection to *poesis* or creative making, the definition of *technē* as both art and science, as two forms of knowledge not unrelated in Greek philosophy. This essay describes technology as "putting exact science to use" in an "enframing" or "ordering-for-use," calling upon the standing reserve of nature as a kind of challenge.[86] Enframing is "nothing technological, nothing on the order of a machine."[87] For Heidegger, such making, bringing forth, revealing used to be grouped together under the concept of technē, which referred not only to technology but to "the poesis of the fine arts."[88] "Technē belongs to bringing-forth, to poesis; it is something poetic."[89] The essay concludes that "modern technology, as a revealing that orders, is thus no mere human doing."[90] And the mystery of technology, too, remains concealed to the last as Heidegger understands it: "The essence of modern technology has for a long time been concealed, even where power machinery has been invented, where electrical technology is in full swing, and where atomic technology is well under way."[91]

Considering the close bond between technē and poesis, Heidegger elaborates on the relation between technology and the "mysterious" essence of art: "Because the essence of technology is nothing technological, essential reflection upon technology and decisive confrontation with it must happen in a realm that is, on the one hand, akin to the essence of technology and, on the other, fundamentally different from it. Such a realm is art. . . . The more questioningly we ponder the essence of technology, the more mysterious the essence of art becomes."[92]

It is this negotiation between art and science that Benjamin ascribes to the cinematograph, not in the mystical terms of a *poesis* or *technē* but in the terms of its capacity to elaborate a real world of detail otherwise inaccessible to the eye. "The Work of Art" argues that

> To demonstrate the identity of the artistic and scientific uses of
> photography which heretofore usually were separated will be one

of the revolutionary functions of the film. By close-ups of the things around us, by focusing on hidden details of familiar objects, by exploring commonplace milieu under the ingenious guidance of the camera, the film, on the one hand, extends our comprehension of the necessities which rule our lives; on the other hand, it manages to assure us of an immense and unexpected field of action. . . . With the close-up, space expands, with slow motion, movement is extended. The enlargement of a snap-shot does not simply render more precise what in any case was visible, though unclear: it reveals entirely new structural formations of the subject.[93]

The political stakes and fates of Benjamin's and Heidegger's work are well known, and the contexts of their writing and reading have been the subject of much debate in the last decade.[94] Responding to a "modern"—if not "modernist"—perspective that is in part represented by Heidegger, Bruno Latour understands the project of modernity as an active, even coercive, attempt to keep the spheres separate: subjects and objects, bodies and machines, politics and science. In *We Have Never Been Modern*, Latour exposes as artificial the separation that he calls "purification," insisting on the proliferation everywhere in the modern world of "hybrid" objects or collectives that de-polarize the political, scientific, social, and cultural oppositions held in place by what he calls the modern "Constitution."

Arguing with Heidegger's nostalgia for the lost unity of technē, Latour finds that the "gods are present" not only as Heidegger said, using Heraclitus's phrase, in art or handicraft, but even in the latest commodities:

And yet, "here too the gods are present": in a hydroelectric plant on the banks of the Rhine, in subatomic particles, in Adidas shoes as well as in the old wooden clogs hollowed out by hand, in agribusiness as well as in timeworn landscapes, in shopkeepers' calculations as well as in Hölderlin's heartrending verse. But why do those philosophers no longer recognize them? Because they believe what the modern Constitution says about itself! . . . The moderns indeed declare that technology is nothing but pure instrumental mastery, science pure Enframing and pure Stamping

[Das Ge-Stell], that economics is pure calculation, capitalism pure reproduction, the subject pure consciousness. Purity everywhere! They claim this, but we must be careful not to take them at their word, since what they are asserting is only half of the modern world, the work of purification that distils what the work of hybridization supplies.

Who has forgotten Being? No one, no one ever has, otherwise Nature would be truly available as a pure "stock." Look around you: scientific objects are circulating simultaneously as subjects objects and discourse. Networks are full of Being. As for machines, they are laden with subjects and collectives.[95]

Whereas Heidegger regrets lost connections between domains, the Being found in beings, the presence of the gods in everyday objects, Latour emphasizes that such connections have not been lost but covered over, hidden expressly, by the rhetoric or rules of a modernity precariously perched on a structure of denial and furiously working at "purification." Forgetful of its ancient roots, anthropological traditions, and pre-industrial collectives, this modernity insists on the "progress" of its technological developments, even while expressing a "nostalgia" for a lost past.[96]

Latour gives the name "hybrids" to machines made up of subjects and collectives, subjects and objects. This book considers dancing machines as hybrids, imagined into being and danced on various kinds of stages before the "great divide" of modernity, or modernism, which has been characterized in different ways by Huyssen and Latour.

Dancing machines represent differences and their leveling. Michel Serres notes that there is no motor without *difference*.[97] Motors function via differences of all kinds: in the first generation of motor, mechanical, it is a difference in the relations of force that causes movement; in the second, thermodynamic, it is a difference in temperature. Serres theorizes that every new form of motor reveals or expresses a particular difference: "There can, however, be no relation without difference. Theorem: to every new motor there corresponds the discovery of a new difference."[98]

Yet the machinification of the laborer in Taylorist scientific management, in Charles S. Maier's view, was meant to erase differences:

What Americanism seemed to promise in its obstinate preaching about productivity, the role of the expert and of optimization, was the means to escape from class confrontation and social divisions. For very different reasons, all the zealots of scientific management and technological supervision sought only one thing: to invalidate the model of ideological conflict of the *avant-guerre* pre-war period, contest its claim to inevitability, and thus affirm a new image of class relations.[99]

Thus between the theory of the science illustrated by the machine and the practice of its application to, or its conjunction with, humans in scientific management, the differences the machine embodies disappear. Dancers dancing machines represent difference in motion, but they also represent the differences erased by machine culture, essentialized in modernist abstraction, suppressed in Taylorist anonymity. Figuring both machines' differences and a machinic reduction of differences, the dancing machine studied in this book reveals the contiguities between human subject and object, high art and low, modernism and mass culture, exposing forgotten or hidden links between live performance and its photographic recording, between science and art, industry and diversion.

# 2.
## Choreocinema

Let us hail the dancer who set the fireworks off, the elemental
force that shaped that ghost of an age in which woman (her
undulating graces and undergarments) reigned to the point of
usurping the place usually reserved for young men on the
marble chariots of the Grand Palais.

The Parisian woman dominates the century, at the giant
gateway to the Place de la Concorde, and everywhere—
music, painting, poetry, theater, furniture design—the froth of
her deep skirts will obfuscate all curves and figures until the
day when African art, sports, Picasso and Chanel sweep away
that fog of chiffon and compel the victress either to return to
her place in the kitchen or to submit to the rhythm of the
stronger sex. It is true that the film-maker will quickly restore
her privileges and allow her to reclaim her aggressive role as
an objet d'art.

JEAN COCTEAU, *Souvenir Portraits: Paris in the Belle Epoque*

### THE DANCER, THE TRAIN, AND THE CINEMA

Recalling the figures of Loie Fuller and "La Parisienne" reigning over the
Paris Exposition Universelle of 1900, Jean Cocteau gives these female
icons pride of place over the competitive marvels of electricity and cinematography yet links them to the future of the cinematograph. Asking "Is
it possible . . . to forget that woman who discovered the dance of her
age?"[1] Cocteau lauds the unforgettableness of Fuller's live performance,
enhanced by electric artifice, but hints that the cinematograph will be-

come crucial to the unforgettableness of women, and dancers, from this moment on. In Cocteau's view, the dancer's encounter with the film-maker, often assumed, like "Picasso and Chanel," to banish the fog of the end of the century, will instead reinforce her iconic position. Inventing a new dance contemporary with the invention of the cinematograph, this icon of the end of century is understood, in Cocteau's eyes, to tame the machine to her own uses.

An 1896 watercolor maquette for a poster advertising the new technology of cinema, attributed to the popular fin-de-siècle poster artist Jules Chéret, had already rendered unforgettable the collision of dance and the new technology: a Fulleresque figure spreads wide her famous skirts to welcome the projection of a film of a train. Merging two staples of the cinematograph's first films, the image suggests an allegory revealing the close connections between dance and cinema at its inception: the most popular dancer in Paris steps back graciously as the cinema lurches forward. Like the screen that will become invisible behind the cinematic image, the dancer here represents the proscenium stage that will give cinema a theater. Fuller's breed welcomes a new audience and holds their attention even as the engine of a new form of entertainment puffs toward greatness. This proto-poster invites dance spectators to give the new technology a try, to become moviegoers.

But in this image Fuller also smiles enigmatically, like a Gioconda conscious of her representation. She seems to accept benignly the cinema that will kill her art, but it is surely because she has already calculated what this new technology can give her, and those dancers like her, who know how to use it. Trains and dancers would be excellent subjects for the early cinematographers in search of movement, and they would both contribute to the construction of the new medium's spectator. Cinema scholars have explored the anticipation of cinematic experience in train travel and the parallels between the two technologies. In *Parallel Tracks*, Lynn Kirby moves beyond the literal "marriage of train and cinema" to consider "filmic" perception inspired by and made possible from the train.[2] For Mary Ann Doane, "the train, and the cinema as well, thus contribute to the detachment or dissociation of the subject from the space of perception—what might be termed a despatialization of subjectivity effected by modern technology."[3]

The Cheret-style poster of Loie Fuller can be understood to sketch, allegorically, two different ideas about perception and spectating in the cinema. With the train both projected onto and coming out of her body, she becomes the terrain for the overlapping of what have developed as two narratives for how cinema works: one suggesting the appropriation of the visual world in a form that the spectator mistakes for real, the other the representation of its infinite veiling or inaccessibility. The parallels set up in the image—between dancing and cinema, on the one hand, and the train and the cinema, on the other—seem to erase the differences between the old technologies and the new. Yet they bring together, over the dancer's body, two radically different notions, whose applicability to early cinema has been much debated: the screen that shows only an image, always veiled; and the potential terror of the image taken for real.

EDISON OPERATES DANCERS

These significant coincidences between dance and cinema's power to veil the image, and the terror and pleasure of spectating they share, were already predicted by writers imagining the cinema just before and during its inception, bringing into sharp focus the intimate connection between this emerging technology and dancers. *L'Eve future* (*The Future Eve*), a work of science fiction by Villiers de l'Isle-Adam published in France in 1886, features a fictional scientist named Edison, who, Villiers admits in a later introduction to the novel, was inspired by his real-life namesake although not modeled on him.[4] Villiers's Edison has a calling that legitimates a sinister quality: he has chosen to devote his considerable resources to the cause of saving men from the destruction brought on by loving beautiful women.

In Villiers's startlingly misogynist text, Edison and his friends are upset by "the non-correspondence of the physical and the intellectual in women"—with their beautiful bodies and annoying minds, such women are to be exposed as theatrical imposters and reconfigured. Edison's significant technological enterprise is given over to the service of "fixing" women by various techniques electrical and visual, including "photo-sculpture" and a proto-cinematography. The Pygmalion-like artist-inventor-scientist engages in detaching women's desirable qualities (such as beauty) from their undesirable qualities (their minds, their voices, their arguments). The targets in this text are actresses and dancers, who are the worst, supposedly, because they have mastered the artifice of beauty that seduces men and gets them into trouble—ruinous debt, destroyed health, and the madness brought on by ruin, syphilis, and manipulation.

Edison's idea is that men will control the future by controlling women, and they will control women's minds by tinkering with their bodies—not coincidentally the bodies of female performers, which, in spite of the stories about licentiousness, are also the most disciplined, the most controlled.

In rewiring women's interiors, Edison makes them into ghostly automata who keep their charming faces and shapes but obey the master's commands. To demonstrate his capacities to the young Lord Ewald, endangered by his liaison with the beautiful Alicia Clary, Edison stages a show. In the novel's most famous scene, Edison brings to life a dancer, Evelyn Habal, whom he holds responsible for his friend Anderson's suicide, attributed to the madness brought on by various kinds of ruin—financial, syphilitic—resulting from his affair with her. Meanwhile, Evelyn herself has died, presumably also from syphilis, but she is resurrected at Edison's underground laboratory through a kind of cinematic projection. Dancing and singing, Evelyn appears before them:

> "The seductive ballerina will dance a variation for you, accompanying her song with her tambourine and castagnettes." Pronouncing these last words, Edison got up and pulled a cord that fell from the ceiling along the length of a wall hanging. . . . A long band of rubberized material, embedded with many tiny pieces of glass of colored hues, hung laterally between two supports of steel in front of the luminous center of the astral lamp. This band of material, pulled at one end by clockwork, began to slide quickly between the lens and the tympan of a powerful reflector which, suddenly—on the great white cloth stretched across from it, in the ebony frame with the golden rose above it—refracted the apparition of a very pretty and quite young redhaired woman in her actual size.
>
> The vision, with transparent flesh, miraculously photochromed, in a sequined costume, danced a sort of Mexican popular dance.

The movements were performed with the essence of Life itself, thanks to the procedures of successive photography that, along the length of a ribbon of six yards, can capture ten minutes of movements of a being on microscopic lenses, which are then reflected by a powerful light-projector.

Edison, touching the molding of the frame's black wreath, sparked the center of the golden rose.

Suddenly a flat voice could be heard, starched, cloying and harsh; the dancer sang the *alza* and the *holè* of her fandango. The tambourine began to hum under her elbow and the castanets clack.

The gestures, the looks, the labial movement, the play of the hips, the lowered eyelids, the smile's intent, all were reproduced.[5]

In the next scene, this seductive, lifelike figure is projected in a second film but, stripped of all her charms, she is shown as the death's head she represented to Anderson. Edison the "electrician" makes the first "living image" disappear, then pulls another cord and makes another band appear, this one presenting the *danse macabre* of a "vaguely feminine" toothless, hairless, wrinkled figure, who sings an obscene song while dancing the same dance. "She is the same," responds Edison to Ewald's question, "only this is the *real one*. This is the one hidden inside the other's semblance. I see that you have never seriously taken into account the progress of the Art of cosmetics in modern times, my dear lord!"[6] Edison revels in exposing to Ewald's eyes the awful truth of feminine beauty, the threat lurking beneath the surface, the lure of female artifice, that the dancer represents. Evelyn embodies the "gold standard" of such evil, and other women are simply copies, scrip or coin, in comparison.[7]

Evelyn's beauty is not natural; her dancing is pathological. Like a pathologist, anatomist, and collector, Edison fetishistically preserves all of Evelyn's charming traits—hair, teeth, breasts, hips, skin—in a drawer as factual "evidence"; he rages that Anderson was driven to abandon his wife and children, become a dishonest businessman, and end his own life "for the contents of this drawer." Resonating with the logic of classification and museification of the species, Edison's rage casts women as closer to animals than humans; they think only from their sex and draw men's attention entirely to sex: "These neutered women whose entire 'thinking' begins and ends at the belt—and who consequently draw ALL men's thoughts precisely to the point where this belt buckles, even when this belt only (and always!) encircles, luxuriously, a wicked and strategic calculus—these women, I say, are less distant, in REALITY, from animal species than from ours."[8]

Edison's analysis of the movements and the body executing them in a kind of haunting physiology is first and foremost a demonstration of the dancer's pathology and the "social pathology" of her kind. In similar terms, the beauty of Ewald's fiancée, the actress Alicia Clary, is described by Edison as self-serving, a "difformité pathologique," a kind of elephantiasis that threatens him and will ultimately kill her.

Anderson's succumbing to Evelyn's charms is part of what Edison calls a "choreographic inclination," a "contagion" that he describes statistically. If his Android catches on, Edison jokes, industrialists will be making them by the dozens in response to this epidemic, whose number of victims in America and Europe is on the rise.[9]

By both idealizing and denigrating the dancer, *L'Eve future* is aligned with nineteenth-century dance reception, which read dancing bodies as figuring or reproducing symptomatic expression, pathologizing both dancing and dancers. Villiers's Edison is an evil genius; in this novel, the pathological behavior of the mad scientist responds to his pathologizing of his female subjects. Yet Ewald finds Edison guilty of a "positivism that makes the One Thousand and one nights pale in comparison."[10] Edison's response is that Electricity is itself a Scheherazade.[11] He marshals electricity, photography, and cinematography in the creation of his "electro-human" creature, Hadaly (a rewired version of the actress Alicia Clary). She is the Future Eve, created by Artificial Generation (a combination of projected photo-sculpture and spiritualist reincarnation), which reproduces a living woman, with her recorded voice, copied face and figure, but—as it turns out—a different, vibrant, personality.

If woman can be analyzed, broken down, and catalogued by Edison's various recording devices and classification systems, his automaton's performance ultimately escapes even his strategic plans. Appearing to Lord Ewald, and fooling him into thinking she is the woman she is copied from, Hadaly moves him deeply by her reflection and generous concern for him.

The machine, in fact, turns out to stir Ewald's emotions more than the real woman whose place she takes ever could have done. More perfect, more seductive because more "spiritual"—with a gentle spirit and poetic mind— the Android Hadaly is the ideal feminine. She serves as the foil to the femmes fatales whom Edison has witnessed destroying his friends.

When agreeing to the experiment that would model the form of Alicia Clary onto the robot Hadaly, Ewald had feared that the Android would do nothing more than imitate the actress, who was herself nothing but imitation; but he finds to his surprise that she has the spark of the infinite in her. Feeling manipulated by Edison's technology and his plan to use Science to arrange affairs of the heart, the cyborg asks Ewald to give her more credit—to imagine her surpassing the intention of her creator. Her long discourse on the "unintelligible and formless" Infinite that is the true reality moves Ewald to consider her request to bestow on her sentient life simply by believing in her as a living being.[12]

Edison's "positivist" mania can also be read as ironic, as Ewald's comment signals, and the text lends itself to a reading as a critique of science. In his portrait of Villiers, Stéphane Mallarmé lauds the irony of *L'Eve future*, especially this passage in which the electro-magnetic Hadaly makes the young lord feel passion that his real lover Alicia never did, thus defining passion as the thing that one feels for machines and not for real women. The greatest irony of the novel is the impassioned use of "science" against passion; attempting to liberate themselves from women, these men remain haunted by their images and dominated by their fantasies. Even as Science seems to free men from the Ideal femininity and beauty to which they are enslaved, it desperately safeguards and reproduces that ideal. Edison promises that in the future, all women will be like Hadaly, transformed into the Ideal.

In *L'Eve future*, a kind of ur-cinematic technology terminates the seductive power of the live performer, but it also *reproduces* or preserves the power of the performance. Before its "official" coming-into-being, cinema is already being imagined as a giver of life, or recorder of death, between performance and pathology.[13]

And if this is one way of thinking about cinema's birth—called into being by the live performance that it would enhance, record, and also destroy—it is also possible to imagine cinema in operation in these live performances before its actual existence. With the invention of the cinematograph, dancing will give up much of its aura to technology, yet from it dancing will gain prolonged life and wider audiences.

Ten years after Villiers's novel was published, a dance film from the real Edison's laboratory, hand-colored frame by frame, would represent a Loie Fuller imitator dancing the famous *Serpentine Dance*. Lumière films would include Spanish dancers whose "holè" could be seen onscreen if not heard. Early cinema relied on live performance as one subject for early films and, with live accompaniment, was an ideal medium for presenting moving bodies dispossessed of their voices.

The culture into which cinema was born in France was one in which dance performance held a central place, a place it would, during the decades studied in this book, cede to cinema. Yet Loie Fuller's dance was also one of many entertainments that anticipated cinema, staging elements that the cinematograph would bring together: stereoscopic photography producing a theatrical three-dimensional effect in a more or less private viewing scene; magic lantern projections; Edison's kinetoscopic films that played for a single viewer in a box; panoramas or dioramas, sometimes moving and sometimes viewed by a moving public.[14] Fuller's performances were described in cinematic terms by Mallarmé, who found her dance cinematic before its time, suspending its images and demanding a new kind of spectating.

Throughout his theater texts, Mallarmé critiques overly fetishistic spectating, the overly visual consumption of performance. Fuller's veiled dancing provoked both anxiety and pleasure: "dance's suspense; fear or contradictory desire, of seeing too much and not enough, demands a transparent prolongation." Different from the kind of show that offers itself to the gaze of fans, Fuller's serial movements raised the question of smooth transition between movements—motion rather than pose—that early cinema addressed, and they provoked a kind of looking that can be analogized to the persistence of vision that makes cinematic projection of the eventually standard twenty-four frames per second appear to present uninterrupted motion. For Mallarmé, what is significant about the cinematograph is not that it presents pictures but their *déroulement*; if the cinema could and would replace books, it is because their images are not still images but moving. In Mallarmé's famous formulation, dancing is a form of writing; but writing itself—books—will, he claims, one day be replaced by cinema: "I am for—no illustration at all, everything that a book evokes needing to take place in the reader's mind: but, if you replace photography, why not go directly to the cinematograph, whose rolling [*déroulement*] images and text will replace many a volume to advantage."[15] What gives the illusion of volume in cinema is the movement of images and of the camera. And the movement-image—as Deleuze calls it—is one that, like Mallarmé's ideal Book, presents not things as such but the musicality or rhythm of things in relation crucial to Mallarméan poetics. If cinema succeeds at making us take its images for real, it is not simply because of the verisimilitude of the image in movement but also the movement of the mind, the connecting of still images, that makes it work.

Fuller's dancing also provoked, in Mallarmé, a kind of spectating that would eventually become important in film theory. By suspending its meaning in its signs, dance produces the simultaneous options of seeing "too much" and "not enough." This viewing scene, of conflicting desire and fear, will come to typify the cinematic spectatorial position in psychoanalytic film studies. Proposing another layer of interpretation of the "lack" and "disavowal" at the heart of cinema, psychoanalytic cinema studies link these elements to questions of visuality and sexual difference, which Jacqueline Rose has summarized as "the image of woman as the very difficulty of cinema."[16]

Mallarmé's thinking is far from what Rose calls the psychoanalytic-imaginary "concentration on the visual as simply perceptual," or the notion of the world as "appropriable through its visibility," which helped to shape the late-nineteenth-century industrialized reproduction of images and their standardization first in photography and then in cinema. His poetics is one of the intellection of forms rather than their perception or appropriation. Yet he is interested in dancing and cinema not because they are simply visual (or perceptual) but because they are complexly visual—bringing into question the compatibility of visibility or visuality and truth. Mallarmé's introspective spectator is trained by watching early modern dance: isolated before the spectacle even while enjoying it, absent from himself while completely absorbed, attentive to Loie Fuller's fluid permutations—and her always-veiled image.

But how much of this ideal viewing experience described the first cinema projections by Louis and Auguste Lumière, which Mallarmé would have attended at the Grand Café in 1895 or 1896? Precursors and competitors to the *cinematographe* experimented with varying speeds of projection that did not produce natural-looking movement, and some of those most invested in the idea of the motion picture camera abandoned it because they believed it would never capture naturalness.[17] In Stephen Kern's view, the early cinema "reproduced the mechanization, jerkiness, and rush of modern times."[18]

According to Tom Gunning, it is the setting-into-motion, the contrast between still and moving projection, that heightened the excitement of early cinema spectating. The scene of an early screening of the Lumière short "Arrival of a Train at La Ciotat," thought to have provoked the screams and even flight of spectators, gave rise to a founding myth of cinema—that early film spectators were naïve and took the image for real: "The absolute novelty of the moving image therefore reduced them to a state usually attributed to savages in their primal encounter with the advanced technology of Western colonialists, howling and fleeing in impotent terror before the power of the machine."[19]

Gunning argues rather that these sophisticated, urban, early spectators responded with delight and terror not to the veracity of the image but to a "cinema of attractions"—short films with moments of revelation, shown to animated crowds, not unlike other "attractions" of the period at circuses or fairgrounds, or the prestidigitation of Méliès's theater.[20] The "cinema of attractions" developed and extended this "disavowal" ("I know, but yet I see"), addressed the spectator "directly," and solicited a "highly conscious awareness" of the film's artifice. While calling attention to the apparatus in every way, especially by showing still frames and then setting the cinematograph cranking, the Lumières' projections amazed audiences by projecting photographic images in motion and produced their "vacillation between belief and incredulity."[21] According to Gunning,

> While such a presentation would seem to forbid any reading of the image as reality—a real physical train—it strongly heightened the impact of the moment of movement. Rather than mistaking the image for reality, the spectator is astonished by its transformation through the new illusion of projected motion. Far from credulity,

it is the incredible nature of the illusion itself that renders the viewer speechless. What is displayed before the audience is less the impending speed of the train than the force of the cinematic apparatus.[22]

For Gunning, cinema forged a new audience through its power as an attraction, appealing to spectators jaded by the boredom of urban industrial life.[23] Their vacillation between shock and excitement at early cinema projections, transforming still images into moving images, "expresses an attitude in which astonishment and knowledge perform a vertiginous dance."[24] Although formal dance performance is cited as partly leading the way in this setting-into-motion that cinema would come to master, dancing would also resist the new technology and its attractions.

TRANSITIONS

Although it arrives in color, with fantastic powers, and full of singing and dancing, the cinema imagined in Villiers's novel anticipates some aspects of the real cinema elaborated in one of the sites of its invention in France only a few years later. Close on the one hand to physiology and on the other to dance and theater arts, cinema is imagined not simply as a technique for producing visual images but as a process with real purchase on real bodies, developing in research on the physiology of movement. These characteristics, which mark chronophotography by Marey and early films by Albert Londe and others, suggest deeper, closer links between dance and cinema at its origins. It was not the cinema of physiological time-motion studies that mainstream modern dance would turn away from but the cinematic song-and-dance that it left other dance forms to embrace.

Dance, it has been argued, was central in pointing the way toward new conceptions of time and space that the cinematograph would confront. In Gilles Deleuze's reflections in *The Movement-Image*, early cinema took on the problem of reconstituting the movement of live performance in the photographic and serial reproduction of the image, and in fact accomplished what Henri Bergson, among others, doubted it capable of. Yet beyond Bergson's lack of appreciation for the cinematograph, Deleuze theorizes its place in the rethinking of time and space that defines Bergsonian *durée*. In Bergson's negotiation between movement, as physical reality in the external world, and the image, as psychic reality in consciousness, between an external or objective reality and an internal consciousness, Deleuze locates not only cinema but also contemporary art forms such as early modern dance. Deleuze goes on to note that dance and other arts were exploring time and motion in ways the cinema would later exploit.

Summarizing Bergson's three theses on movement from the 1907 *Creative Evolution*, Deleuze recasts it as a text about cinema's ability to reconstitute movement. First, "you cannot reconstitute movement with positions in space or instants in time." Second,

> there are two different illusions of reconstituting movement: ancient and modern. For antiquity, movement refers to intelligible elements, Forms or Ideas, which are themselves eternal and immobile, potentialities to be embodied in matter. But, conversely, movement merely expresses a "dialectic" of forms, an ideal synthesis which gives it order and measure. Movement, conceived in this way, will thus be the regulated transition from one form to another, that is, an order of *poses* [exposures?] or privileged instants, as in a dance. The forms or ideas "are supposed . . . to characterise a period of which they express the quintessence, all the rest of this period being filled by the transition, of no interest in itself, from one form to another form. . . . They noted, then, the final term or culminating point (telos, acme), and set it up as the essential moment: this moment, that language has retained in order to express the whole of the fact, sufficed also for science to characterise it.[25]

In Deleuze's view, Bergson was critiquing a "primitive state" of cinema in which movement was attached to people and things, connected to this "order of poses," and only later did it become capable of rendering the movement image. This revolution in image making followed, Deleuze argues,

> a development at work in the arts, which was changing the status of movement, even in painting. To an even greater degree, dance, ballet, and mime were abandoning figures and poses to release

values which were not posed, not measured, which related movement to the any-instant-whatever. In this way, art, ballet and
mime became actions capable of responding to accidents of the
environment; that is, to the distribution of the points of a space,
or of the moments of an event. All this served the same end as the
cinema.[26]

As an "industrial art," cinema follows the scientific revolution in connecting movement not to privileged instants but to what Deleuze calls the
"any-instant-whatever," the instant equidistant from any other. For Deleuze, cinema is the system that reproduces movement by relating it to the
"any-instant-whatever."

> What is the interest of such a system? From the point of view of
> science, it was very slight. For the scientific revolution was one of
> analysis. And, if movement had to be related to the any-instant-
> whatever in order to analyse it, it was hard to see any interest in a
> synthesis or reconstitution based on the same principle, except a
> vague interest of confirmation. This is why neither Marey nor
> Lumière held out much hope for the invention of the cinema. Did
> it at least have artistic interest? This did not seem likely either,
> since art seemed to uphold the claims of a higher synthesis of
> movement, and to remain linked to the poses and forms that
> science had rejected.[27]

If the modern dance revolution in some ways led the cinematograph to
new ground, it also turned from it at a crucial juncture. After dance's
early encounters in anticipation of and collusion with cinematic technology, even as a certain kind of dancing remained a staple of early films, another strain of modern dance would follow the path of hesitation before
the apparatus.

The cinematograph disappointed many of those, like Marey, engaged in
its invention and who felt, for various reasons, that in its earliest forms,
the machine failed to represent the reality of movement.[28]

In his development and ultimate abandonment of the motion picture
camera, Marey, in Dagonet's view, shattered an illusion of "fusion" developed in the philosophy of Bergson.[29] In *Picturing Time*, Marta Braun ar-

gues that although Bergson's philosophy may have made no impact on Marey, Marey's work had a "profound effect" on Bergson, who refers to the chronophotographs in several publications without mentioning Marey by name: "Chronophotography provided a language for representing simultaneity—what was popularly understood to be Bergson's idea of time."[30] But she also notes that Bergson's method of "intuition" and Marey's of machinic measurement meant that their "ideas of the nature of reality were hardly compatible" and "their conclusions could not have differed more sharply."[31]

> Yet Bergson's attack on the camera reveals a hitherto neglected source of one of the most pervasive metaphors he uses in his work to characterize the "normal" perception of time. . . . Marey's images are symbols of an incorrect, insufficient, and invalid way of perceiving movement. . . . Chronophotographs are images not of movement through time, according to Bergson, but of position and succession. . . . Because for Bergson succession or continuity is not reducible to mere instantaneous juxtapositions in space, Marey's models became the perfect examples for demonstrating just what reality is not.[32]

Bergson used photography (and chronophotography) to describe spatialized perception. *Creative Evolution* mentions the cinematograph explicitly and develops *the idea* of cinema (a kinetic cinematics) while criticizing instant photography and cinematography as limited. In a chapter titled "The Cinematographical Mechanism of Thought and the Mechanistic Illusion," Bergson uses the image of the snapshot as a fair translation of a moment of transition but an image that does not represent *movement*. He writes: "in reality the body is changing form at every moment; or rather, there is no form, since form is immobile and the reality is movement. What is real is the continual *change of* form; *form is only a snapshot view of a transition*."[33]

For Bergson, working like a camera, "the mind manages to take stable views of the instability" (and arrives at three things: qualities, forms, and acts); "knowledge bears on a state rather than on a change."[34] Developing the photo metaphor to include the cinematograph, he writes, cinematic apparatus is a way to describe ordinary knowledge and perception.

There are two ways to portray on a screen a living picture, such as the marching past of a regiment: The first is to make cut-outs that function as shadow puppets. The second is to

> take a series of snapshots of the passing regiment and to throw these instantaneous views on the screen so that they replace each other very rapidly. This is what the cinematographe does. With photographs, each of which represents the regiment in a fixed attitude, it reconstitutes the mobility of the regiment marching. It is true that if we had to do with photographs alone, however much we might look at them, we should never see them animated; with immobility set beside immobility, even endlessly; we could never make movement. In order that the pictures may be animated, there must be movement somewhere. The movement does indeed exist here: it is in the apparatus.[35]

Bergson did not admit the possibility of reconstituting movement in duration with the isolated pictures of cinematography. In what is generally read as a reference to chronophotography, he notes that "with these successive states . . . you will never reconstitute movement . . . because every attempt to reconstitute change out of states implies the absurd proposition that movement is made of immobilities."[36] As phrased in *Matter and Memory*, "Images in fact will never be anything but things, and thought is movement."[37]

Bergson describes how it is the "invisible movement of the film" that strings together the successive attitudes of the actors as it unrolls, recovering actors' mobility.[38] The process of abstracting and generalizing movement is the same as the process that the human mind carries out in ordinary knowledge:

> The process then consists in extracting from all the movements peculiar to all the figures an impersonal movement abstract and simple, *movement in general*, so to speak: we put this into the apparatus, and we reconstitute the individuality of each particular movement by combining this nameless movement with the personal attitudes. Such is the contrivance of the cinematograph. And such is also that of our knowledge. Instead of attaching ourselves

to the inner becoming of things, we place ourselves outside them
in order to recompose their becoming artificially. We take
snapshots, as it were, of the passing reality, and, as these are
characteristic of the reality, we have only to string them on a
becoming, abstract, uniform and invisible, situated at the back of
the apparatus of knowledge, in order to imitate what there is that
is characteristic in this becoming itself. . . . Whether we would
think becoming, or express it, or even perceive it, we hardly do
anything else than set going a kind of cinematograph inside us. . . .
the *mechanism of our ordinary knowledge is of a cinemato-*
*graphical kind.*[39]

The cinematographical apparatus mechanized an already existing human function, a spectatorship that had been in part influenced by dance,
and it would also alter spectators and spectating in new ways. For some,
the cinema would re-create a vision that dancing and its spectators had
already experienced: a suspension of time or of the meaning of gestures
in time; a kind of "persistence of vision" before serial motion; a seriality
that also permitted the experience of the moment; a rhythm of images es-
caping the retina or allowing spectators to "see" what could not be seen;
the social and psychological formation of an "attraction" or conflictual
fear and pleasure before the image. For others, cinema—at least in its
current forms—could not capture or reproduce the mental functioning
and effects of time and space. It is an audience trained in, among other
things, dance spectatorship that would become the subjects of new mechanized forms of vision.

FROM DANCE SPECTATOR TO CINEMA SPECTATOR

If, at the beginning, cinema spectating followed dance spectating, it had
partly to do with a general audience moving from dance to newer forms,
from one "attraction" to another. But ultimately spectators chose film, or
film, becoming a resolutely mass art, chose larger and larger audiences.[40]
Debates about cinema's ability to serve as a true representation of the
movement of bodies, to represent a physiological reality, would be abandoned in a larger framework of discussions of film's realism and surrealism. Debates about whether cinematographic technique ultimately pro-

duced a fragmented image, or an image of fusion, would be relegated to film history and aesthetics, tangential to film's raison d'être. By 1924, film would be playing with fragmentation as a *ballet mécanique*.

Rather than a discontinuity, in the move over from the supposedly "natural" spectating of a dance audience to the "mechanized" viewing of cinema, a certain continuity is suggested in the philosophical and poetic texts taking stock of the transition. The "mechanized" viewing that cinema would realize has parallels, Bergson argues, in human cognition. The kind of spectating inspired by dancing like Loie Fuller's suggests a "subjective" vision that, Jonathan Crary has argued, developed early in the nineteenth century and was mechanized by cinematic and other technologies.

In *Suspensions of Perception*, Crary has expanded his account of the development of a new kind of spectator with new visual technologies across the nineteenth century, documenting changes in observation techniques and the emergence of subjective models of vision as well as of machinic objectivity of vision (that is at least suggested, he argues, in work like Muybridge's), in viewing practices that can be considered pre-cinematic.

> Even before the actual invention of cinema in the 1890s, though,
> it is clear that the conditions of human perception were being
> reassembled into new components. Vision, in a wide range of
> locations, is refigured as dynamic, temporal, and composite—the
> demise of the punctual or anchored classical observer begins in the
> early nineteenth century, increasingly displaced by the unstable
> attentive subject. . . . It is a subject competent to be both a con-
> sumer of and an agent in the synthesis of a proliferating diversity
> of "reality effects," and a subject who will become the object of
> all the proliferating demands and enticements of technological
> culture in the twentieth century.[41]

Although Crary argues that radical changes in spectatorship were implemented by visual technologies, he also argues for the importance of user practices in bringing about such changes, in a two-way exchange between viewers and machines. His account stresses the overlapping of innovations in visual modernism and the empirical study of cognition, tracing first the emergence of models of subjective vision in different disciplines (1810–40) and then the rise of "machinic objectivity."[42] In the wake of Helmholtz,

Crary writes, vision by the 1860s was no longer thought of as certain or "objective": "Not only did his exhaustive inventory of the physiology of vision and hearing reveal the undependability of the senses, but it set the ground for the gradual rationalization and instrumentalization of the senses through the transfer of their functions to machinic and technical prostheses of various kinds."[43] The Helmholtzian "relocation of perception (as well as processes and functions previously assumed to be 'mental') in the thickness of the body was a precondition for the instrumentalizing of human vision as a component of machinic arrangements."[44] "Vision, conceived in this way, became compatible with many other processes of modernization."[45] Thus, Crary argues, in the second half of the nineteenth century, any significant qualitative difference between life and technics begins to evaporate.

Crary then explores the development of a machinic objectivity of vision, using photography as an example, and the industrialization of visual consumption in pre-cinematic practices such as the Kaiserpanorama. Definitions of modernity's "camera-reality" by Kracauer and Benjamin or Roland Barthes's concept of photography's "reality-effect" among others serves to illustrate how photography "at least suggested" an automatic machinic perception.[46]

In Crary's account, models of subjective vision reemerge from this mechanized "objectivity" in the late nineteenth century in both art and science. Artistic and scientific images create a new spectator with a new kind of attention: "By the late 1890s the very possibility and value of a sustained looking, of a 'fixed' vision, became inseparable from the effects of dynamic, kinetic, and rhythmic modalities of experience and form."[47]

Rather than simply imitating machines' functioning, as with the motor or mechanics, dance interacted with the elaboration of the motion picture camera, in choreographies anticipating cinema as Loie Fuller's did, and with the presence of dancers before the cameras of Melies or Griffith.[48]

Yet if dance—willingly or not—has come to depend on cinematic technology, it is not only because it makes pictures of dancing that last longer than the dancing itself. Rather it is because the cinematograph made machinic a vision that dancing among other performances was inspiring, or anticipating, before its advent. Dancing fits into a frame of Marey's project for recording machines tracing the body's physiology and the modernity Walter Benjamin described as constituted by photography, allowing the representation of the "unconscious" on the margins of sight. At the same time, even as manifest spectacle, dancing challenges vision, resisting an industrialized machinic "objectivity" and shaping a spectator who would both seek out and hesitate before cinema's invention.

If, for some, dance on film represented what Benjamin describes as a "loss of aura," it also may have made possible the very art-for-art's sake symbolism or naturalism that modern dance—following the lead of Fuller's one-time pupil, and rival, Isadora Duncan—tended toward. One explanation for the justification of a branch of modern dance through a rhetoric of naturalism might be dance's attempt, after its early days at the heart of cinema, to distinguish itself from the mass art that cinema was becoming. In the same way, Benjamin argues, the rise of photography permitted painting to move toward abstraction.

Although an important branch of modern dance would move away from cinema, companies such as the Ballets Suédois in the 1920s would play with, and eventually cede the stage to, the cinematic in their live performances. Dancing continues to shape a certain cinematography—for example, in the geometric choreographic formations of the large-scale musicals—that will ultimately marginalize and minimize the art.

At the same time, early cinema preserved a certain naturalness in certain kinds of dancing even as the mechanics of the apparatus reproduced them artificially. Yet this naturalness, for example, of the African dances recorded by Lumière operators in open-air pavilions at the Expositions Universelles, can be understood as a construct of and for the camera, an artificial performance of "authentic" dance culture within a context of display and entertainment.

In Cocteau's text on the turn-of-the-century Exposition Universelle that opens this chapter, the rhythms and forms of African and modern art will sweep away the femininity of the Fulleresque image, but the filmmaker will restore Woman's objectified role as a work of art. In spite of mainstream film's tendency to fetishize the female figure, some collaborations between cinema and dance would create a dancing subject rather than object, a movement-image rather than a simple image of movement. Innovators continued to make dances for the camera or use the camera as a kind of dancing machine. But this precise and punctual coincidence, of two forms taking shape together, cinema with modern dance, has been erased or buried under a retrospective rhetoric about dance's live presence and cinema's technological apparatus. Although much modern dance moved on from its founding encounter with cinema to reject it, as some of its inventors did, as not true to movement, some dancers continued to negotiate with cinema in its first decades as a new form for the machine age. Even those dancers who would shy away from the camera, such as Isadora Duncan, found themselves described in its image.

### "LOIE FULLER" DANCES FOR LUMIÈRE; ANABELLA DANCES FOR EDISON

Obscure, hidden beneath the masses of fabric swathing her; obscure in that we cannot see her and she (it?) cannot see us; obscure in her (its?) unconcern in returning the camera's gaze, spinning—seemingly—not for the camera's or our eyes. Moving, clearly, with knowledge that we are there, that someone is watching, yet at the same time moving out of our way, out of our eye.

*La Danse serpentine* is the invention of Loie Fuller, whose coquettish skirt-dances, modeled on the music hall dancing of her time, became performances of an obscure and obscured body, a heavy body not aiming to seduce its public, a hidden body giving itself over to the representation of something beyond it; a strong body creating structure within her massive veils. The performance of pure motion and the movement of silk, wings, panels, petals, turbulences—in Mallarmé's words—around and across her body.

In contrast, Anabella—another of Fuller's many imitators—dances for Edison in a sprightly coquettish way. Waving her wings on sticks, which she manipulates like a drum majorette, she dances for the camera and the audience it guarantees. She performs not turbulences or forces of nature but simply "Anabella"—herself—and gives her name to the film. But she is one of the many nameless, anonymous, myriad imitators of a popular style of stage dancing.

The difference between the two imitators—"Loie Fuller" dancing for Lumière and Anabella dancing for Edison—could be described as a difference of focus. Like many of the stage dancers of the nineteenth century,

Anabella dances for someone—in this case her cameraman—as if he were her patron. She dances for her immediate audience. "Loie" dances for an eye that the camera only points toward but that film will eventually make possible: the global market for technobodies, the publics created across the century. Fuller herself, conceiving her dance for the camera, is aware that this eye is greater than dancer, audience, or cameraman: it is historic; it is enormous; it extends in space and time.

Loie Fuller's techno-dancing takes cinema into its future.

# 3.

# Abstraction

One rainy morning I took a two-horse, open carriage, as
there were no autos in those days, and went to the train to
meet Ernst Haeckel. The great man descended from the train.

ISADORA DUNCAN, *My Life*

If you don't live contemporarily, you are a nuisance. . . . If a
man goes along the street with horse and carriage in New
York in the snow, that man is a nuisance; and he knows it, so
now he doesn't do it. He would not be living, or acting,
contemporarily; he would only be in the way, a drag.

GERTRUDE STEIN, *How Writing Is Written*

The idea that a factory, or at least the more highly organized
and organizable parts of a factory can not be "harmonized"
is no sillier in 1927, than the idea that a horseless carriage
could move, was in, let us say, 1880.

EZRA POUND, *Machine Art*

Whereas Loie Fuller can be seen as a fin-de-siècle champion of the new
technology of cinema, Isadora Duncan can be imagined as the poster
child for a more complex or contradictory response to the age of machines in dance that followed fast on the heels of the turn of the century.
Duncan would describe her work as "symbolist" and ally herself alternately with an American spirit and a European aesthetic, with European
science and American industry, with anti-American radicalism and American feminism. In this chapter, rather than attempting to reconcile the

contradictions she represented, I consider the different modernisms that mobilized around her, in writing and performance, in London and Paris, in the first decades of the twentieth century. She becomes an emblem of Victorianism passing into modernism via a particular conception of machines, and the absorption of machines into an aesthetic that declared itself, sometimes, resolutely antimodern.

This chapter takes Isadora as starting point for looking at artists working in many media who thought about "movement" and the representation of "things" in movement in the art of the machine age—about literality and symbolism, objects and energy, photographic cliché and cinematic rhythm. It also traces, through the terms of writers' responses to and uses of dance, the development of the concepts, or practices, of abstraction, both graphic and choreographic. The concepts of "abstraction" and "concretion" refer not simply to a modernist aesthetic of abstraction, often defined as antinarrative or antifigural. Here, under the banner of "abstraction," are practices often ironically announcing themselves against such formal abstraction: sometimes deriving from a practice of image making that appears to reduce or simplify form while encoding more information; sometimes deriving from what is called "a method of science"; sometimes deriving from "cinematic" condensation; or sometimes from stereotyped "Asian" or "African," ancient or "primitive" arts.

Modernist abstraction, if indeed it is partly rooted in Marey's photographic-physiological representations of movement, inherits a complex view of bodies. Across the media of dance, literature, and the theater arts to be examined here, this complexity is often expressed in beguilingly simple forms. But complexity is inherent in a view of human forces parallel to natural ones, dancers saying they move like motors, poets saying their condensed forms reproduce the dancing or cinematic image, "scientific," mathematic, or ancient codes.

Contemporary with the first decades of cinema, modernism's fascination with machines extended beyond form to what mechanization paradoxically made possible: a cinematic sequencing that for some recalled the ancient frieze as much as it did nineteenth-century photography; symbolist and expressionist theater in the face of an industrial daily nightmare; new forms of writing marked by the energy of technological modernity while also shunning it; naturalist plastic and performing arts made possible by technologies of vision and lighting.

What happens to the image of dance within this conflictual movement of modernism both toward machinic and ancient, mythic, or natural forms? In the shift from print culture to a twentieth century dominated by visual technologies, dance's ephemerality becomes both mechanized and mythologized.

## ISADORA'S MOTOR POWER

More than a simple counterpoint to the thinking of the machine age, Isadora's dance embodies a nineteenth-century view of the machine, the human motor, and allies itself with a nineteenth-century romantic science that continues to play a role in the twentieth-century conception of a "dancing machine."

The rumor runs that in the debate about fragmentation and fusion in the cinematic image, Isadora Duncan took the side of Marey, Bergson, and others, distrusting cinema because of its uneven acceleration, its inability to capture and reproduce the essence of movement.[1] In the one short film known to exist of Isadora, she dances informally outside at a gathering in Rodin's garden. Lost in the swaying movements of her upper body toward the earth and sky, she is either unaware of or shying away from the camera. Lasting barely half a minute, the image has the quality of a stolen glance. In life, Isadora was a woman constantly in motion not only onstage but across continents; she was described by those who knew her as always late but never rushed.[2] In her dance, Isadora expressed a radically new fluidity, a weightedness imagined as ancient, and the hovering of the *perpetuum mobile*.

Isadora cast herself as both stirring a pre-technological, slowed-down past and speeding toward a revolutionary future. Immediately in the wake of Loie Fuller's French conquest, Isadora danced against modernity and machines, reawakening, as she saw it, the ancient, sleeping spirit of dance. Her life and her choreography announced her emancipation from Victorian restraints: Isadora danced bare-legged and barefoot, campaigned for dress reform, wore transparent Greek-inspired tunics onstage and, when she could afford to, the latest Poiret fashions offstage.

At the turn of the century, her dancing inspired, and responded to, poetry and choreography with a Greek revival tone. Yet Isadora described her dancing as an output of the "human motor" harnessing what Helmholtz and other nineteenth-century scientists had described as a universal energy. Between a nostalgia for romantic science and her published and choreographed manifestos for the liberated, educated female dancer of the future, Isadora's position illustrates a tension between art and technology in the early twentieth century. She performed the Whitmanesque liberation of the American spirit and the modernity of a lifestyle of sports cars and sexual freedom. In a faster and faster moving world, Isadora's dances were the more remarkable in that the weightedness of her arms and legs often expressed a lightness in movement. Compared with Loie Fuller's techno-body on the stage and in the cinema of her time, Isadora's simple choreographies, revealing her body against her famous blue curtains, passed like the dream of another time.

The publisher of Isadora's memoirs hails her as "the woman who founded modern dance," and this attribution of the place of honor to Duncan rather than to her predecessor Fuller—both expatriates who were equally successful during their nearly contemporary lifetimes—reveals Isadora's more powerful influence on the evolution of modern dance.[3] But the readability of Isadora's memoirs—and the fact that they were guaranteed a readership fascinated by her various successes and scandals—must also be considered as a factor in her posthumous success: Isadora's account of her life and work is far more persuasive than is Fuller's; her description of her technique more poetic and her motivations more compelling.

Because of Isadora's dancing, teaching, and writing, modern dance has been conceived as American and natural. Yet in Duncan's often contradictory accounts of her mélange of sources, American and ancient overlap, European and African collide, and Duncan herself would describe her work as symbolist, taking shelter in European symbolist circles.

Against a continuing trend of mechanical dancing and acting styles, the countercurrent of Isadora's work reveals a subterranean influence in modernism of this alternate form of dancing. In a kind of allegory, this chapter follows the sort of dancer epitomized by Isadora Duncan, who disappears while literary modernism—here considered in the work of two writers, Ezra Pound and Gertrude Stein—moves toward a kind of abstraction; this chapter also suggests how a different kind of dancer, machinic or mystical-mechanical, develops. Even as the figure of Duncan herself disappears, the energy of her dancing is converted into different modernist media and ultimately leads to dance's reconfigured affiliation with the choreography of industry, motors, machine ballets, and cinema.

Isadora's simple lines claimed a double heritage in the British Museum's Elgin marbles and in American nature, from childhood days "by the Pacific Ocean, by the waving pine-forests of the Sierra Nevada," where she "discovered the art that has been lost for two thousand years."[4] But her childhood in the San Francisco Bay Area, where she was born in 1877,[5] was also full of economic hardships that she claimed would later help her "face ferocious managers." Isadora was often sent to charm the butcher when there was no money, and her autobiography, *My Life*, reveals a constant negotiation between the ideals of art and feminism and economic and social realities: "On the one hand I was feeding my mind with sentimental novels, while on the other I had a very practical example of marriage before my eyes."[6] In Isadora's retelling, the Duncans' poverty only sharpened their dedication to their ideals. The family moved East—first to Chicago in 1899, and then to New York, where Isadora got a job dancing in theatrical impresario Augustin Daly's production of *A Midsummer Night's Dream*. *My Life* identifies Isadora's dissatisfaction with her work and with American ignorance of her aesthetic ideals as the reason for their move to London in 1900. Although the family stayed there only a year, for Isadora it was a first step toward a lifelong emigration to Europe.

In London, the Duncans were hard up; yet in the midst of this poverty and deprivation, writes Isadora,

> I spent long days and nights in the studio seeking that dance which might be the divine expression of the human spirit through the medium of the body's movement. For hours I would stand quite still, my hands folded between my breasts, covering the solar plexus. . . . I was seeking and finally discovered the central spring of all movement, the crater of motor power, the unity from which all diversities of movement are born. . . . it was from this discovery that was born the theory on which I founded my school.[7]

Isadora's rhetoric links the nineteenth-century science of the human motor to high modernism. Inspired both by the concept of a universal energy, illustrated by waves, and the serial motion photographed by Marey, which Isadora found in Phydias's friezes, it was a dancing admittedly ancient yet deceptively modern, a dancing that abandoned stillness and pose for "diversities of movement."

In London, Isadora was admired by artists and writers; she was promoted by Charles Hallé and danced at his New Gallery as well as in various salons; she discovered an idol, Ellen Terry, and became a member of the bohemia that brought together artists, writers, and upper-class patrons. Like Loie Fuller, Isadora thus met not only the artists but also some of the philosophers and scientists of her time; her autobiography mentions reading and meeting Ernst Haeckel in Berlin: "I wrote him a letter expressing my gratitude for the impression his books had made on me." Even more surprising was their exchange at a performance in Berlin: "I made a speech praising the greatness of Haeckel, then danced in his honor. Haeckel commented on my dance, likening it to all the universal truths of nature, and said that it was an expression of monism, in that it came from one source and had one direction of evolution."[8] It is likely that Isadora was moved by Haeckel's *Kunstformen der Natur* (1899–1904), with its "cult ideals of the True, the Good, and the Beautiful," corresponding to his "monistic religion."[9]

Isadora lavishly praises the teaching of other "dance masters": "I applied myself to the task of reading everything that had ever been written on the Art of Dancing, from the earliest Egyptians to the present day, and I made special notes of all I read in a copy-book; but when I had finished this colossal experiment, I realised that the only dance masters I could have were Jean-Jacques Rousseau ('Emile'), Walt Whitman, and Nietzsche."[10]

Later in her autobiography, she re-forms the triumvirate: "afterwards, coming to Europe, I had three great masters, the three great precursors of the dance of our century—Beethoven, Nietzsche, and Wagner. Beethoven created the dance in mighty rhythm. Wagner in sculptural form, Nietzsche in spirit."[11] On the same page, she revises her inspirations to include the American Wild West: "It has often made me smile—but somewhat ironically—when people have called my dancing Greek, for I myself count its origin in the stories which my Irish grandmother told us of crossing the plains with grandfather in '49 in a covered wagon." These include stories of children born in covered wagons during wars with Indians and fathers greeting their newborns with smoking guns, part of what she refers to as "taming the wild men, the Indians."[12] Her dancing was born of this grandmother's music and the American melting pot: "into these Irish jigs had crept some of the heroic spirit of the pioneer and the battle with the Redskins—probably some of the gestures of the Redskins themselves, and again, a bit of Yankee Doodle."[13] But black America is significantly missing in this mélange, and in rejecting what she calls jazz's "sensual lilt" in favor of a Helmholtz- or even Haeckel-inspired "striving upward through labour to harmonious life,"[14] Isadora locates herself within a conservative European worldview. In London, she would admire the lifelong servitude, the "extraordinary demeanour of good English servants" who inherit and pass on domestic positions, as creating "the calm and security of existence" threatened in America by servants' "wishing to rise in the social scale."[15] This critique of modernity, social mobility, and enlightenment in the face of race and class—written after Isadora had founded a school in postrevolutionary Russia—figures only as an aside in her autobiography, yet it echoes in significant ways in the modernism created by fellow expatriate artists in Europe.

John Dos Passos, in his portrait of her, "Art and Isadora," describes Isadora's life as Art, and her death—as well as her children's—as the fault of gears.[16] In 1927, like her children before her, Isadora died in a car accident. In Dos Passos's retelling, Isadora was killed by machines not only mechanically but metaphorically.[17]

In Dos Passos's novelization of her story, Isadora's life was Art. She was "afraid of nothing; she was a great dancer," and "the nineties London liked her gall." Living in the world of automobiles did not suit the Duncan style; they had gone to Europe "to escape the materialism of their native America." After an early triumph in Munich, Isadora's carriage was unhorsed and drawn by students. "The Duncans were vegetarians, suspicious of vulgarity and men and materialism. Raymond made them all sandals."[18]

The Duncans' bohemian fashion, and Isadora's stage art, reflected as well as inspired current trends in the European avant-garde movements at their inception. In both the choreography and the poetry of the early years of the twentieth century, sandaled dancers figure a new classicism developed in Victorian art, merging into modernism.

The modernist mandate for newness and invention was paired, in Ezra Pound's phrase, with the artists' mission to "bring back the gods." In this current of modernism, running through the plastic arts and poetry, the-ater and dance, dancers came to figure nontechnologized bodies and to represent the mythic dimension of a preindustrial age. In concert dance, this dimension was apparent not only in Isadora's dancing but in the in-fluence it had on the style, if not the movement, of choreographies for Di-aghilev's Ballets Russes de Monte Carlo, such as Nijinsky's *L'Après-midi d'un faune* or Michel Fokine's *Daphnis et Chloé* (London premiere, 1914), both created in 1912.[19]

Although rejecting the world of the automobile and announcing an antitechnological position, the art of dance—both Isadora's and the Russ-ian Ballet's—was paired with modernist fascination with technology. The European avant-garde's romance with technology depended on myths, on the ancient rather than the Victorian, and like Isadora it imagined danc-ing capable of performing ancientness and modernity simultaneously.

## MECHANICAL GROTESQUES

Announcing Isadora's ancient dancing, and prefiguring its death, poetry both a few years before her arrival in London and in the wake of her de-parture represented the dancer in a mechanized, technologized city. The poetry of high modernism in which ancient dancers appear and disappear, visible, for example, in Pound's volume *Lustra* (1914), published during his residence in London, can be read as a continuation of nineteenth-century British Greek revival typified by Walter Pater and his one-time pupil Oscar Wilde. Bigger than life, and older than time, the images of an-cient dancers appear like the Homeric dawn in poetry in England before and after the turn of the century.

Wilde's most famous dancer was Salomé, the central figure in the play named for her that Wilde wrote in French, in France, under the influence of the many Salomés in the literature and painting of Romantisme, Par-nasse, and Symbolisme. Wilde never saw the play staged in his lifetime, but the role was performed in London by Maud Allen, who had danced with Loie Fuller's troupe.[20] Wilde identified intensely with his Salomé, yet the text of the play includes no stage directions for the dance, and Wilde's intentions for the choreography of the "Dance of the Seven Veils" have remained a mystery.

The play itself represented for Wilde the essence and apex of his art. Both in form and content, *Salomé* speaks of things close to Wilde's heart: "If I were asked of myself as a dramatist, I would say that my unique position was that I had taken the drama, the most objective form known to art, and made it as personal a mode of expression as the Lyric or the Sonnet, while enriching the characterization of the stage, and enlarging— at any rate in the case of *Salomé*—its artistic horizon."[21] In Wilde's work the dancer stands for art and artifice, sexual freedom, resembling Wilde's version of the Baudelairean dandy. Like the dandy, she is the epitome of "being": the central but threatened figure at the heart of Wilde's conception of theater and its potential to stage sexual identity in what Ed Cohen has called the "somatically defined individualism" of Victorian Britain.[22] In Wilde's eyes she represented, with her dance—both the heart of *Salomé* and a black hole in the text—a theater revolution.

Before *Salomé*, "The Harlot's House" was the product of Wilde's life in Paris, where he moved in 1883, on his return from a successful American tour. An otherwise inconsequential poem, "The Harlot's House" draws an ancient sandaled figure, prefiguring Isadora, who moves against contemporary dancing automata:

*The Harlot's House*

We caught the tread of dancing feet,
We loitered down the moonlit street,
And stopped beneath the harlot's house.

Inside, above the din and fray,
We heard the loud musicians play
The "Treues Liebes Herz" of Strauss.

Like strange mechanical grotesques,
Making fantastic arabesques,
The shadows raced across the blind.

We watched the ghostly dancers spin
To sound of horn and violin,

Like black leaves wheeling in the wind.

Like wire-pulled automatons,
Slim silhouetted skeletons
Went sidling through the slow quadrille,

Then took each other by the hand,
And Danced a stately saraband;
Their laughter echoed thin and shrill.

Sometimes a clockwork puppet pressed
A phantom lover to her breast,
Sometimes they seemed to try to sing.

Sometimes a horrible marionette
Came out, and smoked its cigarette
Upon the steps like a live thing.

Then, turning to my love, I said,
"The dead are dancing with the dead,
The dust is whirling with the dust."

But she—she heard the violin,
And left my side, and entered in:
Love passed into the house of lust.

Then suddenly the tune went false,
The dancers wearied of the waltz,
The shadows ceased to wheel and whirl.

And down the long and silent street,
The dawn, with silver-sandalled feet,
Crept like a frightened girl.[23]

The clockwork rhythm and rhyme of this poem contrast the Baudelairean *flaneurs* who "loitered down the moonlit street" with the "din and fray" of a cheap waltz and the expressionistic "grotesques" racing across the blinds of a brothel. The figures have a ghostly beauty: they spin "like black leaves wheeling in the wind"; they are skeletons in a funereal quadrille; they are eerie gypsies in a "stately saraband." They become puppets miming a delightful, horrible love tale.

The appearance of one of these marionettes on the steps outside destroys the illusion: from the realm of the dead, one dancer comes out and smokes like a "live thing." The poet narrates to his companion: "The dead are dancing with the dead, / The dust is whirling with the dust." But already under the spell, the girl leaves him for the hellish, enchanted "house of lust." Her departure and his disillusion end the dance; the tune goes false, the dancers acknowledge their human fatigue.

Out in the street, the dandy-poet conjures an image of true beauty: the image of the ancient dancer, Dawn, announced against the deathly, mechanical dancing of the brothel puppets. The dandy and the products of his imagination triumph over the seedy world of the dancers in "The Harlot's House," making clear the poet's preference for the ancient image of classical beauty, the "silver-sandalled" dancer over the fascinating but hawkish figures of modern times. This is the Wilde who in the next few years would make his bride into this Greek ideal, designing her gowns and using her as an image to promote notions of classical beauty.

It is easy to associate Isadora with the sandaled dancer and difficult to align her work with an essay published by her partner Edward Gordon Craig, in 1907, calling for a simultaneously ancient and hypermodern mechanization of performance. In "The Actor and the Uber (or Super-) Marionette," Craig joins the ranks of those who complain about actors' attempts to mime or copy a banal, material reality. While praising the actor's potential power, and some real actors' skill, Craig maintains that acting cannot be an art until it ceases to be a chaotic, accidental, improvisational, or mimetic exercise. Craig insists that the bad actor, like a camera, only shows "clichés" of modern life, "slavishly, photographically" copying a "life" that is uninteresting compared with the calm rhythms and powerful beauty of "Death" as it can be rendered in other theater traditions.[24] Emotion must be banished, along with stage sets, fixed gesture, and the "mechanical perfection" of mimetic realism, in order to achieve this new sacred art, celebration of the ancient joy of ceremony, hymn to Life, divine invocation of Death.[25]

Wishing for the stage to become again the terrain of ancient rites, where a nonhuman idol reigns, Craig points out that Asian and African theatrical traditions are founded on the puppet or marionette as a descendent of the idol Buddha or other symbolic figure, housed in theatrical architecture and revered in ritual. His closing image, a fable recounting how bad theater began, imagines two women, jealous of the enlightened, ecstatic worshippers before such a statue-god, planning their own parodic imitation of the scene. True worship, Craig argues, has disappeared from the theater; the two women have taken over. With Eleonora Duse, Craig calls for the death of acting (or even actors) as he knows them and a reconstitution of the theater through revolutionary new forms that are simultaneously ancient and global.

Craig proposes a theater he defines in Western terms through a comparison to Flaubert's "style indirect libre"—the "méthode inflexible" both of narrative and of physical science. In fact, Craig's vision suggests ultimately a further mechanization of acting as called for by such a theater, but one that would come under the guise of the sacred and not the psychological. Its effects can be seen in the dance writing, by Marinetti and Yeats among others, that he published and influenced.

THE DANCER DISAPPEARS IN A STATION OF THE METRO

Although she is not dancing in "The Harlot's House," dawn is dressed as an ancient dancer and moves with the emotion that Isadora's dancing will champion against the mechanical or "automated" music-hall dancing of her generation. Pound's early London poems repeat this image, explicitly making dawn a dancer in "The Garret," in which "Dawn enters with little feet / Like a gilded Pavlova." Across three poems not usually considered a series, a dancer disappears in Pound's verse, and the dance is refigured as a poetic operation, as poetic modernism itself. In Pound's 1914 volume *Lustra*, "Dance Figure" evokes the omnipresent sandaled dancer:

Dark eyed,
O woman of my dreams,
Ivory sandalled,
There is none like thee among the dancers,
None with swift feet.[26]

As with many of Pound's lyric poems of this period, "Dance Figure" reads like a Homeric translation with its adjectives ("dark eyed," "ivory sandalled") and antiquated language ("none like thee"). In *Lustra*, a certain kind of dancing—not ballet but the kind of dancing Isadora had performed in London living rooms—serves Pound with its ability to recreate ancient forms, to "bring back the gods."

But if ancient dancers populate Pound's early poems, dead dancers—or more precisely dancers who have disappeared—offer his poetics something more interesting and ultimately more modern. Pound's *Lustra* contains a short lyric homage to a dead dancer, "Ione, dead the long year":

Ione, dead the long year

Empty are the ways
   Empty are the ways of this land
   And the flowers
         Bend over with heavy heads.
They bend in vain.
Empty are the ways of this land
       Where Ione
Walked once, and now does not walk
But seems like a person just gone.[27]

Although nothing here tells us that Ione was a dancer, this poem speaks in memoriam of a woman who also appeared in *Lustra*'s "Dance Figure" in an earlier unpublished version,[28] and who reappears seven years later in Canto VII (1921): "Knocking at empty rooms, seeking for buried beauty / . . . The wilted flowers / Brushed out a seven year since, of no effect / . . . Ione, dead the long year."[29] This dancer's—and her poem's—reappearance in the project of the *Cantos* marks a continuity in Pound's transition from lyric to epic via the concept of the ideogram; it is her disappearance, and her reappearance as a citation of Pound's own 1914 verse—that is, a repeated disappearance—that figures a modernist turn, linking dancing to the poetic image that Pound will call ideogrammic or imagine as a vortex of energy between 1912 and 1914. In the space emptied by the dancer's disappearance, modernist poetry is reconceived as technological energy.

The emphasis on apparition in "Ione" recalls that of the ideogrammic "In a Station of the Metro," the cornerstone of Pound's Imagism. "In a Station of the Metro" marked a revolution in poetry described—and in some ways made possible—by the experience of mass transit. The influence of Pound's edition of Fenellosa's work *On the Chinese Written Character* and Chinese and Japanese verse forms is well known. But in the writing of this poem, beyond the poetics of the pictogram, the condensation and displacement that took Pound a year to complete intensely re-create the "metro experience" that gave birth to its overlapping images:

The apparition      of these faces in the crowd;
        Petals on a wet      black bough.[30]

Pound's Imagism excised and condensed into the spare framework of the two-line poem an implicit rather than explicit metaphor, created by the juxtaposition of images whose relationship is not explained. The story of this poem is, of course, not only the overlay of images, the faces of the crowd and the petals in rain; the story is Pound's poetic experience and the transformation of that experience, via Imagist theory, into innovative English verse with ancient Asian precedents. Perhaps the two lines of "In a Station of the Metro" would not be so interesting if we did not read into the blank spaces Pound's narrative about the epiphany at La Concorde, about the year of scribbling and the triumph of cutting it all away to the core of the matter, and the rigorous Imagist tenets set down in 1913.[31]

The Imagist guidelines for poetry are included with the vorticist material in Pound's appreciation of the sculptor Gaudier-Brzeska but date from the movement begun several years before: "The tenets of the Imagiste faith were published in March, 1913, as follows:—I. Direct treatment of the 'thing,' whether subjective or objective. II. To use absolutely no word that does not contribute to the presentation. III. As regarding rhythm: to compose in sequence of the musical phrase, not in the sequence of the metronome."[32]

The metro poem's play with visibility and invisibility is its way of treating the "thing"—in this case an experience, an emotion, and a poetics—both musically and "directly." Rhythm and meaning are created not only by words but by the spaces on the page and by their silences. The direct presentation of images in nouns and adjectives is made abstract by the lack of connectors. What is missing here are the verbs that would tell us what this apparition, these faces or petals are *doing*—in relation to each other, or by themselves. And this is precisely the point of the new poetics: they are not *doing* anything, moving in a ghostly way through the poet's memory, blurring, soaking through onto the page. This implied movement of images, re-created by the reader who connects them, relies on methods of direct presentation and of abstraction recalling, if not borrowing from, dancing.

"Ione, dead the long year" uses many of the same strategies as the haiku-like "In a Station of the Metro," although its images are less condensed and more grammatically connected. Although "Ione" is longer and more regularly versed, its shape is not unlike that of the shorter poem. In both, the typography sets spaces between the units of meaning: full phrases in "Ione" and noun clusters in "Metro." The spaces, expressive of poetic activity in "In a Station of the Metro," are expressive of poetic emotion in "Ione"; the poem itself is largely empty of visual imagery, and in its structure and presentation it echoes the absence of the woman herself. Certainly the main image it is missing is Ione, who is not depicted, not described. Invisible, Ione's apparition moves through the poem and out of it, and her disappearance (did she ever actually *appear*?) ends it.

In his commentary on the *Cantos*, Carroll Terrell notes that there was, "among the *New Freewoman* group, a beautiful nineteen-year-old French-born dancer, Jeanne Heyse, who used the alias Joan Hayes and the professional name Ione de Forest. She committed suicide at her home in Chelsea, London, on August 2, 1912, which can be fairly described as a "long year" before the first publication of Pound's obituary poem" in *Poetry and Drama*, in December 1914.[33] It is curious that the woman in "Ione, dead the long year" is not recognizably a dancer and that her identifying name dropped out of the final draft of "Dance Figure." Without Terrell's excavation, we might not know that the woman evoked had been a dancer, or that she was the same woman who inspired "There is none like thee among the dancers / None with swift feet," and possibly other poems in *Lustra*. A similar female presence permeates many of its poems—"April," "Gentildonna," "The Spring" ("She, who moved here amid the cyclamen / Moves only now a clinging tenuous ghost"). These spirits stand in contrast to *Lustra*'s images of real women—the women in the tea shops, restaurants, and streets of contemporary London—and the dance figure is distinct from the contemporary Ballets Russes unappreciated by the anemic, bourgeois "little Millwins." In "Les Millwin," the

Russian ballet drives the crowd of students from Slade, "the turbulent and undisciplined host of art students," to exult at its splendors.

These Ionesque presences, removed from contemporary life, are nymphs from Pound's private mythology. Ione is not spoken of as a dancer who lived and danced; she "seems like a person just gone." In many ways "Ione, dead the long year" is a conventional poetic lament, heavy with repetitions, with three refrains of "empty are the ways," which slows the verse to a halting progression. Although "Ione, dead the long year" moves through verbs, the only active ones are markedly inactive: past tense ("walked once"), negative ("now does not walk"), or uncertain ("seems"). Where the missing verbs told the whole story of the poetics of "In a Station of the Metro," the verbs in "Ione" tell the story a bit more explicitly. The subject of the poem is dead, invisible, ungraspable. The verse does not describe how she does what she does; rather it shows what she does *not* do and tries to repeat that non-action in its language—the halting, repetitive phrases, its lack of explanatory detail, the depiction of an empty space and futile floral imagery.

In this way, the poem's presentation of the persona of Ione works not unlike movement or music. Pound may have been following not only the sequence of the musical phrase but music's "condition" in the measured silences matched with the dancer's visual quality of immanence and self-consumption. "Ione, dead the long year" uses the rhythm and meaning of the silences created by the typographic design in presenting the image of a woman who moves now only through the poet's memory. The death of Ione can be read as an image for the disappearance of the figure of the dancer from poetry—and her replacement by a force field of energized absence. If dancing embodies ancient poetics for Pound, its potential for what Pound conceives of as abstraction "in the concrete" is made possible by the idea of dance rather than the presence of dancers. The concept of dance as motion, speed, the play of the image, figures more significantly in Pound's poetics of the Imagist and vorticist years, in what he would call "the dance of the intellect among words."

DANCE OF THE INTELLECT

Music and poetry were, for Pound, not only related; they had been, until the end of troubadour poetry, inseparable. In *Antheil*, Pound points out that "music and poetry had been in alliance in the twelfth century, that the divorce of the two arts had been to the advantage of neither, and that melodic invention declined simultaneously and progressively with their divergence."[34] Even postdivorce, words and music are submitted to the same editorial criteria: "There is musical rhetoric,"[35] Pound writes; "There is in music a fault corresponding to the fault of verbosity in writing."[36] In this way a chord is not unlike a vortex in its precision: "Let us say that chords are like colour. They are a complex of sound occurring at a given instant of time, a minimum audible of time."[37] This is not far from the notion of presenting "an emotional or intellectual complex in an instant of time," or the "radiant node or cluster" of vorticism.

For Pound, music and movement are crucial to the poetic image, and because performed poetry is impossible, these elements must be embodied within the language of the poetic image. In *ABC of Reading*, Pound outlines three ways "to charge language with meaning to the utmost possible degree": "I. throwing the object (fixed or moving) on to the visual imagination. II. inducing emotional correlations by the sound and rhythm of the speech. III. inducing both of the effects by stimulating the associations (intellectual or emotional) that have remained in the receiver's consciousness in relation to the actual words or word groups employed."[38] The strategies of phanopoeia and melopoeia, informed as they are by music and movement, are subsumed by logopoeia, what Pound called "the dance of the intellect among words." These techniques restate as a manifesto Pound's observation that "Music rots when it gets *too far* from the dance. Poetry atrophies when it gets too far from music."[39]

What does Pound mean by the "dance of the intellect among words"? How are the musical and visual components of dance integrated into the medium of words in Pound's poetry of this period, and how do they affect the tension between abstraction and representation?[40] Pound's modernist poetics reconcile the musical, the visual, and movement in vorticism; he used abstraction not only as a technique of "arrangement" but as a power of language itself. Dancing describes the work of poetic language, coding into the condensed form of the moving image the larger experience, idea, story; the way that intellection comes into words—the essentially rhythmic, musical expression that is modernist language. The dancer's fusion of rhythm and visual images, and the way dance engenders meaning in the presentation of an image, makes it a model for modernism's poetic and visual codes, the tension between representation and abstraction.

Modernist poetry stages the disappearance of a certain kind of dancer in a technologized world even before the automobile kills Isadora.

## MODERN DANCE AND MODERNIST ABSTRACTION

Exploring Pound's use of music in his Imagist and vorticist poetics of 1913–14 ("to compose in sequence of the musical phrase, not in the sequence of the metronome"),[41] David Antin finds a contradiction between the impetus for abstraction and for "direct" representation: "Anyone who in 1914 could combine the notion that 'all arts aspire to the condition of music' with the first proposition of Imagism, which advocated 'direct treatment of the "thing" would have to be either a fool or a provincial. The first notion promotes total abstraction. Music envy is the mark of the abstractionist. . . . The Imagist proposition advocates total commitment to representation." When Pound says "music is an arrangement of tones, painting is an arrangement of colors and forms in three dimensional space, and poetry is an arrangement of images," Antin notes, "Pound has not placed the action of poetry on a structurally equivalent plane with music. Tones in music are distinctive and totally nonreferential—we would now probably say phonemic—while images are nothing if they are not referential or representational."[42]

Antin's substitution of Pater's much-quoted fin-de-siècle remark about the "condition of music" for Pound's more specific "to compose in sequence of the musical phrase" should not pass unnoticed. Antin speaks of the "music envy" of the writers influenced by Pater as a naïveté about what musical form could offer to literature—the reduction of musical form to "an arrangement of tones." Pound's involvement with music may be seen to have taken two paths: a Paterian interest in the abstract "condition of music" and a prosodic interest in the concretion of musical rhythm and structure.[43] In the *Cantos*, for example, Pound used rhythm, patterned silence, and the repetition, development, and variation of a phrase in a musical way not only to create what T. S. Eliot called a "musical pattern of secondary meaning" but to structure the text musically, in some ways not unlike a fugue.[44]

Antin argues that Pound reconciled the contradictory impulses: arranging the elements specific to the medium in a "modernist" way, promoting an arrangement of "traditionally representational linguistic elements for poetry while appearing to advocate much more radical possibilities for painting and sculpture and believing that he was a thoroughgoing modernist across the board." In terms of modernist abstraction, Pound was "too far from the action to know where the battle was, he was just standing in the way of the shrapnel. Gertrude Stein was our only pure modernist."[45]

Rather than simply attempting to pinpoint in their poetic practices the abstraction that Antin specifies as modernism's most significant innovation, in this section I explore the way in which both poets use the terrain of dance to work out the problems of abstraction and representation that haunt modernism. Antin's formulation of the problem is valuable in illustrating how the tension between abstraction and representation in modernist poetry is played out, for Pound and Stein, in the world of rhythm, music, and dance.

Because it puts the figure into motion, modern dance has often served as the image of abstraction. Antin frames his disappointment with modernists other than Stein in an example taken from the dance world: Martha Graham's explanation of how she began her innovative work in dance is read as typical of modernists who claimed to be looking for abstract universals when in fact they were simply trying to fulfill a specific, representational program for their art. In Graham's account, Antin finds at first an absolute statement about what she wanted—to liberate the medium from what he calls "an arbitrary system of representation, in this case the cooch dance exoticism of Ruth St. Denis." But he decides he has misread her intention when he reads that Graham wanted, "by correcting what looked false," to create "significant movement . . . fraught with inner meaning." As Antin notes, Graham and others may well have been after "a kind of universal openness," which has little to do with "whether we really understand their intentions" as expressed in their rhetoric.[46]

But modern dance poses the question of abstraction and representation in a particular way that modernist literature does not. Antin considers Graham's written account of her work as if it were the work itself. When he asks what she can mean by "false," or wonders what a "true" walk might be, he raises the point that the justifying rhetoric of intentions may have little to do with choreographic content. Antin says that false walks or true ones can only exist within a representational—or dramatic—structure in which a dancer plays the role of a liar or a hypocrite who walks. As any artist might, in expressing or explaining a new project, Graham uses absolute terms in a relative way.[47]

Antin concludes that it was Pound's composition and not his medium that was modern in 1914, and it is worth noting that "Ione, dead the long year" is a "modernist" or abstract arrangement of typically representational words. For Antin, Gertrude Stein puts modernity into practice not only in composition but in content, at the level of words and the uses they are put to. Stein herself describes this as the technique of the cinema, but it is legible in two of her word portraits of dancers.

Stein's "Susie Asado" is of interest in studying the tension between the representational and the musical or abstract, inspired as it was by a dancer who is never named in the poem and by Stein's experimentation with exactitude. Carl Van Vechten notes in Stein's *Selected Writings*: "There is reason to believe that these two poems ['Susie Asado' and 'Preciosilla'] paint a portrait and make an attempt to recapture the rhythm of the same flamenco dancer."[48] The writing Stein produced around 1913–14, now referred to as the Spanish period because of the influence Stein's travels there had on her work, marks a break with her earlier writing.[49] In *Lectures in America*, she formulates the abstraction question in terms of music and her desire for "direct description": "The strict discipline that I had given myself, the absolute refusal of never using a word that was not an exact word all through the *Tender Buttons* and what I may call the early Spanish and *Geography and Plays* period finally resulted in things like Susie Asado and Preciosilla etc. in an extraordinary melody of words and a melody of excitement in knowing that I had done this thing."[50]

In *The Autobiography of Alice B. Toklas*, Gertrude-as-Alice writes: "We finally came back to Madrid again and there we discovered the Argentina and the bull-fights. The young journalists of Madrid had just discovered her. We happened upon her in a music hall, we went to them to see spanish dancing, and after we saw her the first time we went every afternoon and every evening." Stein continues: "it was there and at that time that Gertrude Stein's style gradually changed. She says hitherto she had been interested only in the insides of people, their character and what went on inside them, it was during that summer that she first felt a desire to express the rhythm of the visible world. It was a long tormenting process," she adds. Trying to resolve the problem of the internal and external, Stein writes that she worried about whether "after all the human being essentially is not paintable": "These were the days in which she wrote Susie Asado and Preciosilla and Gypsies in Spain. She experimented with everything in trying to describe. She tried a bit inventing words but she soon gave that up. The english language was her medium and with the english language the task was to be achieved, the problem solved. The use of fabricated words offended her, it was an escape into imitative emotionalism."[51]

Stein writes in 1923 about the Spanish period: "it was my first conscious struggle with the problem of correlating sight, sound, and sense and eliminating rhythm."[52] Yet in "Susie Asado," it is the rhythm that so powerfully renders present the flamenco dancer who is otherwise invisible in the text:

Sweet sweet sweet sweet sweet tea.
   Susie Asado.
Sweet sweet sweet sweet sweet tea.
   Susie Asado.
Susie Asado which is a told tray sure.
A lean on the shoe this means slips slips hers.

     . . .

This is a please this is a please there are the saids to jelly. These are the wets these say the sets to leave a crown to Incy.

     . . .

Sweet sweet sweet sweet sweet tea.[53]

Amid this barrage of unexplained objects, the rhythm is the unifying thematic element. The poem seems to exist separately on the visual and rhythmic planes, presenting its subject, Argentina, as the audience experienced her; in one view, Stein "doesn't write about it, or at it, or around it. She writes *it*."[54] At the same time, the poem erases its subject, who is never named: if we did not have her explanation of her method of depicting, her narration of the Argentina story, and Van Vechten's information, we might never know that the poem was inspired by her. Clearly, Argentina's inspiration for her portrait was not visual, in the way that the singer who inspired "Preciosilla" is visible in the title and in the "diamonds bright" of the text. In "Susie Asado," the relation between the dancer observed and the text passes from performance to a word portrait: in the staccato accents of the opening, it is the shoe against the floor that we are hearing. As if taking her cue from Stein's commodification of her sound, La Argentina would later market a recording of her feet and castanets.[55]

On the page, we see all kinds of things: household objects, the images attached to the nouns Stein uses: tea, tray, shoe, light, silver seller, jelly, incubus, pot, trees, vats, bobbles, pups, sash, bobolink, pins, nail. The nouns, extracted from the piece, tell a story while slipping away from meaning. Although Stein argues for exactitude, standard English, and dislike of nouns, in this poem, they are suggestive, inventive, and associative. Commentators have noted that the word "wets" links a chain of metonymic associations that creates a sexual code within the language of the poem. Others consider the word as a verb out of place in a syntax that asks for a noun at that spot ("These are the _____"). In another reading, the word is a reference to alcohol; *Webster's Third New International Dictionary* gives multiple meanings for "wet" as a noun, some of which appear most often in the plural.

The aural qualities of "Susie Asado" distract the reader from anchoring meaning in nouns or in visual images, in language imitative of the reality of the dance—a kind of aural Cratylism—an aurally motivated language. La Argentina, in this text, is represented through rhythm. Her image is not embedded in the words' representational function but in their sound or "acoustic image." Like the "lean of the shoe," the dancing that is as aural as it is visual, that slips away from meaning, the poem mobilizes objects by making its nouns move.

ISADORA DANCES FOR GERTRUDE STEIN

In "Orta or One Dancing," Gertrude Stein pays homage to Isadora, similarly disguised by the name Orta Davray. Like Isadora's dancing, Stein's prose plays with conventions of representation but also challenges with a kind of monumental, radical, classicism. Stein's writing, like movement, builds on a physical foundation of rhythm, repetition, and variation, driving home the dancer's life with the recurrent "she was dancing," a refrain that is both hypnotic and exhausting. The simplicity of Stein's sentences, with their simultaneous clarity and obscurity, echoes the beguiling simplicity of Isadora's steps with their profound resonance. Yet like Duncan, playing with and flouting convention, Stein always wanted to be "historical."

Stein's Isadora is a heroic "one"—uniquely singular and multiple. Introducing the piece, Ulla Dydo writes that "Isadora Duncan came to represent fluid, creative expression of complete physical experience that included thought. Her free, expressionist dancing is shaped into the rhythmic repetitions and permutations of the portrait, which embodies what it says in what the language does." For Dydo, "Isadora is what she does—dance—just as Stein is what she does—write"; Duncan's "thinking, never stiff and sterile, is never apart from dancing."[56]

Stein describes Duncan as unique and yet changing; although she is repeatedly described as "one," she embodies both distinction and multiplicity or fluidity: "she was one having come to be one of another kind of a one."[57] Far from simulation, Isadora's was a multiple "becoming," a strong identity with the ability to represent many things. Isadora, in Stein's portrait, stands for being-by-doing and doing-by-dancing: "She is one doing something. . . . That one is dancing." Isadora's dancing is not nothing but something; not the frivolous pastime that F. T. E. Marinetti would call it but a statement of belief. Isadora dances with great intention, with ambition and with ideas, and in Stein's prose, the dancer's intention, or meaning to dance, becomes meaning *in* dance. Isadora is capable of "believing anything," "meaning anything," "thinking of anything," and ultimately "meaning everything." Isadora is "believing something and meaning something and dancing." And in a later development, this meaningful, intellectual and emotive dancing becomes simply "meaning dancing."[58]

Like Marey's chronophotographs or Phydias's freize on the Elgin marbles that Isadora took as her inspiration, Isadora becomes, in Stein's portrait, a figure in motion who moves out, extends into the space of affirmation and existence. For Isadora, as for her talented family and artist friends, "meaning is existing." Rather than seeking the meaning of existence that "very many" other people need, Isadora's exceptional and eccentric tribe understood that "dancing was existing."[59]

For Stein, Isadora's dancing was thus both intellectual and emotional; she was driven to dance "exceedingly," and she was "exceeding in affirming everything." Her dancing was an affirmation and also, somehow, a contradiction without being contradictory; a challenge to conventions. "She was one who would be contradicting any one if she had not been one exceeding in affirming everything." "She was affirming dancing." Stein describes her working hard, under strain, worn out, from thinking and dancing, from "moving in every direction in meaning being existing." Isadora's work radically integrated feeling and intellect; she understood that emotion has significance that dance can express: "She was dancing in feeling that feeling has a meaning."[60] Her dancing was an active re-membering of being, expressing a triad of meaning-being-existing. Stein's portrait presciently suggests that failure, age, or death would not stop Isadora, because her art was not about completion but about possibility: "She was dancing. She had been dancing. She would be dancing."[61]

Robert Bartlett Haas considers Stein's change (or changes) in writing style as moving toward capturing movement so intense as to be a thing in itself.[62] This "thing in itself" is embodied, for Haas, not in a style dominated by nouns or adjectives—which Stein said she didn't like—but in a style emphasizing more active parts of speech. In a 1935 essay "How Writing Is Written," Stein claims as one of her writing's greatest achievements "getting rid of nouns" and follows with the comment, "In the Twentieth Century you feel like movement. The Nineteenth century didn't feel that way."[63]

Stein conceives her work as "a whole made up of its parts."[64] In a response to nineteenth-century writers' focus on the "pieces put together to make a whole," Stein sees this wholeness as the hallmark of twentieth-century creation, invented in and by the United States:

> The United States . . . had the conception of assembling the whole thing out of its parts, the whole thing which made the Twentieth Century productive. The Twentieth Century conceived an automobile as a whole, so to speak, and then created it, built it up out of its parts. It was an entirely different point of view from the

Nineteenth Century's. The Nineteenth Century would have seen the parts, and worked towards the automobile through them.[65]

This view of the nineteenth and twentieth centuries informs Stein's *The Making of Americans*, a work reminiscent of the photographic composite, used for typing (and stereotyping) human variation by, for example, Francis Galton. Stein claims William James as the inspiration for this project: "I had an idea that I could get a sense of immediacy if I made a description of every kind of human being that existed, the rules for resemblances and all the other things, until really I had made a description of every human being." From confusion ("I made so many charts that when I used to go down the streets of Paris I wondered whether they were people I knew or ones I didn't. That is what *The Making of Americans* was intended to be"), Stein arrives at the conclusion that the project could be done. With enough patience, Stein argues, anybody "could literally and entirely make of the whole world a history of human nature." Once she reached this realization, Stein says, she lost interest in the project and decided to try for a "more complete vision," "to see if I could hold it in the frame in writing with a faster tempo."[66]

Stein also aims for exactitude:

> Ordinarily the novels of the Nineteenth Century live by association; they are wont to call up other pictures than the one they present to you. . . . I wanted to get rid of anything except the picture within the frame. While I was writing I didn't want, when I used one word, to make it carry with it too many associations. I wanted as far as possible to make it exact, as exact as mathematics.[67]

Later in the essay this writing is described as cinematic, as Stein explains that in telling a story over again, "there is no such thing as repetition. . . . There is always a slight variation." It is this slight variation, rather than repetition, that structures her writing so that there is "no essential difference between prose and poetry":

> All my early work was a careful listening to all the people telling their story, and I conceived the idea which is, funnily enough, the same as the idea of the cinema. The cinema goes on the same

principle: each picture is just infinitesimally different from the one before. If you listen carefully, you say something, the other person says something; but each time it changes just a little. . . . You will see that when I kept on saying something was something or somebody was somebody, I changed it just a little bit until I got a whole portrait. I conceived this idea of building this thing up. . . . What I was after was this immediacy. A single photograph doesn't give it.[68]

Stein's portrait effectively makes "cinema" of Isadora, guaranteeing the slowly built-up fluidity that the dancer feared the motion picture could not. From this cinematic vision, Stein moved on, in the later portraits, to condensation: "I used three or four words instead of making a cinema of it. I wanted to condense it as much as possible and change it around, until you could get the movement of a human being."[69]

Abstraction is often defined by moves away from the figure. But in Stein's and Pound's poetics, and in the poems considered here, dance is arguably influential in shaping abstraction in modernist poetry. Dancers seem to disappear as figures here, but they are encoded or absorbed into concepts of modernism: for example, in Pound's Imagism or vorticism, fields of energy, and the "dance of the intellect" that deciphers or uncodes them, Pound makes poems that shift dancing from figure to ground. Stein makes cinema of Isadora while erasing her name, like other nouns, from view; in Stein's cinematics, slightly varied frames move sequentially to portraits, and the prose recalls the friezes inspiring Isadora's dancing.

In a 1930 essay, "How to Write," five years before Stein's "How Writing Is Written," Pound announces that the project during the previous decades had been an ongoing "struggle against 'abstraction.'" In this struggle, the enemy is "abstract terms, ideas that are merely 'imperfect inductions from fact.'"[70] Publishing this and other previously unpublished texts from Pound's Italian period, Maria Luisa Ardizzone has revealed the extent to which Pound opposed what he saw as the syllogistic logic of the abstraction inherent in Western metaphysics and set up against it an idea of *technē*—art and language based on nature, organicity, the science of matter. Against the metaphysical and cognitive thinking that he saw as "abstract," because, in Ardizzone's words, it "reduces the manifold of experience through a general abstraction,"[71] Pound propounded not "representation" but the concretion represented by the ideogrammic method.

Following both Ernest Fenellosa's essay "The Chinese Written Character" and Rémy de Gourmont's *Physique de l'Amour*, Pound posits a language based on the ideograph, on the instinct unopposed to the intellect. For Pound, "the ideograph abstracts or generalizes in the known concrete,"[72] and following Fenellosa, Pound sees this as a scientific method. In Fenellosa's definition, the ideograph brings together signs in the "method of science" because it compounds known quantities, rather than stringing signs and referents along in an increasingly abstract signifying chain. In "How to Write," Pound quotes Fenellosa's argument:

> Ask an occidental what red is and he will tell you that red is a colour; and ask him what colour is, and he will tell you colour is a refraction of light. Skip refraction and ask him what light is and he will tell you that it is a vibration of something or other, and ask him what vibration or other or electro-magnetism is and he will plunge still further into incognita. When, on the other hand, a Chinese man wishes to write down the ideograph for red he puts together the sign pictures for: cherry, rose, iron-rust and flamingo.[73]

For Fenellosa to say that "this latter is the method of science" and for Pound to accept it as such is both a denial of the scientificity of one kind of systematic explanation (Western metaphysics) and the substitution of a different explanation.

In ideogrammatic poetics, "the thing is what it does." "The eye sees noun and verb in one, things in action, action in things." This language depends on the eye, and "the word as eye-memory" rather than "the word as ear-memory."[74] Pound locates this poetics not only in the Chinese kanji but also in "good" Western poetry and the "stimulus" of Africa—"not so important for our purpose but it is not negligible. Lévy-Bruhl points out the savage's lack of power to generalize. He has forty verbs where we have two or three verbs and some adverbs. The savage language grades down into pantomime and mimicry."[75] Pound's compounding of African and Asian art and poetics reveals both an idealization of ancient culture and a reductive view of "the primitive."[76]

The challenge for Pound's modern poet is to invent a logopoeia that could encode this ideogrammic method in words rather than pictographs. The verb will become all-important to this project, the "epicenter" of the modern era; in Ardizzone's summary of Pound's "Ogden and Debabeliza-tion," "Substituting verb for noun, plural (unity) for the One, biologic logic for the syllogistic, Pound banishes from language the predicates of Aristotelian substance of metaphysics, which is one and immobile." For Pound, "the demon of our age is uniformity," and thus he looks to the multiplicity of nature and to science.[77] This "science" that Pound wants poetic language to reproduce in the "ideogrammic or scientific method," Ardizzone variously defines as "the new science of matter" centered on "the cells studied by the scientist in his laboratory, "Gestalt psychology" influencing biology and physics in the 1920s, the mathematics of "strain" (calculating change in material made by applied forces), as well as the Erasmus Darwin–inspired natural philosophy of Gourmont, the biochem-istry influencing Fenellosa's idea of scientific code, and the Baconian (or Newtonian?) experimental subject, revealed in such statements as "at the focus of the 'poEm' he [Pound] wants to put, not 'the KNOWABLE,' but that which 'I KNOW.'"[78]

In other words, to create a "logopoeia" essential to modernity, the in-tellect's dance among words, the poet must borrow from the scientist. But the science Pound refers to is itself multiple, variable, and in flux. Using the concept of dance to describe the complex new language that must be realized in the West to cope with the new realities, describe the "discov-eries" of science and the truth of nature (in which there is "agreement be-tween things and words,"[79] Pound slides away from the Victorian dancer who peopled his early poems and toward a mechanistic conception of movement and music that the dancer (invisibly or implicitly) stands for. The ideogrammic "scientific" language, like the dancer, concentrates and releases energy, encodes the multiple into the one. The ideogram deper-sonalizes the action, but like dancers it abstracts *in* the concrete. Dancers themselves are not important.[80] But the space previously occupied by them, the place where once they walked, is filled by something else.

THE SYMBOLS AND NOT THE REAL THING

The work of the three Americans in exile in Europe that anchors this chapter reveals complex responses to the influence of technology on art, the disappearance of some antiquated forms, and their rebirth in new forms in the first decades of the twentieth century. In their responses to "things" and their representation on the page, in a century in which "you feel like movement," Pound and Stein seem to take opposite approaches. Pound's Imagism and vorticism describe force fields energized around "direct treatment of the thing" provoking a "dance of the intellect." Stein describes "getting rid of nouns" to write movement itself, the "rhythm of the visible world." The first poetics announces itself against abstraction, and the second is often held up as a model of abstraction. Yet in both cases, writing turns toward dance for models of how to write "things" mobilized or mechanized in the machine age.

Dance history has not imagined Isadora in the terms of a dancing machine, nor does it identify her with the modern world of "things." It is Isadora herself who, allying herself with the human motor, located her dancing with a nineteenth-century conception of the machine, against the "mechanical grotesques" of the turn of the century and the machine ballets that would become fashionable in the 1920s.

With her two countrymen, Isadora is often identified with an "American" outlook, with the "movement" that Stein expresses. And as Stein's attempts to establish the "being" of the subjects of her portraits, that is, the presence or consciousness of people rather than their external aspect, have been linked to the influence of her teacher William James and his work on radical empiricism,[81] dance historian Ann Daly links Duncan to Jamesian theories of mechanical will, the idea that mechanisms of reaction produce emotional states, that movement induces emotion.[82]

Isadora allied herself with European literary and theatrical symbolist doctrine. In *Done into Dance*, Daly writes that Isadora was described as a "symbolic dancer" by the American press because her pieces "clearly meant something beyond their material existence." Daly argues that Duncan was "at heart a symbolist long before she had ever read the poetry of Maurice Maeterlinck, or met with producer/director Lugné-Poe, or seen actress Suzanne Despres" and that unlike Loie Fuller's, Duncan's aesthetic was "an expression of effect, not form."[83] Yet Isadora's dancing was far from the stylized performance of symbolist theaters of Paris at the fin de siècle, and it was even further from Lugné-Poe's cartoonlike, marionette-inspired staging of Jarry's *Ubu Roi* in 1896. In her autobiography, she staunchly rejects pantomime: "Movement is lyrical and emotional expression, which can have nothing to do with words, and in pantomime people substitute gesture for words so that it is neither the art of the dancer nor of the actor, but falls in between the two in hopeless sterility."[84] Duncan describes friendships with a wide range of performers and directors; allied with Ellen Terry and Eleonore Duse, with Terry's son Craig and Stanislavsky, as well as with contemporary performers in France, Russia, and Italy, Duncan and her circle embraced a range of acting styles.

In *My Life*, Isadora laments that although her influence on the avantgarde theater of her time was enormous, it rarely bore her imprint: "theater managers were unable to understand my art, or to understand how my ideas might have been of benefit to their productions. This is strange when one considers how many bad copies of my schools have appeared since in the productions of Reinhardt, Gemier, and others of the Advanceguard of the Theatre."[85] Identifying her art with symbolist theater, Duncan complained that critics took her work too literally.

Citing an anecdote told by Duncan to a reporter, Daly writes that "Duncan had realized the advantage of the symbolic over the literal when she was just five years old." Isadora's anecdote goes as follows: "I recited 'Ten Little Niggers' and made a great hit. I see, now [laughing merrily], that it was a very inartistic performance. I had bought 10 little nigger dolls and had them sitting up in a box, and at the end of each couplet stuck one in my pocket. Now I see I shouldn't have had the dolls. One must have the symbols and not the real thing."[86]

From this vignette, Daly concludes, "Like the symbolists, Duncan looked for the suggestion of the thing rather than the thing itself." But Duncan's self-critique in this anecdote from childhood does not mask the reductivism of this conception of the symbol. In this formula, Duncan begins by equating the figures of the dolls with the "Ten Little Niggers" described in the poem and ends up equating the dolls with "the real thing"; in between, the process of symbolization is denied both to the "Ten Little Niggers" poem and to the dolls. To the reporter, Duncan says in retrospect that she should have relied on the representational content—the symbols—of the poem rather than the "real thing"—the dolls. But the symbolicity of the dolls, and of the figures of the "little niggers" in the story, is erased. For Duncan, the story of "Ten Little Niggers" can only be a story about literality, even in retrospect: one in which dolls are too easily confused with the characters, and the real people, they represent.

From this anecdote it is important not only to conclude, as Daly does, that Duncan saw herself as a symbolist but also to ask why. It is important, too, to consider Duncan's association of literality with photography. In a remark made in the same interview quoted by Daly, concerning the interpretation of her dances, Duncan notes, "The notion that every gesture has some precise meaning is all wrong. It is mood, not photography."[87] The same kind of "real thing" that the black dolls represent is also embodied by the too-precise art of photography.

In Amy Koritz's summation of Isadora's symbolism in the context of its interpretation by Arthur Symons and Craig,

> Duncan does not attempt, as Symons does, to maintain an
> opposition between nature and art while unifying them at the
> same time. Rather, the whole point of Duncan's strategy is to
> overcome this dichotomy. She does not, however, consistently do
> so; instead, Duncan frequently adopts the terms of the symbolist
> dichotomy, particularly as it was expressed by Craig. The body
> becomes a problem to be overcome on the path to Art.[88]

The symbolism described in the story just related justified a rejection of the too-literal issues of body and representation in America as figured by blackness. But symbolists such as Mallarmé or Villiers, inspiring Symons and Craig, would have insisted on the repercussion of the symbol's echoing resonance of meanings. Here Isadora rejects what she understands as an American literalness for an abstraction without such symbolic resonance.

The politics it performs in hiding, condensing, or erasing figures raises the stakes of modernist abstraction. The association that Isadora makes, for example, between American blackness and literalness, between Europe and symbolism; the way that Pound ascribes to "African" and "Asian" cultures a coded language, a "primitive" poetics that machines and the machine age recapture; or the way that Stein describes her attempt to document every kind of human being that existed in *The Making of Americans*, all suggest the importance of figure, body, and color within different modes of modernist representation and their erasure, disappearance, or re-figuration in modernist abstraction.

In concert dance considered in the next chapters, machine ballets share the stage with ballets inspired by African, Afro-Brazilian, and Asian dance, and one effect of more references to the cinema, to technological modernity, and to artistic primitivism in these ballets is the erasure of dancers. This simultaneous disappearance of dancers and reappearance as mechanicals or "primitives" unexpectedly finds roots in the high modernism and the avant-gardes of the 1910s, in the twin operations of "abstraction" and "concretion." The hesitation of a certain kind of dance in the face of cinema—a certain kind of modern dance turning away from cinema after Isadora (even if admitting the camera)—proves to be one source of the *ballet mécanique* of animated technology in which "things themselves" take center stage and dance.

### ISADORA DANCES FOR MARINETTI

In *Water Study*, set to a Schubert waltz, Isadora's choreography is not only an "emotional" response to water or a representation of water but a movement study of the mechanics of water movement transposed onto the body. In this solo the body moves like water, exploring water's different kinds of forces and rhythms and representing them with different body parts and different kinds of steps.

The opening sequence challenges the dancer to move backward with the legs while moving forward with the torso, as a receding wave pulls out from the shore while on the surface it is still rolling in. Thus the dancer's feet, moving underneath, take the body stage right as the upper body bends forward and sideways, arms extended over the legs, floating stage left. At the end of the passage, the two currents represented by arms and legs crisscross as the feet cross in a turn and the arms wrap around the body. The twisted line runs from feet through the torso and ultimately uncrosses the arms as they reach up into the air.

In the second sequence the dancer's small jumps suggest water spurting from the ground, and the same turns finish the sequence as the wave runs through the body and up out through the arms and hands. The choreography's final sequence before the series repeats has the dancer crouching to the ground and then rising up with arms extended upward like a fountain. The final ornament has the dancer leaning to one side and then the other, as if buffeted by currents on both sides, before a final wave runs through the body, and arms, hands, and head are thrown back.

The simple steps belie the complexity of this dance, appropriately called a "study": sometimes they are generated from the center or solar plexus and articulated out through the limbs in sequential movement; sometimes they are a whole body movement such as a jump. The dance explores the two radically different kinds of movement possible for bodies: the axial movement of a limb or head and the rotary movement of the whole body around itself; in the first, the body represents some movement of the water, and in the second, the body moves as if carried by water. In this spread of movement, the possibilities of the human body are sounded—although the movement qualities, rhythms, and steps remain limited. *Water Study* choreographs both dancing like water—that is, the representation of the movement of water—and also dancing in water—or the passive movement of the body as if taken by a water current or wave. As beguilingly simple as this little dance appeared to onlookers such as Marinetti, danced in Isadora's studio to her mother's piano accompaniment, it was a technical revolution. It was undoubtedly partly because of Isadora that Marinetti would go on to imagine dancers not only representing metaphorically but themselves becoming the movement forces they represent—in his case, projectiles. It is an idea taken directly from Isadora, whose modernism he could not appreciate.

# 4.
## Ballets Without Bodies

In his "Manifesto of Futurist Dance" (1917), F. T. E. Marinetti writes of
preferring the cakewalk, and Loie Fuller, to Isadora's dancing, weighed
down by its feminine emotionalism:

> Isadora Duncan creates the free dance, with no preparatory mime,
> that ignores musculature and eurythmy in order to devote every-
> thing to emotional expression, to the aerial ardor of its steps. But
> fundamentally she merely proposes to intensify, enrich, and
> modulate in a hundred different ways the rhythm of a woman's
> body that languidly rejects, languidly evokes, languidly accepts,
> and languidly regrets the masculine giver of erotic happiness.
>
> Isadora Duncan, whom I often had the pleasure of admiring in
> her free improvisations among the veils of mother-of-pearl smoke
> of her atelier, used to dance freely, thoughtlessly, as if talking,
> desiring, loving, weeping, to any sort of little tune no matter how
> vulgar, like "Mariette, ma petite Mariette" strummed on a piano.
> But she never managed to project anything but the most complex

feelings of desperate nostalgia, of spasmodic sensuality and cheerfulness, childishly feminine.[1]

Marinetti notes later in the same essay that "We Futurists prefer Loie Fuller and the 'cakewalk' of the Negroes (utilization of electric light and mechanisms)." Yet the Futurist's ideal dance would be independent of music: "Music is fundamentally and incurably passéist, hence hard to employ in the Futurist dance." Dalcroze's work is interesting to Marinetti as a "rhythmic gymnastics," but it doesn't move beyond "muscular hygiene and description of the work of the fields."[2] The goal then for Futurist dance is not only to kill romantic social dances like the tango but also to stage dancing as technology and bodies as machines.

Marinetti's childishly masculine program for Futurism proposed everything from less pasta in the diet to new ways of walking that would shape bodies along the guidelines of Futurist aesthetics. In Marinetti's history of dance, its first liberation from Isadora's Wagnerian sensibility, from tango and tea dancing, came with Nijinsky's dancing: "With Nijinsky the pure geometry of the dance, free of mimicry and without sexual stimulation, appears for the first time."[3]

Edward Gordon Craig's review *The Mask* had published Marinetti's earlier manifesto "The Variety Theater" (1913) in 1914. Like Craig, Marinetti calls for a new theater and expresses disgust with the contemporary theater, which "vacillates stupidly between historical reconstruction (pastiche or plagiarism) and photographic reproduction of our daily life." The "Variety Theater" that Futurism exalts is born, like the Futurists themselves, from "electricity" and "fed by swift actuality." By inventing "new elements of astonishment," the Variety Theater creates what Marinetti calls "'the Futurist marvelous,' produced by modern mechanics," which includes a range of ironic, witty, and hilarious caricatures, and "dynamism of form and color . . . jugglers, ballerinas, gymnasts, colorful riding masters, spiral cyclones of dancers."[4] Variety Theater presents a range of genres at a fast pace: "a cumulus of events unfolded at great speed, of stage characters pushed from right to left in two minutes ('and now, let's have a look at the Balkans')" reminiscent of *Ubu Roi* or cinema newsreels.

Unlike Craig's, however, this theater is modeled explicitly on the cinema: "The Variety Theater is unique today in its use of the cinema, which enriches it with an incalculable number of visions and otherwise unrealizable spectacles (battles, riots, horse races, automobile and airplane meets, trips, voyages, depths of the city, the countryside, oceans, and skies)."[5] The theater's practical goal, Marinetti insists, is to "distract and amuse" the public. It is "synthetic"—by which he means "very brief"—"dynamic, simultaneous. That is, born of improvisation, lightninglike intuition, from suggestive and revelatory actuality." The collaborative manifesto "The Futurist Synthetic Theater" (1915) argues that "with this essential and synthetic brevity the theater can bear and even overcome competition from the *cinema*."[6]

Marinetti's program is confused; although he argues again, in "The Pleasure of Being Booed," that "dramatic art ought not to concern itself with psychological photography," the manifesto on the "synthetic theater" calls for Futurists to "fraternize warmly with the actors who are among the few thinkers who flee from every deforming cultural enterprise."[7] But whereas various theater tendencies are praised or rejected in a whim, and the cinema is both imitated and rejected, the theater manifesto clearly articulates the importance of theater-going for Italians ("90 percent of Italians go to the theater, whereas only 10 percent read books") and for Futurists ("The greater number of our works have been written in the theater").[8]

Some critics, such as Roselee Goldberg, have seen the Futurists as realizing Craig's call for inhuman, Ubermarionette, performance. Various Futurist artists were involved in performances sponsored by Diaghilev, including the 1917 *Feu d'artifice*, a light show with no dancers set to a Stravinsky score and conducted by Balla at a Ballets Russes concert in Rome. Marinetti's own choreographies reflect the contemporary taste for "machine ballets": imagining the dancer as capable of machinic impossibilities and sexing the machine as female, they are in some ways conceived as impossible to perform.

In the fantastic soirées of Futurist dance, and then in the concert dance of two major ballet companies in Paris in the later 1910s and 1920s, this chapter explores the collaborative work of teams of composers, choreographers, writers, and painters and the diverse themes and dancing of what are here called "machine ballets." The artistic and political stakes of the mechanization of bodies are considered, from the marionette praised by

Craig to the "savageness" of dancer Jean Börlin praised by Blaise Cendrars, from the mechanized feminine of Futurism, bordering on science fiction, to cinematic and technological Americanness, representing the everyday fantastic. The concept of the "dancing machine" proves useful to modernisms representing the political spectrum from left to right.

This chapter traces two lines of the development of "dancing machines," which the following chapters explore further. The first is the highly visible mechanization of performers in the machine ballets popular in Paris in the 1920s. Developing out of a prevalent machine aesthetic in avant-garde movements of the 1910s and 1920s, these choreographies would make mainstream what Martha Graham referred to a decade later as the omnipresent machine ballets of European dance companies.

The mechanization of the performer and the mechanics of emotion and performance loom large in avant-garde performances and on European stages in the 1920s, inspired by Jarry's machinic fin-de-siècle *Ubu Roi* and by performance theory of the first decades of the twentieth century,[9] including Craig's "The Actor and the Uber (or Super-) Marionette." Yet two very different kinds of dancing, representing two contradictory and yet complementary energies, are identified under the label "dancing machines" in this as in previous chapters: the mechanical dancer, whose work, like that of Babbage's automat, is hidden, and the "human motor," who expresses the energy of physical labor—the dancing often identified as "savage" or "primitive."

In some of the dancing studied here, bodies are mechanized in a machine aesthetic; in other dancing, an imagined "savage" energy—sometimes identified with Russian dancers, sometimes with African American ones—drives the machine. The connection between "savages" and machines is accomplished via the metaphors of mechanization or motors, images of puppets or animals. The Ballets Russes's 1911 *Petrouchka*, a half-hour staging by Fokine of the carnivalesque life of three puppets, continues this fascination with the automated and mechanistic aspect of acting, of human life, and emotions.[10]

Sometimes choreographies by the Ballets Russes or Ballets Suédois become machine ballets through references to a cinematic modernity, usually identified with American life: jazz, cars, the big city. But sometimes choreographies become machine ballets by referencing a fantasy of pre-technological "primitiveness": if there is a "savage" energy that serves as a source to keep machines going, there is also a savageness that mechanization brings on.

Within these two categories of dancing machines, this chapter explores the "disappearance" or abstraction of dancers onstage and onscreen in forms in which machines or mechanized objects take over the leading roles, either through the backgrounding of dancers to a set imagined as a rhythmic ensemble of elements or to a cinematic image. Beyond choreographies with cinematic references, the range of possibilities for "dancing machines" is expanded in interactions and mutual influences between concert dance and cinema, explored here in two examples from 1924. The first is René Clair's *Entr'acte*, filmed and screened as part of the Ballets Suédois's *Relâche*. The second is the collaborative *Ballet mécanique* that followed Fernand Léger's 1922 designs for the Swedish ballet's *Skating Rink* and for the 1923 *La Création du monde* based on African myths, with a scenario by Blaise Cendrars.

Dance's capacity to merge the real and the unreal, the quotidian and the technological, in ways that would quickly become the province of cinema suggests that, even while citing the cinema and adapting to it, choreography was also in some ways, for some artists, still showing cinema what it could do. In turn, avant-garde cinema offered the means to stage the ultimate disappearance of dancers into animated, mechanized objects in motion, in ballets without bodies.

THE DANCER BECOMES A (WAR) MACHINE

Marinetti's manifestos glorify machines and imagine dancers closely connected to them: the Futurist love of speed and admiration for the automobile are cast in the language of male heterosexual desire; and if machines are women, then female Futurist dancers can become machines. Specifically, Futurist dancers can represent the machines of modern war:

> One must go beyond muscular possibilities and aim in the dance for that ideal *multiplied body* of the motor that we have so long dreamed of. One must imitate the movements of machines with

gestures; pay assiduous court to steering wheels, ordinary wheels, pistons, thereby preparing the fusion of man with the machine, to achieve the metallicity of the Futurist dance. . . .

In this Futurist epoch of ours, when more than twenty million men form with their battle lines a fantastic Milky Way of exploding shrapnel stars that bind the earth together; when the Machine and the Great Explosives, cooperating with the air, have centupled the force of the races, obliging them to give all they have of boldness, instinct, and muscular resistance, the Futurist dance can have no other purpose than to immensify heroism, master of metals, and to fuse with the divine machines of speed and war.

I therefore extract the first three Futurist dances from the three mechanisms of war: shrapnel, the machine gun, and the airplane.[11]

Marinetti's writings on technology, war, and performance raise over several decades the question of what Walter Benjamin described as the Fascist "aestheticization of politics."[12] In the context of their conception during the First World War, Marinetti's three choreographies glorify both the human motor and the machinery of destruction, male enthrallment to and domination of feminized objects.

In *Dance of the Shrapnel*, the action is divided into two parts; both feature a female dancer who at times plays the role of the projectile, at times the role of the explosion or force of nature, and at times the role of commentator. At the beginning of each part is visible a "mountain soldier who carelessly sings beneath an uninterrupted vault of shrapnel" and marches with a "slow, casual, thoughtless gait." In distinction to this bumbling figure, the dancer performs a finely honed war machine. In part 1, the danseuse impersonates (with the feet) the sound of the "projectile coming from the cannon's mouth," the parabolic trajectory of the shrapnel (with arms spread apart), and its "proud, blessed, silvery explosion," with the hands wearing "very long silver thimbles." After these movements, the dancer holds up signs: after the first explosion, a sign printed in blue: "Short to the right"; after the second, "Long to the left." As the dancer's movements become more and more abstract, representing the forces of armament in motion, the signs she holds up become more detached from the action. In the third movement, after her representation of the explosion and the sign "Long to the left," the dancer holds up another sign, printed in silver: "Don't slip on the ice. Synovitis." In the fourth movement, "With the whole body vibrating, the hips weaving, and the arms making swimming motions, give the waves and flux and reflux and concentric or eccentric motions of echoes in ravines, in open fields and up the slopes of mountains." After this movement, the dancer holds up three signs printed in black: "Water duty," "Mess duty," and "The mules, the mail." In the fifth movement, her movements express "the indifferent and always idyllic calm of nature and the *cheep-cheep-cheep* of the birds. The danseuse will hold up a sign printed in disordered letters: *300 meters to camp.* Then another in red: *15 degrees below zero. 800 meters red ferocious suave.*"[13]

In part 2, the dancer puts down her signs and takes up a cigarette, "while hidden voices sing one of the many war songs."[14] In the final four movements, the "undulations" with which the dancer expresses the war song are interrupted by the four movements from part 1: the whistling parabola of the shrapnel; its explosion; the waves of echoes; the cheep-cheep-cheep of the birds.

In the second choreography, *Dance of the Machine Gun*, Marinetti aims to "give the Italian carnality of the shout *Savoia!* that rips itself apart and dies heroically in shreds against the mechanical geometrical inexorable rolling-mill of the machine-gun fire." Again the dancer represents both with her body and by holding symbols. With the feet, she sounds the hammering of the machine gun, holding a sign "Enemy at 700 meters." Then with one hand full of white roses, the other of red roses, she imitates the fire pouring from the machine-gun barrels. Her third movement, made with open arms circling and sprinkling, describes the fan of projectiles. The fourth movement repeats the hammering feet with a slow turn of the body; the fifth uses forward thrusts of the body to accompany the cry "Savoiaaaaa!" In the final movement of the piece, "The danseuse, on hands and knees, will imitate the form of a machine gun, silver-black under its ribbon-belt of cartridges. Stretching her arms forward, she will feverishly shake the white and red orchid like a gun barrel in the act of firing."[15]

The third dance in the manifesto, *Dance of the Aviatrix*, features a female dancer imitating the movements of an airplane rather than those of an aviator. She dances on top of a "violently colored geographical map

(four meters square)." She wears "on her chest, like a flower, a large cel-
luloid propeller that because of its very nature will vibrate with every bodily movement. Her face dead white under a white hat shaped like a mono-
plane." This costuming is problematic in view of the choreographic
program Marinetti envisions for the piece. In the first movement, the
dancer lies on her stomach on the carpet-map, simulating the efforts of a
plane trying to take off. She rises to hands and knees and eventually
stands, shivering all over. In the second movement, she shakes two signs:
"300 meters—3 spins—climb" and "600 meters—avoid mountain." In
the third movement, the dancer piles green fabric together to simulate a
mountain and leaps over it. In the fourth, she waves a cardboard sun in
front of her as she chases after it in "frenzied, mechanical" movement. In
the final two movements, the ballet concludes with the baroque figures of
two framed paper representations, the first of the sky at sunset, the second
of the night sky. The dancer is required both to hold the representation
and jump through it like the plane.[16]

Between her embodiment of the forces of nature (abstract or representational) and of the machine, the dancer covers the entire range of images
imagined by Marinetti. She is a perfect figure for both the material and
fantastic aspects of war, for its sounds and symbolic choreographies. Yet
these dance texts, despite their vehemence, reveal both an idealization of
dance as the form that can do anything and an ignorance of the dance and
of dancers' limitations. Marinetti imagines spectacles staged by dancers
who are never real people. Ultimately the dancer, as powerful a machine
as she can be, remains a representation only; she is not a Futurist. She is
the entertainment at a Futurist spectacle rather than one of its organizers.

Giovanni Lista has documented, under the heading "ballets and choreographies," Futurist theater both performed and unperformed, published
and unpublished. Most could be considered mechanical ballets in the train
of thought that Marinetti sketched as "the new possibilities for dance suggested to us by mechanical rhythms": Depero's *Ballets plastiques* (1918)
and *Aventure electrique* (1917); Balla's *Machine typographique*, imagined
in 1914, performed in 1916 in Diaghilev's salon in Rome (he chose *Feu
d'artifice* instead); Marinetti's *Les Poupées electriques* (1909), inspired by
*L'Eve future*; and Vasari's "synthèse tragique en trois temps," titled *L'An-*

*goisse des machines*, staged in Paris in 1927. Many are predictably positive mise-en-scènes of technological utopias: Marinetti writes of Depero's *Enicham du 3000* that it stages a future when "man will live in perfect symbiosis with machines."[17] They reveal Futurists' professional interest in ballet; Lista relates Depero's meeting with Massine in New York in 1929, the four ballets that Depero had planned and never realized, and then a fifth, conceived with Massine in 1930, titled *New York, New Babel* and also never realized.

Other performance-texts represent the madness of the machine. Balla's ballet about the *machine typographique* includes the mechanical shocks and simultaneous gestures of twelve dancers; several other ballets represent technologized pathologies.[18] In Depero's *Aventure electrique*, a typically bourgeois setting of train station and restaurant is turned upside down with electrified characters, including two "black servers." In Marinetti's *Poupées electriques*, American engineer John Wilson and his wife live with two *automates électromécaniques*, but it is the real woman and the female automata who are the dolls of the title. For Lista, the subject of the play is the "non-liberty" of woman, her "fragility facing every form of electro-physical or electro-psychical energy acting on the nerves."[19]

Lista emphasizes that the postwar Futurism of the 1920s turned increasingly toward "l'art mécanique" influenced by De Stijl, the Bauhaus movement, and Léger's "purisme français" in France. A parody of Futurism's technological idealism, the *Ballet mécanique futuriste*, first performed in Rome in 1922, staged the "attraction-repulsion between man and machine."[20] This ballet mécanique referred to a theatricalized Taylorism, which for Lista was similar to Meyerhold's, with streamlined gestures, red, black, white, and metallic gray figures in cardboard, projections, the sound of motorbikes, and a choreography characterized by "surprises spatiales" in which dancers circulated in the theater. Panaggi's mechanical costumes for the ballet's Russian dancers were, Lista notes in *Théâtre futurist italien*, countered by Paladini's costume for a "pantin humain." All of the ballets reflect the influences of silent cinema, pantomime, or music hall.

In somewhat idealizing terms, Lista sees Futurism as a movement in movement, taking its rhetoric as a substitute for its contradictory practice. In *La Scène futuriste*, he writes: "The nonstop mobility of Futurist research, its mythologizing of art imagined as work-in-progress—that is, as a material image of becoming and thus as an ephemeral concretization of Heraclitean flux—impose the model of a protean Italian avant-garde on the historian's work."[21] In his work on Futurist photography, Lista has also emphasized the group's early rejection of photography as a "fixing" art, in line with its repugnance for stillness. In *Futurism and Photography*, Lista explains that whereas Marey sought to trace continuous movement and its physiological mechanisms, the Bragaglia brothers invented "photodynamism" to capture the voluntary and brusque gesture with its psychological motivations. He goes on to argue that in spite of Marinetti's commitment to Fascism, "Futurist photo-performance, in fact, coincided with a stage of cultural militancy that could no longer be practised in a country dominated by Fascism."[22]

In spite of Futurism's praise of performance, performative Futurism is not the work of actors or dancers but that of the "great men" who design it. Its more important choreographies are those of the "Futurist stroll. Studies of new ways of walking," the "Interventionist walk," or the "Futurist march interpreted by Marinetti, Settimelli, Balla, Chiti, etc." Admiring dancers and imitating them, the Futurists simultaneously sideline dancers and dance performance as too close to symbolist, sentimental, idealization of femininity. Futurist "lyricism, essentially mobile and changeable," adopts rhythmic, gymnastic, choreographic elements but absorbs them into rhetoric and posturing. Futurist aesthetics ultimately prefers the movement of "words-in-freedom" to liberated bodies and the dancing of machines to that of any body.

THE BALLETS RUSSES: PUPPETS AND SAVAGES

In his program notes for the Ballets Russes's 1917 *Parade*, Guillaume Apollinaire applied his new term "surrealist" to the collaborative work by Massine, Satie, Picasso, and Cocteau. Apollinaire called the work a "stage-poem" representative of an "esprit nouveau," which he called "surrealist" to counter the realism of the contemporary theater. This "new spirit," Apollinaire wrote, "will not fail to seduce the elite, and it hopes to change arts and manners from top to bottom, to the joy of all. For it is only natural to wish that arts and manners should attain at least the level of scientific and industrial progress."[23]

Reflecting on the company's early years in Paris, and its various succès de scandale, Diaghilev later wrote: "for the Parisians, we were savages; then we became savage and refined, and it took twenty years of work to be able to occupy a place equal to theirs, Westerners, or even, sometimes, a preponderant place. And today the Parisians often regret seeing us become less and less savage and, perhaps, even far too refined."[24] One critic who had called the Ballets Russes "savage" was André Levinson, but he also noted the "mechanized," "geometric," movements of the ballets *Noces* and *Parade*, and how, in some cases, Picasso's costumes hid the human motor.[25]

One way the Ballets Russes became more "refined" was in producing contemporary ballets that staged modern themes. The Ballets Russes was touring with *Petrouchka* in Rome in the spring of 1917, while Picasso and Cocteau were developing *Parade* there with Diaghilev. In her study of *Parade*, Deborah Rothschild notes that there are several points of comparison between the two ballets: the Pierrot character—reflected in Picasso's interest in Harlequin—the *pantin* (puppet), and the circus figures manifest in *Parade*'s opening curtain; the story that "elevated and transformed a popular fairground idiom into high art"; and the Moor—a standard, exotic, feature in puppet shows—who slays Petrouchka and appears turbaned on the *Parade* overture curtain as well.[26] The production has been described also as "indirectly applying Jarry-style tactics."[27]

The production team of Satie, Picasso, Cocteau, and Massine was inspired by many forms of popular entertainment: American and French cinema, Mary Pickford and Méliès, vaudeville, circus, Neapolitan comedy, and *images d'Epinal*. Picasso's Cubism with its African influences and Cocteau's scenario also took cues from Italian Futurists, some of whom, including Balla, worked on the curtain and constructions with Picasso.

Yet *Parade* is also generally acknowledged as the first of the twentieth-century ballets on a modern theme, in this case often described as Americanness, which is epitomized by the hawking charlatans outside fairground or boulevard theaters. The ballet features two managers in Cubist constructions: one American, wearing a skyscraper construction and cowboy outfit; one French with a stylized top hat, tuxedo, moustache, pipe, and cane. A third, originally conceived as a "Negro minstrel manager," was first imagined in blackface and wearing a dummy horse; then he became a papier-maché figure "modelled on blackface cakewalk dancers," attached to a two-man horse costume typical of vaudeville; and then he disappeared

entirely from the horse.[28] The managers, for whom Cocteau originally envisioned speaking roles, present the music hall headliners: the Chinese conjurer, the American girl, and the acrobats.

The setting, in Cocteau's description of the action, is "a street in Paris,
on a Sunday," where the managers

> in their atrocious language, try awkwardly to attract the crowd,
> but are unable to convince the people sufficiently to draw them
> into the theatre. The Chinaman, the American girl, and the two
> acrobats come out onto the street from the empty theatre, and
> seeing the failure of the managers, they try the power of their
> charms; but all their efforts are to no avail. In short, the story of
> *Parade* is the tragedy of an unsuccessful theatrical venture.[29]

Because of its contemporary setting and theme, Cocteau subtitled it a
*ballet réaliste*, staging "daily truths and rhythms" and illustrated by Picasso's "true realism" of volumes, matter, and shadow. The American
girl, writes Cocteau, "mimicked one thing after another, jumped on a
moving automobile, flew in it over a road, swam a river, trembled like the
flickering of a 'movie,' chased a robber with a revolver and imitated
Charlie Chaplin."[30] The spectators of *Parade*, Apollinaire concludes, will
be fascinated to find how graceful modern movement can be; among the
wonders, "the American girl, by turning the crank of an imaginary automobile, will express the magic of their everyday life."[31] Like the cinema,
and the cinematic muse Mary Pickford, whom her character was based
on, the American girl makes magic.[32]

In his memoirs, Cocteau relishes a comment about *Parade* by a gentleman
he overheard remark, "If I had known it was so silly, I would have brought
the kids."[33] Cocteau was pleased to imagine that the work, like his favorite
clowns Footit and Chocolat, remembered from the Nouveau Cirque of
1899, might mesmerize children. With his "blend of baby, nurse, and
British noblewoman" with "cruel makeup," grimacing "bloody lips," and
"mad duchess's voice," Cocteau remembers, "Footit brought to the ring
the atmosphere of a devil's nursery, in which children recognized their own
cunning malice and to whose grandeur the grownups surrendered themselves." Footit's fall guy, Chocolat, plays the simple servant in "clinging

knee britches of black silk and a red tailcoat" and the colonial returning from Paris singing "Tararaboumdihé, la grammair' ça m'fait suer!"[34] The clowns should be considered an important inspiration for *Parade*: they were filmed by the Lumière brothers in their first films, and a photo postcard of the team shows portraits of the two clowns with an image of "Footit dans une des ses farces" seated on a bench next to a two-man horse.[35]

Cocteau records that "five years later, in 1904, that same Nouveau Cirque was to be the scene of a historic theatrical event: the arrival of rhythm from America," when "the first blacks (we had only known poor Chocolat) brought the solemn 'Cake.'"[36] Praising the dancers and their cakewalk, Cocteau says that not the first jazz band, nor the Black Birds, nor "any trendy, glittery show [could] be compared to that apparition."[37] These first black dancers in Europe are dancing machines:

> On its feet, the audience stamped, and in the center of that delirious hall, Mr. and Mrs. Elks danced. They danced, skinny, wiry, beribboned, glittering with stars and splashed in white light, hats cocked over eyes or ears, knees higher than their thrown-back faces, hands twirling flexible canes, tearing their movements from themselves and hammering at the artificial floor with the taps of their patent-leather shoes. They danced, they slid, they reared, they broke themselves in two, in three, in four, they drew themselves up, they bowed. . . . And behind them, an entire city, all of Europe, started to dance. And, through their example, rhythm took over the new world and afterwards the new world of the old world, and the rhythm spread to the machines and from the machines back to men and it was to go on forever and the Elks are dead, dead are Chocolat and Footit, dead the Nouveau Cirque and, dead or alive, the procession goes on with its dance, led by the little canes and beribboned skeletons of the Elks.[38]

Although the Elks here become skeletons in a kind of *danse macabre*, the life brought to Europe by these dancers and this dance continues in Cocteau's memory, and in the rhythm that they spread across Europe. The continuation of this dance and these dancers, "dead or alive," is also the result of the cinematic images of the Elks and the "Nouveau Cirque" made by Lumière operators in 1902.[39] Their rhythm, taken up by the cinematographic machine, continues "forever." Yet the images of African and African American dancers, in many examples considered in this and later chapters, vanish in formalist abstraction, imitation.

THE BALLETS SUÉDOIS: A CRITIQUE OF THE SNAPSHOT;
AN HOMAGE TO CINEMA

Modernist erasure of dancers in concert dance, and collaboration with the cinema, reached an extreme in Rolf de Maré's Ballets Suédois, which was performing choreography by the company's leading dancer, Jean Börlin, in Paris seasons between 1920 and 1925. Significantly, the all-European company provoked some critics to describe their dancing in racial terms, stereotyping the dancers in unexpected ways. And in its highly formalist stage works, the influence of "primitivism" in the plastic arts can be seen along with the influence of the cinematic.

De Maré's entrepreneurship took the collaborative multimedia forms engineered by Diaghilev even further. His company presented choreography characterized by "strong pictorial emphasis,"[40] or in the words of a contemporary critic, choreography staged to show "how far modern dance can after a time extend beyond the elements of dance itself."[41] Dance historian Lynn Garafola comments that "the approach was an extension of cubofuturist ideas that had circulated within the avant-garde since the early 1910s, and that Diaghilev had explored during the war, not only in 'Feu d'artifice' which eliminated the dancer entirely, but also in Fortunato Depero's unrealized 'Le Chant du rossignol,' where the artist described the chief interest of the dances as being the 'movement of volumes.'"[42]

The company has more often held historians' attention for its choreographic justification of painterly sets and movement integrated into or subordinated to them rather than for the dancing per se. This was apparently de Maré's preference ('I have hoped that something of the beauty that can be found in these paintings can be recreated in dance').[43] After the first season, which had featured more dancing and in which the influence of Fokine's teaching and choreography was apparent, Börlin's work suffered from the company's emphasis on the pictorial. In his own words, Börlin claimed not to be making *tableaux vivants* but to be inspired by old and modern masters: "each picture gives birth in me to an impression that immediately transforms itself into dance."[44] According to some historians, Börlin was given little choice, and the approach favored by de Maré and carried out by the choreographer would exasperate and exile the company's dancers and ultimately lead to its dissolution.

The absorption of dancers into sets and costumes, into full-scale stage-pictures influenced at least in part by cinematic projections, was justified by a logic of "unity": in de Maré's terms, a kind of Wagner-esque total artwork; in Fernand Léger's terms, a kind of rhythmic synthesis related to cinema, a figureless, mechanized movement: "a spectacle must be fast-moving for the sake of its unity."[45] At stake in this idea of unity or synthesis is the erasure of individual bodies as well as a reimagining of the rhythm of the collective. This thinking reached its apogee in Léger's comment in "Functions of Painting," that the dancer could function as part of a larger ensemble of movable scenic parts.

Although de Maré worried about the divide between cinema and stage, his ballet company pushed the use of cinema within choreography to an extreme. "There is too big a gap between dance and screen," he said in 1921. "We are faced with the question of rhythm and timing which is difficult to sort out. It would require the reel to be run by an invisible conductor."[46] Yet across four ballets choreographed by Börlin in four consecutive years, the Ballets Suédois collaborations manifested a growing awareness of the cinema as one of the visual techniques that dance performance was in dialogue with and that dance audiences were interested in. Cinematic references and cinematic form facilitated the staging of ballets of technological modernity. From the photographic metaphor used in Cocteau's libretto for *Les Mariés de la Tour Eiffel* (1921), to cinematic references in Léger's designs for Canuba's *Skating Rink* (1922) scenario, and Gerald Murphy's *Within the Quota* (1923), as well as the inclusion of a short film, *Entr'acte*, in the company's final production, the 1924 *Relâche*, these authors and designers used references to photography and cinematography to focus on social issues, technology, Frenchness, and Americanness in choreography; in the process, they parodied, commented on, and competed with cinema. Contemporary critic André Levinson described the "apotheosis of Americanism" in *Within the Quota* and the "gestes mécaniques" and the "pulsation de la machine" in *Skating Rink*.[47]

In *Les Mariés de la Tour Eiffel*, against the quaintness of the wedding-party photographic portrait on Paris's most famous monument, Cocteau stages the chaos of contemporary life by featuring technology with both mythic resonance and menacing potential: "To the right and the left of the stage the human phonographs, like an antique chorus, like the compère and commère of the music hall stage, describe, without the least sounding like 'literature,' the absurd action which is unfolded, danced, and pantomimed between them."[48]

*Les Mariés de la Tour Eiffel* represents an allegory of the camera and the photographic event, the souvenir, set at the Eiffel Tower; Cocteau claimed the set by Irene Lagut "brings to mind those Parisian postcards at the sight of which I have seen even little Arabs sigh in Africa."[49] For Cocteau, metropolitan technology may dazzle the colonials, but the artist exposes his position as magician: "A remark of the Photographer might do well for my epigraph: 'Since these mysteries are beyond me, let's pretend that I arranged them all the time.'"[50] In Walter Benjamin's observation, "Cocteau's *Les Mariés de la Tour Eiffel* can perhaps be considered a 'critique of the snapshot,' insofar as in this piece the two aspects of shock—its technological function in the mechanism and its sterilizing function in the experience—both come into play."[51]

The camera, human-sized, functions significantly as the initiator of the action, producing the characters and eventually swallowing them up. The phonographs Un and Deux speak all the roles, narrate the action onstage, and read the "dépêches" that arrive at the Eiffel Tower announcing imminent events. *Mariés* is thus both a ballet in which the characters—ostrich, general, little boy, bathing beauty—move and do not speak, and a sort of music-hall or even radio drama, with its speaking cast reduced to two. The banter of the phonographs includes wry commentaries on contemporary life in Paris: the Eiffel Tower used to be "queen of Paris" but is now "a telegraph girl." A picture of the wedding at the Eiffel Tower is critiqued: "it could be called a primitive"; and the camera walks off at the end to catch a train.

Meanwhile, when the child issues forth from the camera, the phonograph clucks, "Here is yet another of the dangers of photography." He attacks the party, presumably in order to get macaroons.[52] In Cocteau's summary: "Everything is seen from afar, in perspective—modern antiquity, people of our childhood, wedding parties that are dying out—an episode on the Eiffel tower which, having been discovered by the painters becomes again what it should never have ceased to be—a charming person in mittens whose one function was, formerly, to reign over Paris and who has now become a telegraph operator."[53] Cocteau goes on to describe how the "little boy, armed with ingratitude from his birth in the camera, slaughters his people with balls,"[54] a scene that Judi Freeman sees as a "retort to *Parade*," parodying French rather than American culture.[55]

Joan Acocella has questioned how great an effect Cocteau had on the choreographies with which he is associated, but Ramsay Burt, Lynn Garafola, and others have argued that his influence extended to the movement shaped for his libretti.[56] Garafola has written that the impetus for Börlin to draw on "extratheatrical movement idioms," as Massine had done in *Parade*, most likely came from Cocteau, whose stated aim was to "rehabilitate the commonplace,"[57] and who worked closely with the choreographer for *Mariés*: "The work's few dances all derived from this world of familiar pastimes—the polka for the Trouville bathing beauty (a role that Börlin himself sometimes danced), the quadrille and wedding march for the guests, and the two-step for the 'telegrams,' who looked like Tiller girls."[58] *Skating Rink* and *Within the Quota*, Garafola notes, also "drew on vernacular idioms," respectively, of the *apache* dances and the shimmy.[59]

In Gerald Murphy's libretto for *Within the Quota* (1923), a Swedish immigrant steps off the boat in New York and encounters a parade of characters representing American stereotypes:

> A millionairess, bedecked with immense strings of pearls, ensnares him; but a reformer frightens her away. Then a Colored Gentleman appears and does a vaudeville dance. He is driven away by a "dry agent" who immediately thereupon takes a nip from his private flask and disappears, to the immigrant's increasing astonishment. The Jazz Baby, who dances a shimmy in an enticing manner, is also quickly torn from him. A magnificent cowboy and a sheriff appear, bringing in the element of Western melodrama. At last the European is greeted and kissed by "America's

Sweetheart"; and while this scene is being immortalized by a movie camera, the dancing of the couples present sweeps all the troubles away.[60]

Gail Levin writes that "many of Murphy's character types and their costumes were borrowed directly from American cinema" and that the score also "cleverly parodied the music playing in silent-movie theaters."[61] In addition to cinema, the ballet also refers to two other forms evoking, without representing, black Americans: vaudeville in the blackface character of the Colored Gentleman, and jazz in the character of the Jazz Baby and omnipresent in Cole Porter's score for the ballet.

The submission of dancers to a rhythmic set was elaborated in a Léger-designed ballet, *Skating Rink*, and in cinema, the collaborative *Ballet mécanique* took Léger's ideas to their filmic fulfillment. *Skating Rink* originated as an idea for a ballet with that title by the writer and critic Ricciotto Canudo: in de Maré's words, summarizing Canudo, the ballet would be about "the awkward melancholy of the pleasures of skating, the sort of intimate bestiality that one feels in the slippery balancing, the slow motion of popular couples, all the types that evolve in this milieu; in short a synthesis of all these instincts." In a 1911 essay, Canudo had called for synthetic stage spectacles in the Futurist vein: "the perfect harmony of all elements of performance" was to be engineered via "an art of synthesis and not solely choreographic entertainment."[62] The libretto was published as a "futurist poem" in the *Mercure de France* of May 15, 1920: "Skating-Rink at Tabarin/Ballet-on-Skates." The ballet, influenced by Charlie Chaplin's 1916 film *The Rink*, had music by Arthur Honneger (of the group Les Six), who had worked on *Mariés*, and curtain, costumes, and decor by Léger. It opened on January 20, 1922.

Freeman notes Léger's interest in the rink as a social forum: "As a place of leisure, an essential feature of a world dominated by work and the machine, the rink for him was a place where all types of people convened to share a common pastime. His backdrop for the ballet unified this diverse crowd in a mélange of geometric forms and blocks of bold color, which closely resembled his contemporary paintings called *Elements mécaniques*." The dancers were meant to animate the empty lower half of the curtain as "moving scenery," but they were eventually integrated as static figures with the geometric shapes.[63]

The ballet's story of a crowd investing its energy in the skating rink and a trio in conflict at its center has been read as both an endorsement of popular culture and an exposé of continuing class conflicts. One plot summary focuses on the radiating energy of the Poet/Madman triumphantly carrying off the woman as the crowd swallows up the rival lover; other versions describe a fight, fall, and possible death of the woman, who is carried off as a victim.[64] Ramsay Burt claims that in *Skating Rink* Börlin choreographed the "disturbing new spaces of modernity" but also an antibourgeois Americanness that made the ballet more than elite entertainment.[65] Like *Parade*, Burt argues, *Skating Rink* was "modern" because of its American references: Hollywood, jazz, mechanical modernity, the desire for financial rewards and a better life.[66]

In his stylized tramp costume with top hat askew and asymmetrical jacket, Börlin's main character resembled Charlie Chaplin and the animated Charlot figure Léger would use to open and close *Ballet mécanique*. But beyond these references to Chaplin, *Skating Rink* was also cinematic in its choreography. Commenting on a reconstruction of the ballet by Millicent Hodson and Kenneth Archer, Burt writes:

> Like the crowd in "Petruschka," the gliding skaters are not anonymous but each have their different roles and characters, and, just as the three main roles in "Petruschka" are puppets, there is something puppet-like about the skaters. Their abstracted circles and arcs blend with mimetic gestures as they react to the events that take place. The style of the dancers' reactions, as Archer and Hodson's research revealed, should be that of early silent film actors. . . . Everything is overdone for effect just as in a silent comedy. There are other more serious moments when the dancers look like a crowd in a German expressionist film—*Metropolis* or *The Cabinet of Doctor Caligari*.[67]

Burt describes the movements that Hodson labeled "cubist gestures" as "highly Expressionist," resembling photographs of Dalcroze and Laban movement choirs.[68] Burt cites Archer and Hodson's description of the ballet's male dancers, whose torsos remain stable in oversized and asymmetrical jackets and whose "legs skate nimbly underneath, in the manner of marionettes," while the women's skirts keep "stiff geometrical shapes that hold their line as the torso moves freely above," rendering, for Burt, not only puppetlike movement but also the quality of a frieze, "occasionally reminiscent of 'L'Apres-Midi d'un Faune.'"[69] Combining elements of the tradition of European mechanical dancing with American films, the snapshot, and the frieze, *Skating Rink* serves as a link in the chain between machine ballets and avant-garde cinema.

INSTANTIST BALLET

In July 1921, Derain and Satie had put before de Maré's assistant Jacques Hebertot an idea for a cinema-ballet:

> This would be a parody of the Cinema. The backdrop would be created by a projection on a screen that would fill up the entire background; the sides would be of dark fabric. The characters would have the appearance of emerging from the screen, all in black and white, to create a truly cinematic scene. There would be seven or eight different scenes, easy to obtain by simply changing the projection; and we would mock the cinema through exaggerated gestures, speed, and music which would never be in sync with that which was represented.[70]

Freeman notes that this idea was "daring and unprecedented": "The ideas of combining film and performance on stage and playing with the emergence of one form from another were radical ones."[71] But this idea never made it onto the stage, although elements of it, she says, were incorporated into Derain's *Jack in the Box*, with music by Satie and choreography by Balanchine, staged by Etienne de Beaumont's Soirées de Paris in May 1926 at the Théâtre des Champs-Elysées.[72]

Some of these ideas also made their way into the collaboration between Satie and Picabia for the Ballets Suédois's final production, *Relâche* (Theater Closed), in 1924. With a more elaborated cinematic ambience than *Within the Quota*, *Relâche*, with its black, white, and gray set and intense lighting, moved beyond cinema references toward a merging of the two media. Sometimes described as the first ballet using film, *Relâche*, with its inclusion of Clair's *Entr'acte*, can be understood as both following in the tradition of live entertainment like the danced prologue to a film screening and leading the way for future experimentation with dance and film. The film's director, René Clair, writes in "Picabia, Satie and the First Night of 'Entr'acte,'" that this final Ballets Suédois production, *Relâche*, was announced as follows:

*Theatre Closed*

> An instantist ballet in two acts and a cinematic interlude and the Dog's tail by Francis Picabia. Music by M. Erik Satie. Décor by M. Picabia. Cinematic interlude by René Clair. Choreography by M. Jean Börlin.

> For the sake of future historians of the theatre, I must add that no one has ever known exactly why this ballet was "instantist." As for the dog's tail, no one saw the shadow of it. Picabia, one of the great "inventors" of the day, felt that one invention more or less would make no difference. When I met him, he explained that he wanted to have a film projected between the two acts of the ballet, as was done, before 1914, during the interval at café concerts.[73]

The film was screened to live music by Satie, which was, Clair maintains, "the first composition written for the cinema 'shot by shot' at a time when films were still silent."[74]

Clair was asked by the creators to make a short filmed prologue: "an unforgettable vision of Satie: white goatee, pince-nez, bowler hat and umbrella—descending from the sky in slow-motion and firing a cannon shot which signalled the beginning of the show."[75] In fact, there are two figures in the sequence: Picabia's notes for the curtain-raiser say, "Slow-motion loading of a cannon by Satie and Picabia; the shot must make as much noise as possible. Total length: 1 minute."[76]

Picabia's few lines on the project speak of the film in terms of the "pleasure of life" and the "pleasure of inventing" with respect for "nothing except the desire to burst out laughing."[77] *Relâche* is "life as I love it . . . automobile headlights."[78] In an interview with de Maré published on the day of the premiere, Picabia took aim at the theater's "pretentious absurdities" and argued that in *Relâche* "I want only a joy comparable to that . . . of doing 120 in an auto."[79] In reference to this desire for speed, in the ballet's finale, Picabia drives Satie around in a miniature Citroën onstage.

After the "Projectionette" sequence in the prologue, in which Satie and Man Ray on the roof load a cannon that points directly toward the camera, the interval film, *Entr'acte*, begins with shot 28 in the shot sequence described by Jacques and Hayden, the English translators of the film's screenplay. After dots of light, we see Paris upside down: "a series of eleven different long shots of houses and roofs seen diagonally or completely upside down."[80] The next shot (no. 40) introduces what might be the most enigmatic figures of the film: "Medium close-up of three little dolls—one male, two female—against a background of painted flowers. Their heads are balloons with faces painted on them. Through an aperture behind them, which looks like the back window of a car, roofs and houses can be seen passing rapidly from left to right."[81] All three of these balloon faces give the appearance of dark skin: with short curls painted onto her cheeks and almond-shaped eyes, the biggest one looks strikingly like Josephine Baker. A series of shots of the dolls leads up to a dance image:

> 43. Close-up of one of the female dolls whose head slowly deflates and flops onto its shoulder.
> 44. Resume on medium close-up of the dolls, all their heads deflated.
> 45. Close-up of the male doll whose head reinflates and swells to its original size.
> 46. Medium close-up of a ballerina in a tutu shot directly from below, twirling round on a sheet of glass.
> 47. Resume on the three dolls, all their heads reinflated.[82]

In succeeding scenes, Duchamp and Man Ray play chess, and then "white discs" of light, which appear abstracted from the street lamps burning brightly on the street, expand as the camera loses focus.[83] The effect is one of a medusa-like flying saucer appearing above Paris rooftops with the atmosphere of Feuillade's *Vampires*.

A series of shots of a ballerina seen from beneath, with side shots of her arms and legs, arrive finally at her head; stills here show her wearing a false beard and pince-nez; other images substitute Picabia in tutu.

In the second half of the film, a narrative of two marksmen or hunters, which makes various magic turns, ends with one hunter shot by the other and then gives way to a funeral cortege. In the film's most striking footage, this parade of mourners, walking behind a camel-drawn hearse, suddenly begins to march in slow-motion leaps, as if in a parody of Marey or Londe's time-motion studies. This mad slow-motion leaping of mourners in top hats and tail coats eventually gives way to normal-speed movement, as they walk, and then run, after the cart: "Resume on tracking shot of the mourners in top hats, racing along the avenue."[84]

A long chase scene ensues, down a boulevard and out into the countryside, with the hearse losing both camel and driver and picking up speed on its own, and the mourners running after the runaway coffin: "233. Close-up of the mourners at waist-level, arms and legs going like pistons, camera tracking left."[85] Tracking shots move down winding roads and eventually to a sequence of Luna Park roller coaster shots.

Eventually the coffin falls off the wagon into a field, and the crowd gathers around it. When the lid opens, Börlin emerges as a conjurer who makes everyone, one by one, disappear with his magic wand. Then with a final flourish, he makes himself invisible. In a final joke, a sign with the word FIN is held off camera; Börlin breaks through it and bows as if to applause, before he is kicked and then pushed back through the sign in reverse by de Maré.[86]

*Relâche* took the Dada-inspired experimentation of *Entr'acte* as far as stage performance could, and it marked a point at which, de Maré said, the company could now go neither backward nor forward. When the opening night was cancelled because of Börlin's inability to perform—because of illness or addiction—Clair writes, the audience in evening dress exclaimed: "We might have known . . . that's what the title meant . . . *Relâche* . . . It's the apotheosis of Dada."[87] The ballet was the fulfillment not only of Dada but of the longer tradition of experimental theater from Jarry on, with the performers performing machines and ultimately becoming mechanized by and in cinema.

André Levinson, who often complained of the Ballets Suédois's mechanics, lambasted the piece. In his diatribe against Picabia and the publicity materials for *Relâche*, he writes: 'Instead of going to the box office,

I run over to the rue du Quatre-Septembre to buy myself an electric iron. And in presenting the ballet *Relâche* before lighting the fuse of this infernal machine, he promises us life as he loves it: automobile headlights, pearl necklaces, the lithe, curvaceous female forms."[88] Levinson sees it as the same old take on the latest thing, not true invention.

But if dancers, choreographers, critics, and even the impresario saw *Relâche* as an end point for dance, it also suggested a future for new forms of multimedia. Other collaborators with the Ballets Suédois, Léger and Cocteau, would turn to cinema.[89] Léger's next project, *Ballet mécanique*, can be understood as the fulfillment of this impetus to mechanize dancers and the role of the cinema in that mechanization.

MECHANICAL BALLET

The "rhythm of the visible world" that Gertrude Stein represented in poetry as an invisible but audible dance takes visible shape as the dance of objects, as a mechanical ballet in the rhythmic editing of Dudley Murphy and Léger's film, *Ballet mécanique*. The film's operations were conceived by filmmaker, painter, and composer alike as a choreography. Murphy describes the film he wanted to make as a "stop motion dance": in one sequence, he envisioned using the artificial legs that exhibit silk stockings and "decided to do a stop motion dance with these legs around a clock. In bringing the legs to the studio, I drove through Paris in an open cab, with a leg over my shoulder, screaming."[90] Léger planned to remake the film in the final years of his life, in a version he intended to call "Ballet des couleurs." The consistent use of the term "ballet" suggests dance's inspiration for the rhythm of montage in which the "eye and spirit of the spectator will no longer accept" the spectacle and find it unbearable.[91]

Léger wrote in "The Machine Aesthetic: Geometric Order and Truth" (1923) that "the cinema of the future" lay in the *personification of the enlarged detail*, the individualization of the fragment, where the drama begins, is set, and stirs. The cinema competes with life in this way. . . . The object by itself is capable of becoming something absolute, moving, and dramatic."[92] Léger imagined making a film inspired by Abel Gance's use of rapid montage in his 1922 film *La Roue* (*The Wheel*) in which the "machine becomes *the leading character, the leading actor*."[93] About

Gance's film, Léger wrote in 1922: "The fragmentation of the object, the intrinsic plastic value of the object, its pictorial equivalence, have long been the domain of the modern arts. With *The Wheel* Abel Gance has elevated the art of film to the plane of the plastic arts."[94] Léger's description of his own work, cited in Gance's promotional materials for the film in 1922, states: "Fernand Léger is the modern French painter that first considered the *mechanical element* as a possible plastic element; he has incorporated the concept of *equivalences* into numerous pictures."[95]

Léger's abstraction, fragmentation, and rhythmic composition of forms, depicting pictorial "equivalents" of material objects, have been linked to a twentieth-century machine aesthetic. Léger explained that "if one wants to create and obtain the equivalence of the 'beautiful object' sometimes produced by modern industry, it is very tempting to make use of its elements as raw material."[96] For Matthew Affron, Léger illustrates the tension between abstraction and representation in modernist art in his "ambition, defined in a text of 1914, 'Contemporary Achievements in Painting,' to make abstract art that would be 'representative, in the modern sense of the word, of the new visual state imposed by the evolution of the new means of production.'" Léger's paintings of machines and machine parts represented what Affron calls "the extraordinary spectacle of the material quotidian"—a quotidian defined "by the industrialization of work and leisure, by the rationalization of resources and time, by a speeding up of feeling, thought, and perception."[97] Negotiating between the representation of machine life and the abstraction and fragmentation created by machines, Léger's work follows in a modernist tradition of using dance—or the idea of dance, especially without dancers—to figure the motion of machinic modernity.

Although there is disagreement about whose idea it was, Pound collaborated with Léger on the 1924 *Ballet mécanique*. Léger had wanted for some time to make a film that would animate some of his paintings of machines, and Pound connected him with filmmaker Dudley Murphy, who shot the footage, Antheil, who wrote the music, and Man Ray, who consulted on the film at an early stage.[98]

Judi Freeman argues that the film follows Léger's interest developed in the 1910s to paint machines, then in the early 1920s to paint 'life in the

machine-dominated era," and by 1924 to return to the more abstract machine forms as in the canvas *Elément mécanique* (1924); in Freeman's summary, "the imagery became the machine, then the machine closeup, then
the closeup of everyday life."[99] In between, *Ballet mécanique* animated

> swinging Christmas ornaments and saucepan covers, incessantly
> pumping pistons, whirling gelatin molds, gyrating pieces of
> corrugated sheet metal. It appears that Léger instructed Murphy
> to shoot many of these images, along with other images Murphy
> already had shot with Man Ray or, in several instances, chosen
> with Pound or on his own; many of the refracted and fractured
> images, such as Kiki's face, the owl, or the corrugated sheet metal
> resulted from Pound's ideas on film inspired by his experience
> with the vortographies of Alvin Langdon Coburn and from Man
> Ray's rayogram experiments.[100]

The sequences of *Ballet mécanique* show everyday gestures edited into
mechanical sequences and everyday objects animated through film editing and collage. The effect of the movement created by the montage is at
times meant to be painful to watch. In the sequence "The Woman Climb-
ing the Stairs," a washerwoman burdened with a heavy basket labors up
a flight of stairs. The film stops before she reaches the top and then repeats the sequence without variation until the audience becomes uncom-
fortable. Léger writes:

> in "The Woman Climbing the Stairs" I wanted to *amaze* the audi-
> ence first, then make them uneasy, and then push the adventure
> to the point of exasperation. In order to "time" it properly, I got
> together a group of workers and people in the neighborhood, and
> I studied the effect that was *produced* on them. In eight hours I
> learned what I wanted to know. *Nearly all of them reacted at
> about the same time.*[101]

This experimental method, with its echoes of ergonomic studies, can
also be identified in Léger's canvases. Freeman has noted that "the wish to
challenge the spectator and to juxtapose images, speeds, and rhythms in
order to establish equivalences characterize Léger's approach to his painting."[102] In another sequence from the film, the rapid alternation of a trian-

gle with a circle, positioned in the same spot on the screen, makes the replacement of one shape by the other look like an animated movement. In the substitution of triangle for circle, the form appears to sprout legs, which then disappear, or are lifted up, when the triangle is in turn replaced by the seemingly "legless" circle. In this animation of the forms, the audience sees not so much triangle and circle but the movement that the shape onscreen seems to be performing in order to transform itself. Léger writes:

> The particular interest of the film is centered upon the importance which we give to the "fixed image," to its arithmetical, automatic projection, slowed down or accelerated—additional, likeness.
> No scenario—Reactions of rhythmic images, that is all.
> Two coefficients of interest upon which the film is constructed:
> The variation of the speeds of projection:
> The rhythm of these speeds.[103]

The rhetoric does not sound unlike Pound's 1912 Imagist principles. But Léger's goal is not the condensation of meaning into word-pictures that transport the reader emotionally, intellectually, in an instant of time. His goal is rather to batter the viewer with repeated gestures and figures, to put the image in motion in such a way that it disturbs the viewer, fixes him or her to the spot, to the site of viewing where s/he is transfixed.

In *Ballet mécanique*, modernity is represented as objects in maddening motion, taking on a life of their own; a revolution of the animated inanimate or abstraction of the human labeled dancing. As if dancing had been made obsolete, technology and cinema absorb its functioning.

Significantly, when another seemingly abstract sphere floated across the screen three years later, in the opening frames of Jean Renoir's 1927 *Charleston*, it carried African American dancer Johnny Higgins, a bowler-hatted scientist captaining this spherical space ship, who spies a single white woman in an "unknown land" below. In Renoir's recap of this avant-garde "never quite finished" film that he considered his "gesture of farewell to the cinema," "A black scientist from another planet pays a visit to the earth, where all civilization has been destroyed by an inter-planetary war . . . and is found by a savage woman who, not knowing his language, can only communicate with him by dancing. When the dance is over, the visitor returns to his own planet, taking her with him.'[104] As the dancer teaches Higgins the steps he first awkwardly imitates, and then performs with great sophistication, and as the couple sail off together into the heavens, it is tempting to read the film as an allegory for the detachment, erasure, or abstraction of dancers, white and black, "savage" and urbane, American and European, across the decade.

### JEAN BÖRLIN DANCES FOR BLAISE CENDRARS

In a text signed Blaise Cendrars and titled "Jean Börlin," in de Maré's archive, Cendrars calls for a great "sports ballet," but one that would be "democratic": "When can we expect the OVERSEAS-ATLANTIC ballet, the great ballet of DEMOCRATIC CROWDS, the great open-air SPORTS ballet?"[105]

Cinema represents one medium for creating ballets without bodies; another is the arena of the stadium and sport, featuring and aestheticizing bodies but also promoting anonymity in the mass.[106] The merging of stadium and theater in spectacles organized under German and Italian fascism of the 1930s, and the political goals and content of these spectacles, can be read as one outgrowth of the kind of machine dancing fantasized in Marinetti's Futurism and as inspiring another tendency for representation of bodies in motion in film, for example, in Leni Riefenstahl's *Olympia* or *Triumph of the Will*.[107] The usefulness of the image of a technologized body, or body-machine, to what Walter Benjamin identified as the aestheticized politics of European fascism is well documented.[108] But the dancing machine also serves what Benjamin identified as the politicized art that would oppose fascist aestheticization of politics.

Praising Börlin's "three great creations"—*Skating Rink*, *Les Mariés de la Tour Eiffel*, and "le ballet nègre," *La Création du monde*—Cendrars praises Börlin's dancing as American at heart and technological in spirit. Lauded simultaneously as a natural and an inventor, Börlin is praised as a "dancer who does not know how to dance" and for being "at the antipodes of Russians and the French tradition emigrated to St. Petersbourg, the ancien regime, the Regency, and Italianism." On the contrary, "he hovers over the great heart of Whitman that bursts like a giant gramophone and takes off in the arms of the members of the Union of voiture-aviation."[109]

André Levinson critiqued Ballets Suédois's dancing as mechanical. He saw Börlin as the Nordic man and argued that the Swedish "race" did not produce good dancers.[110] For Levinson, dancing summarized palpably and immediately an age's "manière d'être," "the state of a civilisation or originality of a race," and he stereotyped bad dancing in the following terms: "The dancer who is nothing more than the slave and the ape of rhythm is reduced to nothingness."[111] The obvious Africanization of the model of bad dancing, echoing Levinson's distaste for the jazz forms arriving in Europe, is in direct contrast to Cendrar's reception of Börlin's dancing.[112]

For Cendrars, Börlin's dancing is not mechanical but embodies the spirit of technology in the model of the human motor. Börlin's naturalness, his "not knowing how to dance," is identified in terms of class and race: "Jean Börlin is at the level of the sailors, soldiers, mulattos, negroes, hawaiians, savages." And Cendrars sees him as a key figure in a renaissance of popular dance based in the "places where one dances in Paris": the boulevards, the railway stations, the port of Bourget, the Vel' d'Hiv, the Wagram, the Linas-Methléry autodrome, where "posters and loudspeakers make you forget the teaching of the Académie de la Danse, static and time, measure and taste, affected grace, and virtuosity. When you have forgotten all this, you've got it, you find the rhythm, today's beautiful rhythm that brings the new five continents, discipline, balance, health, force, speed."[113]

Although Cendrars's program at times sounds like Marinetti's, Cendrars here insists on the natural and democratic elements of such a program, on technologies mobilized for popular entertainments, on the "savage," indigenous or American, rather than elite or artificial, basis for such technologies. In this text, the choreographer takes off with the union members of experimental aviation rather than turning the dancer herself into a plane, or worshipping the car as a woman. In the service of both the left and right, aestheticized politics and politicized art, the "dancing machine" continues to embody different energies and different ends encompassing the broad spectrum of modernisms and avant-gardes, offering to all sides a rhythm that could take them in.

# 5.
# Labor Is Dancing

TAYLORISM: SPEED AND NATURAL ABILITY

At the same Exposition Universelle in 1900 at which Loie Fuller had made such an electrifying impression, Henri Le Chatelier, author of the introduction to the second edition of Jules Amar's *Le Moteur humain*, admired another American import, Frederick W. Taylor's cutting machines. Le Chatelier became a defender of Taylor's inventions and practices, and arranged for translation of his writings.[1] Contemporary with the machine ballets considered in the last chapter, arriving from the United States and then taking over European work-science after World War I, Taylorism must be counted as a central choreography of the machine age. With the single goal of maximum "productivity," Taylorist scientific management focused on two elements also found in contemporary reflection on dance: first, the essential gesture, calculated to help the worker work at his "best speed"; and second, group coordination. Both depended on a kind of anonymity, with the worker's body being subsumed by the rhythm of his own gesture and that of the group, and the effect of both was an erasure of individual identity. Reflection on the "economy of gesture" marks a host of avant-garde theaters, theorists, and practitioners, from the schools of the Bauhaus, Laban, Dalcroze's eurythmy, and Meyerhold's "Taylorism for the theater." Aside from these well-known and well-studied examples, elements of Taylorist thinking, and responses to it, can be found in dance practice and theory in Europe in the 1920s.

Taylorist scientific management is based on the idea that the true interest of employees and employers alike is maximum prosperity and that "maximum prosperity can exist only as the result of maximum productivity."[2] Its goals are accomplished by training the worker so he can perform "at his fastest pace and with the maximum of efficiency" the highest class of work his abilities permit.[3] In Taylor's 1911 *Principles of Scientific Management*, the basic recipe for maximum productivity depends on both the refinement of the individual gesture and the choreography of the group in the shop or plant. At the intersection of work-science and workers' raw energy, the essential gesture is determined by time and motion studies, and once adopted by the worker, it allows him to move to the capacity of his "natural ability."[4]

The anonymity or anti-individuality imposed on workers by Taylorism and their characterization as "natural" are applied to dancers in a range of dances and dance texts explored in this chapter and the next. Whereas the choreographies of the Futurist soirées or the Ballets Suédois traced the fascination with machines' movement, rhythm, and speed, in dances about cars, airplanes, or missiles, the big city or cinema, this chapter considers dances or dance texts in which dancers do not so much look like machines as internalize their functioning. In very different dance styles, dancers responded to machine culture and machine art in forms ranging from parodic mimicry to inspired imitation. Such dancing—internalizing the machine into the body—often implies a critique of technology even as it encodes or responds to Taylorist thinking. This chapter traces, across the first decades of the twentieth century, in choreographies other than those of the central companies appearing in Paris, and in very different kinds of texts central to modernism, dancers mechanized in the ways that Taylorism aimed at, with streamlined gestures, anonymous detachment, and group synchronicity.

The list of writers and dancers considered in this chapter reads like a strange who's who of modernism, representing all sides of the political spectrum, some witnessing and writing about dance performances (Kracauer on the Tiller Girls, Artaud on the Balinese dancers), others writing dance-plays for the stage (Yeats, Brecht), and still others developing dance philosophies in poetic or prose texts (Yeats, Valéry). As a group these commentators, most but not all writing in France, share neither a language nor ideological or aesthetic backgrounds. They represent readers and audiences of modernism ranging from elite bohemia to popular culture.

What brings these texts into conversation is the way they can be read in response to the rhetoric and practice of Taylorism. Against a discourse of maximum productivity, unproductive dancing can carry the banner of the avant-garde; reconceived as differently productive, it can serve to critique the choreography of labor. Some of the texts argue for an idealized fusion of dancer and dance, or individual in the group, or the worker with the object produced. Idealized as an art of fusion, dancing can inspire scientific management, or transcend the reality of the fragmented, repetitive motions that subtend its principles. But other texts considered here point out the disparity, detachment, or alienation in dancing as in labor. Some texts argue for dance's meaningfulness as a model for labor and others for its meaninglessness, like labor. What this chapter finds is that modernist dance texts—for example, Yeats's famous "Among School Children" or Valéry's "Philosophie de la danse"—are in fact in dialogue with texts of mass culture.

In *After the Great Divide*, Andreas Huyssens describes the interaction of modernism and mass culture as a dance: "ever since their simultaneous emergence in the mid-19th century, modernism and mass culture have been engaged in a compulsive *pas de deux*."[5] Huyssens explores "the extent to which modernism and the avantgarde as forms of an adversary culture were nevertheless conceptually and practically bound up with capitalist modernization and/or with communist vanguardism, that modernization's twin brother."[6] With a few examples, this chapter ranges from the historical avant-garde with fascist tendencies to communist theater practice; it focuses less on the differences in the ideological components of the texts explored and more on the unlikely similarities in their estimations of dance and its relevance to modernization. Without always openly articulating the terms of a debate between high and low culture, between leftist and rightist politics, or between modernization and idealization, these texts identify dance as significant to reconceptions of work, value, identity, and meaning in the machine age.[7]

Taylor's two basic movements—individual gesture and group coordination—repeat aspects of the fragmentation and fusion familiar from Marey's chronophotographs, time-motion studies, work-science, and early cinema. The individual worker's gesture, in the service of a smoothly ordered industry, becomes a mechanical part that lends itself to the operation of an unstoppable productivity. These movements also replay, in a slightly different way, the mechanized movement of the automata and the raw energy of the human motor, the worker's potential labor power and its commodification by industry.

The work of two dancers not affiliated with ballet companies, but finding differing degrees of success in Europe and in the United States, exemplify these two models: the first was embodied by Japanese dancer Michio Ito; the second by an African American dancing in France, Josephine Baker. These two dancers, whose work might seem far from the staging of technology or the popular machine ballets, and has been more often associated with high modernist aesthetics, in fact stage important elements of the choreography of the "industrial" age.

Stereotypes of race run alongside modernist conceptions of the machine and mechanized modernity; in some texts considered here, they are not disguised, but in others they are cast in terms of energy and output. Stereotypes of dancers such as Ito and Baker, considered in this chapter and the next, had not only to do with the appearances of performing bodies but also with the culture of industry and productivity. The perceived Asianness of Ito and Africanness of Baker contribute to the typing of their bodies and dancing as mechanical or motorized.

According to Taylor's *Principles of Scientific Management*, an individual's speed and submission of the individual and the group to management are central to a management science that confronts what it identifies as a culture of sluggish workers who believe that working too hard takes work away from others. Management has to point the way toward productivity through cooperation—understood here as the opposite of unionization.[8] Thus, although the worker has to be trained to realize his "natural ability," even the best workers are "incapable of fully understanding this science,"[9] and management has to take over the preparation (formerly left to the workers themselves), which allows the worker to do his job better. Taylor insists that a close coordination between management and workers is necessary even while the hierarchy between them is firmly established, as his concluding summary of the principles of scientific management makes clear:

Science, not rule of thumb.
Harmony, not discord.
Cooperation, not individualism.
Maximum output, in place of restricted output.
The development of each man to his greatest efficiency and prosperity.[10]

Under the rubrics of harmony and cooperation, efficiency and prosperity, workers' individuality is erased. Yet the end result of productivity, Taylor concludes, distinguishes "civilized," goal-oriented cultures from those that are "uncivilized": "Those who are afraid that a large increase in the productivity of each workman will throw other men out of work, should realize that the one element more than any other which differentiates civilized from uncivilized countries—prosperous from poverty-stricken peoples—is that the average man in the one is five or six times as productive as the other."[11]

Thus workers' submission to management's choreography of a coordinated whole guarantees them a "civilized" identity that only the prosperous can claim. Such conclusions, of course, belie the very terms of Taylorist organization, which creates a hierarchy of management with "scientific" knowledge and a workforce with "natural" ability and nonproductive tendencies. Taylorism's drive toward the abstraction of labor accomplished the erasure of workers' subjectivity and their disappearance into anonymity, along with the stereotyping of their identities.[12]

SWINGING IN CITIES

Giving Taylorist logic an avant-garde twist, Pound argues in "Machine Art" that the coordination of effort and action in the factory would be best choreographed with the help of music: "Nobody has yet heard a New York street corner plus excavation plus steel construction conglomerate, harmonized, and so far as I can perceive, no one will. Construction work is done only once and without rehearsal. Factory work is done day after day, and people can and do practice the best way of doing it." But Pound's interpretation of Taylorist productivity includes lessons learned from the supposedly unproductive "uncivilized." The acoustic potential of machines, Pound argues, has not been exploited; they can—as George Antheil's compositions such as *Ballet mécanique* had suggested—make new music, but they can also orchestrate industry and create a climate in which workers thrive and productivity is increased. In Pound's view, "Modern man can live and should live in his cities and machine shops with the same kind of swing and exuberance that the savage is supposed to have in his forest"[13]; "there is no reason why the shop noise shouldn't be used as stimulus and to give swing and ease to modern work, just as the sailor's chantey or any working song has been used, by lumbermen, or by savages."[14] A closer look shows that this industrial "music" is based on rhythm and rooted in the low frequencies that are used by the "Japanese and Africans" and in jazz.[15] Pound even sees Ford as having "experimented in tempo" and suggests that a "harmonization" of industrial noise synchronizing the speeds of machinery and establishing proportion between the duration of noises, including silences "in tune" with noise, would increase productivity.[16]

Pound's elaboration of the ideogram discussed earlier, a poetic formulation in which "the thing is what it does," also identified Asian and African elements as fundamental: the pictogram represented by Chinese kanji or the "stimulus" of African languages' "lack of power to generalize"—that "grades down into pantomime and mimicry."[17] Associated with these poetics, yet adapted from what he calls the "method of science" and applied to industry, the ideogram also serves Pound as an image of the way machines work: condensing energy and coding information. Pound cites Léger's idea that real machines were better than "ideal" machinelike forms, "that their actual functioning was conducive to better form."[18] Thus, although Pound contemplates forms "*interesting* in themselves, and in their combinations,"[19] it is machines' functionality that makes their forms interesting: "we find a thing beautiful in proportion to its aptitude to a function. I suspect that the better a machine becomes AS A MACHINE, the better it will be to look at."[20]

Inspired by Pound's early work on Chinese characters, his ideogram serves as scientific concretion, poetic rhythmic complex, and movement of machine functioning, linking ancient civilizations to modernity. Pound shared his work on Ernest Fenellosa's *The Chinese Written Character* with Yeats and edited *Certain Noble Plays of Japan* with an introduction by Yeats in 1916. Both together discovered the Japanese dancer Michio Ito, who would choreograph and dance in Yeats's first Noh-inspired play in that year. Living in poverty and "lacking the gasometer penny," as Pound would remember in the *Cantos*, Ito was introduced by the poets into London salons, where he danced in Isadora's footsteps.

Yeats's interest in the dancers of his time has been studied less than his obsessive interest in dance as a metaphor of cosmic unity. Although an unlikely dance amateur, Yeats was familiar with the dancing of the stars of his day as well as with that of the innovators, and he worked closely with Ito and later with Ninette de Valois. In Paris in the 1890s, Yeats would have been taken by his then-roommate Arthur Symons—a noted dance patron and author of *The Symbolist Movement in Literature*, published in 1899—to see the dancer of the moment, Loie Fuller.[21] Although named in Yeats's poem "Nineteen Hundred and Nineteen," it is not Fuller herself but her "Chinese dancers" who are seen by Yeats as a link between the modern world and his Byzantium. Like many of his colleagues, Yeats was largely uninterested in the late-century London theater: "I hated the existing conventions of the theatre."[22] A great admirer of Edward Gordon Craig, Yeats was inspired by his productions and by his call, in the first issue of his review *The Mask* in 1908, for a new theater of "Beauty" with an Oriental emphasis.[23] Like Craig, Yeats disliked the theater's "photographic realism."[24]

Yeats considered Ito indispensable to his "Noh plays," for which the dancer created the role of the Guardian of the Well in *At the Hawk's Well* in 1916: "My play is made possible by a Japanese dancer," he wrote in *Certain Noble Plays of Japan*, and indeed Ito's movement, making reference to the Noh tradition, and tailored for Yeats's text, made the staging of the plays a reality. The Noh conventions famously downplay observation of real-life phenomena; yet Yeats frequently accompanied Ito to the London zoo to watch the hawks as part of creating his role in *At the Hawk's Well*, and Yeats worked closely with Ito during this first production.[25] The simultaneous use of naturalist observation and formalist performance techniques echoes Yeats's paradoxical position in using the Noh while attempting to build a national theater for the Irish "people"—a particular political, if not necessarily populist, use of theatrical symbolism.

Ito's dancing, in these plays and in his later repertory, often staged themes from nature, including animals; yet his dancing was received or understood as mechanistic or mechanical because of its movement quality—a blend of Ito's training in Japan and with Dalcroze in Europe. His dances combine elements of Noh (although historians disagree about the degree of his training and interest in the form)[26] with eurythmy: many feature a slow sustained continuity typical of many Asian movement forms and highly stylized gestures, performed with an expressionless, masklike face.[27]

In his introduction to *Certain Noble Plays of Japan*, Yeats writes that the Japanese dancer "was able, as he rose from the floor, where he had been sitting cross-legged, or as he threw out an arm, to recede from us into some more powerful life. . . . Because that separation was achieved by human means alone, he recedes but to inhabit as it were the deeps of the mind."[28] Yeats goes on to reveal his organic conception of dance's power in his distaste for jarring or avant-garde performance: "as a deep of the mind can only be approached through what is most human, most delicate, we should distrust bodily distance, mechanism, and loud noise."[29] We only believe in those thoughts which have been conceived not in the brain but in the whole body."[30]

Embodiment would be a crucial concept for Yeats and associated with dance's cosmic power; paradoxically, it would also be a significant part of his admiration of Ito's detachment. Although he eventually founded a school in Japan, after teaching and performing in the United States and Europe, and passed on his repertory, Ito is often described as unique. Ito's Japanese heritage and references to classical traditions led Yeats to characterize his dancing as trancelike and superhuman. In Yeats's text, Ito is the epitome of the mystical mechanical, reminiscent of the Orientalized automata of an earlier century and pointing the way toward Yeats's cosmically controlled dancer.

Using the same Chopin waltz to which Isadora danced a gypsy dance, Ito danced his 1927 *Ladybug*. Suspended on half-toe or flying low with weighted jumps, Ito dances with the magnetic tension that also marked his Hawk in Yeats's Noh play. Sharp wings are shaped by overhead arm gestures, to left and right, on the music's opening notes; then hands are brought together as if clapping, the head goes back as the leg extends forward, exploding the design of the first two side poses into a beating and opening of wings and legs that melts into a balancé waltz step under the arched upper body. This opening sequence is repeated before giving way to travel around the floor in circles etched over one another. The balancé and three following steps are executed entirely on half-toe, allowing the body to appear to be skimming the surface rather than dipping down and up in space. In this tense, droning flight, Ito circles stage right, settles for a moment in arabesque, and closes the circle with a spin; then after repeating the opening figures, he circles left again, finishing with a spin. The circle patterns, right and left, are then repeated in jumping sequences in which rapidly circling arms beat like wings over small quick skips, hops, and running steps. Ito's tension is not released in the jumps but allows the body to appear to hover rather than bounce up and down, matching the piano's pyrotechnics with fast footwork and the illusion of flight. The jump sequences accelerate toward their end with élan that follows the accelerando of the piano, in a series of skips in place in which the leg swings forward and backward in attitude and the arms circle together across the body like propellers. In a bravura final sequence, Ito executes a series of jumps and bourrées moving backward on an upstage diagonal, hovering on half-toe as the arms—now slowly and heavily—circle and drape the head and then open out in a movement familiar from Michel Fokine's *Spectre de la Rose* (1911). Another short jumping sequence that settles in arabesque gives way to a repetition of the jump sequences, again retracing the circle patterns and finishing in a final spin that settles into a front-facing version of the opening *Ladybug* side-poses: left leg forward, right back, knees bent, hovering on half-toe, with arms in opposition to the legs, right forward and left back, bent at the elbow and wrist, torso twisted sideways left and head forward, looking out over the right hand. References to Nijinsky's Rose and Faune connect Ito's choreography to its historical context in the West while pointing the way toward some of the movement qualities that Japanese Butoh dance would explore later in the century.

Ito's dancing is evocative: the legs do not make presentational gestures, as in ballet; the arms hold shapes but they are fluid and tense, rubbery and transforming, dynamic rather than static. The body dancing Ito's dances does not look like it is working, but in this way it eludes its audience, receding, even as it moves forward, into the space of "deep mind."[31]

## LABOR IS DANCING

Yeats's most famous dance poem, published in 1926 and thought to exemplify the cosmic dance of *A Vision*, the volume he had published the previous year, raises the question of how the dancer's identity is revealed or concealed in the dance, and how the dance's construction or erasure of identity is imaged as labor. "Among School Children" famously asks, "How can we know the dancer from the dance?" This final line has been read over the course of the century as both idealizing and challenging the unity of dance and dancer, the fusion of artist and art work made possible by dance, the modernist code in which "the thing is what it does." It has been read as commentary on the philosophy of cosmic dance, mind-body relations, aesthetic form, and modernist poetry.

It has not been read as commentary on the dancers Yeats saw and worked with or on its contemporary dance or movement culture, in the context of early cinematic, Mareyan "fusion" and "fragmentation." Nor has it been read as commentary on the question of dance and work, or productive versus nonproductive action. Yet it was written in a decade when debate about the possibility of choreographing labor was addressed in dancing that played with or mocked the drive for synchronizing movements and codifying gestures that fueled productivity. Yeats's question about "knowing"—identifying or separating—the mover from the movement was in fact the question brought on both practically and philosophically by the rise of industrialized labor, the question being posed in ergonomics and in Taylorist work-science about the increased drudgery of physical labor augmented by machines, the erasure of identity that factory work demanded, and machines' negative impact on productivity.

"Among School Children," in its final stanza, directly addresses this question of work in tandem with the question of dance's fusion or synthesis of movement and mover:

Labour is blossoming or dancing where
The body is not bruised to pleasure soul
Nor beauty born out of its own despair
Nor blear-eyed wisdom out of midnight oil.
O chestnut-tree, great-rooted blossomer,
Are you the leaf, the blossom, or the bole,
O body swayed to music, O brightening glance,
How can we know the dancer from the dance?[32]

Critics have generally claimed that the dancer in "Among School Children" is a symbol of the notion of "unity of being" expounded by Yeats in *A Vision*. Frank Kermode's commentary on how this image of the dancer embodies the "unity of being" Yeats wanted in his work is typical; it underlines dance's usefulness as a model for poetry because it is "nondiscursive": "There is no disagreement from the fundamental principle that dance is the most primitive, non-discursive art. . . . Thus it is the emblem of the Romantic image. Dance belongs to a period before the self and the world were divided, and so achieves naturally that 'original unity' which modern poetry can only produce by a great and exhausting effort of fusion."[33] If dance's interest for poetry lies in its ability to represent the fusion of mind and body, artist and artwork, self and world, such fusion is achieved only through the erasure of the dancer's identity and discursive subjectivity. Easily eliding dance's nondiscursivity into a form of primitivity, Kermode also implicitly links dance's "primitiveness" to its effortless nonproductivity. Dancing—and by extension, dancers—accomplish "naturally" what other arts—and artists—must work at with "great and exhausting effort."

In a rare critique of the poem, Ivor Winters raises the question of the idealized labor the poem represents: "The term *labour* seems to mean fruitful human labor or ideal labor, and a labor which costs no effort. But where does this kind of labor exist, except, perhaps, in the life of a tree? The body is always bruised to pleasure soul; wisdom is always born out of midnight oil or out of something comparable. The diction in these lines is abominable." Winters ends his argument with an antifusion statement reflecting the realities of dance practice: "When we watch the dancer we may not discriminate, although a choreographer could; but if the dancer and the dance could not be discriminated in fact, the dancer could never have learned the dance."[34]

Yeats was familiar with different dance traditions and with the newest developments in modern dance; he knew dancers outside of their work and was fascinated by their ability to fuse disparate traditions and suggest multiple meanings in dancing. The question of the dancer as an individual will and not a machine, a thinking body and not an automaton, is familiar to Yeats from the philosophical tradition, posed in one of Yeats's sources for the poem, and addressed in his other poems, such as "Michael Robartes and the Dancer," that include conversations between the poet's stand-in and dancers.[35]

One source for "Among School Children" was Stephen MacKenna's translation of Plotinus.[36] In *Ennead IV*, Plotinus makes a comparison bringing together a Neoplatonic theory of the dance of the stars and the dance of the theater. In the stars' cosmic dance:

> They pass from point to point, but they move on their own affairs
> and not for the sake of traversing the space they actually cover;
> . . . moreover each of them journeys, unchangeably, the same
> unchanging way; and again, there is no question to them of the
> time they spend in any given section of the journey, even suppos-
> ing time-division to be possible in the case. . . . [Their movement
> is] the movement of a single living being whose act is directed to
> itself, a being which to anything outside is at rest, but is in move-
> ment by dint of the inner life it possesses, the eternal life. Or we
> may take the comparison of the movement of the heavenly bodies
> to a choral dance; if we think of it as a dance which comes to
> rest at some given period, the entire dance, accomplished from
> beginning to end, will be perfect while at each partial stage it

was imperfect; but if the dance is a thing of eternity, it is in eternal perfection. And if it is in eternal perfection, it has no points of time and place. . . . it will therefore make no measurements of time or place.[37]

Because "the leading principle of the universe is a unity" or "Reason-principle of the living whole," this unity is present even in the subordinate parts that "by their varied rhythmic movements make up one total dance-play"[38]:

> In our dance-plays . . . the dancer's mind is on his own purpose; his limbs are submissive to the dance-movement which they accomplish to the end, so that the connoisseur can explain that this or that figure is the motive for the lifting, bending, concealing, effacing of the various members of the body; and in all this the executant does not choose the particular motions for their own sake; the whole play of the entire person dictates the necessary position to each limb and member as it serves the plan.[39]

The aim is an organic whole: the dancers' subservience to the plan, and the limbs' to the mind.

This is precisely what Yeats found of interest in the Noh: a certain cosmic continuity linking together its "series of positions and movements": "the interest is not in the human form but in the rhythm to which it moves, and the triumph of their art is to express the rhythm in its intensity. . . . They cross the stage with a gliding movement, and one gets the impression not of undulation but of continuous straight lines."[40] This divine geometry, the rhythmic movements that lead to cosmic fusion, has been read as part of Yeats's elitist, private cosmology. But the mechanics of this machine that drives the Asian dance, or the heavens, sets Yeats's cosmology at one end of a spectrum that includes the unlikely examples of the chorus line and Taylorist choreography of work. The idealism of a coordinated geometry apparent in texts as widely divergent as those of Taylor and Yeats is belied by the fragmented movements of industrial labor.

Two different kinds of dances, in most ways dissimilar, are brought together by this particular concept of the machine as automata and the automatized performer who is, like a machine, controlled by external forces.

In the case of Ito, the external forces that he represents are described as cosmic or mystical and are linked to the performer's Asian identity, even as that identity is said to disappear in his dance. In the second case, the external force that chorus line dancers are seen as subject to is capitalism itself, the prevailing economic system, and the dancers' drill is considered as a staging of Taylorist principles in which individuals are subsumed by the group functioning. Between the avant-garde soloist dancing in London salons and the popular chorus line a few years later, there is a huge gap. That this gap is bridged by machine-thinking—if not the machine aesthetic— suggests dance's continued presence across the range of texts inventing and taking inventory of machines' power.

### THE CHORUS LINE

The epitome of the modern chorus line in the mid-1920s, the Tiller Girls, staged both idealized, group coordination and the loss of identity that comes with it; in this early version of the chorus drill, the individual dancers' identities were insignificant as they vanished into the smoothly functioning whole. Like factory workers, the Tiller Girls were appreciated as a unit, and their dancing as the expression not of an individual will but of a team. Yet in Siegfried Kracauer's commentary on them, their apparent unison conceals the fragmentation and dissociation of their bodies.

If the Tiller Girls are featured in an argument linking high modernist conceptions of dance to mass culture and technological fantasy, it is not only because of their successful formula, which would become a staple of live and cinematic entertainments in the decades following, but also because of the level of critique their spectacle inspired. In Kracauer's essay "The Mass Ornament" and another essay, "Travel and Dance" (1925), contemporary with Yeats's "Among School Children," Kracauer analyzes the danced spectacle of burgeoning mass culture. In contrast to the flow and the unity of Yeats's Neoplatonic dance, or Ito's choreographies, in Kracauer's writing people are reduced by technological modernity to "mere spatio-temporal points" in their movements.[41] Dance and travel serve as substitutes for spheres to which people have been denied access, and in the modern world it proves "imperative to master in every sense the spatio-temporal realms opened up by technology (albeit not by technology alone)." But such mastery is elusive and illusory: "Despite or perhaps precisely because of the humane foundations of Taylorism, they do not become masters of the machine but instead become machine-like."[42]

For Kracauer, the Tiller Girls stage the current Taylorist choreography of labor: "The hands in the factory correspond to the legs of the Tiller Girls."[43] Their spectacle also comments on Taylorism because their coordinated movement does not add up to a Platonic whole: "Admittedly it is the legs of the Tiller Girls that swing in perfect parallel, not the natural unity of their bodies, and it is also true that the thousands of people in the stadium form one single star. But this star does not shine, and the legs of the Tiller Girls are an abstract designation of their bodies."[44] The dancers in fact become mere abstractions, and in Kracauer's critique, abstractness is the characteristic of ambivalent capitalist thinking.

The "mass ornament," of which this chorus line is a prime example, is, for Kracauer, a mythological cult masquerading in the garb of abstraction; this sport—rather than art—represents the "aesthetic reflex" of the *ratio* to which the economic system of capitalism aspires. From abstraction follows anonymity:

> Precisely because the bearer of the ornament does not appear as a total personality—that is, as a harmonious union of nature and "spirit" in which the former is emphasized too much and the latter too little—he becomes transparent to the man determined by reason. The human figure enlisted in the mass ornament has begun the exodus from lush organic splendor and the constitution of individuality toward the realm of anonymity.[45]

And the group is thus, in Thomas Y. Levin's words, a "new type of collectivity organized not according to the natural bonds of community but as a social mass of functionally linked individuals."[46]

Although the chorus line is organized like a machine, by linkage facilitating function, it has no meaning in itself. For Kracauer, it manifests geometry but nothing else: demonstrations of mathematics; straight lines, "mere linearity"—not organic or spiritual.[47] As ballet traditionally arranged ornaments in kaleidoscopic fashion, these "girl-clusters" are in a vacuum and have no meaning beyond themselves. Like the mass ornament, the capitalist production process is an end in itself.[48]

And like the mass ornament, travel and dance are void of meaning in the modern world. Self-referential meaning and movement reign in dances that do nothing more than mark time; in the same way, travel is pure experience of space. In both examples, technology becomes an end in itself.[49]

The Tiller Girls, Ramsay Burt has written in *Alien Bodies*, represented to contemporary cultural critics such as Kracauer both the driving rhythms of modernity and the possibility—although not the reality—of a utopic social totality forged out of the abandonment of individuality and the choreographing of the group. Their performance imitated Taylorist ideas of efficiency, "expressing the logic of mass production through the precision of their dancing."[50] In one 1926 cartoon described by Burt, the Tiller Girls come out of a factory on a conveyer belt; beneath the cartoon is the caption, "Ford takes over the production of Tiller Girls."[51] Yet in staging technologized efficiency, the chorus line was also mocking Taylorist "motion economy" by energetically performing these coordinated movements in an ostentatiously nonproductive, that is, entertainment, context, called by Kracauer "commodified distraction."[52] The chorus line diffuses and disperses the energy condensed in the movement for efficiency even as it brings the assembly line onstage.

In the name of cosmic unity, as in Yeats's text, or capitalist distraction, as in Kracauer's, individual identity is subsumed into a rhythmic fusion in dance that echoes the aspirations of scientific management. Other variations on the mechanization of performers construct race as a fundamental quality that contributes to the disappearance of the dancer into the dance. Yeats speaks about Ito's retreat into depths of mind that defy mechanism, "achieved by human means alone," yet the Noh that Ito in part stands for moves beyond the human form to a rhythmic intensity and geometry. In a similar way, an Asian model of mystical-mechanical, automatic performance influences two of the most significant texts of theater theorists of the twentieth century: Artaud on the Balinese dance and Brecht on the alienation effect. Both admire certain Asian forms of theater and find a certain mechanization in their performers. Before considering Brecht's critique of Taylorism-in-dance, however, a brief look at Artaud's well-known text and a longer look at Paul Valéry's contemporary dance texts will reveal surprising responses to the rhetoric of productivity.

In his famous text "On the Balinese Theater," written after he had seen Balinese dancers in Paris at the Exposition Colonial in 1931,[53] Artaud describes the dancers as robots and puppets:

> Everything about these dancers is just as disciplined and impersonal; there is not a movement of a muscle, not a rolling of an eye that does not seem to belong to a kind of studied mathematics which governs everything and through which everything happens. And the strange thing is that in this systematic depersonalization, in these purely muscular facial movements that are superimposed on the features like masks, everything works, everything has the maximum effect.
>
> A kind of terror grips us as we contemplate these mechanized beings, whose joys and sorrows do not really seem to belong to them but rather to obey established rites that were dictated by higher intelligences.[54]

Like many of his predecessors, including Yeats, Artaud admires dance's metaphysics and dancers' divine geometry. Like Mallarmé, Artaud reads the dancers' gestures as a kind of depersonalized writing or code, hieroglyph or pictogram: "a new physical language based on signs rather than words. These actors with their geometric robes seem like animated hieroglyphs."[55] Artaud links this metaphysical-physical theater to its Asian roots, with its "quality of true physical absoluteness which only Orientals could possibly conceive of."[56] They reveal an "other" reality: "the actors with their costumes form true hieroglyphs that live and move around. And these three-dimensional hieroglyphs are in turn embellished with a certain number of gestures—mysterious signs which correspond to some fabulous and obscure reality that we Westerners have definitively repressed."[57] Their theater "has invented a language of gestures which are designed to move in space and which can have no meaning outside of it. . . . One senses in the Balinese Theater a pre-verbal state, a state which can choose its own language: music, gestures, movements, words."[58]

In Artaud's appreciation of the Balinese, the "preverbal" hieroglyphic sign is valorized, and gesture reaches maximum expressivity. Artaud describes the dance's effect—one of terror and hallucination—in the terms of maximum productivity: "tout porte, tout rend l'effet maximum."[59]

The same unusual combination occurs in a contemporary text of dance theory by Paul Valéry, who was also influenced by Mallarmé and the interpretation of dance as a living hieroglyph, as well as the poetics of signification in dialogue with the rhetoric of productivity.

ORNAMENT OF DURATION

A different definition of dance as "ornament" and its relation to work is proposed by Paul Valéry in *Degas, danse, dessin*.[60] Published in 1934, the volume collects texts connecting the nineteenth-century painter's passions for dancers as well as photography and horses with Valéry's own reflections on a stubbornly antimodern dance. In Valéry's dance philosophy, inspired by Degas, Mallarmé, and Bergson, dance's nonproductive or nonsignifying potential carries forward the banner of an art-for-art's-sake avant-gardism.

In Valéry's "L'Ame et la danse," an allegory of dancers' automatism, with a spiritual cast not unlike that of Yeats's "Among School Children," the central figure dances herself into an ecstasy that ends in her collapse. But in myriad other texts on dance, Valéry takes on the questions of productivity, meaning, and rhythm of movement that marked contemporary reflection on mechanized labor.

In "Philosophie de la danse,"[61] presented as a public lecture before a performance by La Argentina March 5, 1936, the metaphysical cast of Valéry's definitions of dance reemploy physical and physiological terminology, as if his dance aesthetics were inserted into the frame of thermodynamics and work-science. Valéry refers to what l'Ame et la Danse represent as a metaphysical state, as the ecstasy of fatigue, of motor *dépense*: "Dance is only the action of the whole of the human body" transposed into a different space-time; man realized he had the capacity for movements leading to ecstasy, the "total draining of his forces; only a sort of ecstasy of draining could interrupt his delirium, his exasperated motor expenditure."[62]

In the same pages, Valéry concludes that the dancer could also be compared with a flame, or "any phenomenon visibly maintained by the intensive consumption of a superior-quality energy."[63] In quasi-scientific terms, Valéry establishes the non-scientific-ness, the irreality of the dancer's world, the non-utility of her movements: "In the dancing state, all the sensations of a body both mover and moved are linked and in a certain order." In the world where the dancer is, "there is no endpoint external to the acts; there is no object to seize, to catch up to or reject or flee, an object that precisely terminates an action and gives movements first a direction and external coordination and then a clear and certain conclusion."[64]

Dancing is directly opposite to our action in the world of economy of gesture: "le monde pratique," in which our being "always proceeds along the most economical, if not the shortest, path: it seeks return. The straight line, the minimum action, the shortest time, seem to inspire it."[65] Only fatigue stops dance, which goes on like a dream—making it possible to consider dance as a *vie intérieure*—giving to this psychological term a physiological weight.

Yet in the same pages, Valéry remarks, in reverse, on the resemblance between work and dance; the work of creation is itself a dance, a rhythmic realization, "successive operations leading toward realization in commensurable beats, that is to say, with rhythm," because dance is a generalized poetry of human actions.[66] Like science, art tends toward making something "useful" out of the "useless."[67]

Valéry defines dance not only as action in (rhythmic) time but also as an anti-Taylorist, Bergsonian form of time, "a time whose nature is different and unique." The dancer is enclosed in a *durée* she creates, in a "state that is only action, a permanence that is created and consolidated by means of an incessant production of work" that is not (only) goal-oriented or object-producing but a constant hovering like that of the bumblebee.[68]

In "De la danse," a version of "Philosophie de la danse" published in *Degas, danse, dessin*, Valéry contrasts movements with an external goal, ordered by a certain economy of limit, achievement, and resolution, with those that have no external object or goal: "The majority of our voluntary movements have an exterior action as their end: it is a matter of attaining a place or object, or modifying some perception or sensation at a determined point." Such movements are finite, finished once their goal is attained, and conceived and executed with this goal as their limit. "This kind of movement always follows a law of the economy of forces, that can be complicated by diverse conditions, but that cannot regulate our expenditure. We cannot even imagine a finished external action without having a certain minimum [shortest/quickest] come to mind."[69]

But, Valéry continues, there is another class of voluntary movement not motivated by a goal but by a state or condition; dance is the art of such movement. The examples given for this second kind of movement include the leaps and skips of a child or dog, "la marche pour la marche, la nage pour la nage"—movement for movement's sake—which "are activities that have as their end only to modify our sense of energy, to create a certain state of this sense." They are driven by no object, "no *thing* which, once attained, brings on the resolution of these acts." They stop only because of some interruption, intervention, fatigue, and "instead of being subjected to the conditions of economy, it seems, on the contrary, that they have dissipation itself as their object."[70]

Such movements, "which have their end in themselves, an end which is to create a state," can be brought on by different situations, produced by need or impulse, and are most often disordered. They "do not have direction in space." Just as an animal moves to flee a feeling and not a thing, "a man, in whom joy or anger, or an uneasy soul, or the brisk effervescence of ideas" fulminates, gets up and goes walking with an energy that no precise act can absorb. Space is only where such actions take place, and it does not contain their object.[71]

It is this kind of movement, with the added dimension of organized time, that dance epitomizes. It is "a remarkable form of this expenditure" that orders or organizes our "movements of dissipation."[72] Valéry defines dance as the ordered linking of one movement to another, which he suspects would find a neuromuscular analogue in what physicists call resonance. Such movements, which contain their end in themselves, these "alternative fundamental functions of life,"

> are accomplished by a cycle of muscular acts that is reproduced, as if the conclusion or ending of each one of them engendered the launching of the following one. In this model, our limbs can execute a suite of *figures* that follow one after the other and whose rate produces a sort of drunkenness that goes from languor to delirium, from a sort of hypnotic abandon to a sort of furor. The state of *dance* is created.[73]

Thus from individual gesture comes a linked continuum, and from individual bodies and movements come not only "duration" but also "extension"—the Bergsonian notions of continuous and fluid time and space. Limbs composing, decomposing, and recomposing their figures form an "ornement de la durée," just as the repetition of patterns in space forms an "ornement de l'étendue."[74]

> Sometimes these two modes change one into the other. One sees, in ballets, instants where the ensemble is immobilized, during which the grouping of the participants offers to the gaze a fixed but not durable decoration, a system of living bodies stopped short in their attitudes, that gives a singular image of instability. The subjects seem to be seized in poses far removed from those in which mechanics and human forces permit [one] to stand . . . to dream of something else.
>
> This marvelous impression results: in the Universe of Dance, rest has no place; immobility is a thing constrained and forced, a state of passage and almost of violence, whereas leaps, pas comptés, pointe, entrechat or vertiginous turns are perfectly natural ways of being and doing.[75]

Valéry concludes with the musing that there are two realms: "what is likely in one of these Universes is in the other the rarest occasion."[76] Dance offers the "inspiration" of a state far away or beyond ourselves, in which the unstable subtends us and the stable is only there by accident.

In another text from the *Cahiers*, Valéry finds dance to be a generalizable example of movement and signification that applies both to work and to poetry. In contradistinction to Yeats and Plotinus, Valéry imagines dance as an activity that has its end within itself, in which the limbs are not at the service of some external force or plan. In addition, they do not mean through external reference but carry their meaning in themselves. For Valéry, dance does not produce meaning; meaning inheres in it, making it a model of self-sufficient signification to be appropriated by the poem:

> To say that a thing signifies is to say that it leads to something else, not to some state where it is intermediary. There is a functional inequality between the sign and the thing signified. It is to

say that in poetry—the nature of the distinction between the sign
and the meaning changes—As in dance, the actions of the limbs
are no longer defined by exterior things. . . . In poetry, then, a
change in values (of language).[77]

Dance becomes a model for the action or artifact that has sense in and of
itself, that does not mean in the usual way, by "leading to" something
else. "Every action that does not lean toward utility . . . gets associated
with this simplified stereotype of the dance."[78] But this lack of object in
fact renders dance's movement more interesting. For Valéry, the work
performed by the artist is itself a dance, a performance rather than goal-
oriented production:

Consider an artist at work, eliminate the intervals of rest or
momentary lapses; watch him move, freeze, energetically take
up the exercise again . . . in rhythm; you can then see the realization of a work of art, of which the material object that is being
fashioned by the artists' fingers is no more than the pretext,
the accessory, the subject of the ballet.[79]

For Valéry, the poem is produced by a dancelike action, but the fabric of
the poem, its images, are also dancelike: "What is metaphor if not a sort
of pirouette of the imagination to which diverse images and diverse
names get attached?"[80] All kinds of figural language "remove us from the
practical world to form us, and our particular universe, a privileged site
of spiritual dance."[81] The poem is itself a thing in movement:

A poem, for example, is action, because a poem only exists at the
moment of its pronouncing: it is thus in action. This act, like a
dance, has as its only end creating a state; this act creates its own
laws; it also creates a time and a measure of time that fit it and
are essential to it; we cannot distinguish it from the form of its
duration. To begin to speak verse is to enter into a verbal dance.[82]

For Valéry, dance is action transposed to the world of a Bergsonian
space-time: "this art, far from a pointless diversion, far from a speciality
limited to the production of spectacle, to the amusement of watching eyes
or performing bodies, is very simply a general poetry of the action of living beings."[83]

Valéry thus argues simultaneously for dance's non-utility and its sentialized usefulness as an image for human action, including labor; it makes a case for the general significance of its particular signifying. Firmly situated in the nineteenth-century French culture in which dancers were central figures, Valéry's dance philosophy resists and critiques a twentieth-century insistence on the productive gesture and its claims to meaning.

ALIENATION

The very diverse performances considered in this chapter had qualities that made viewers see them as machinelike, even when the dancing did not fit the machine aesthetic: an automated detachment, the submission of individual identity to anonymity or a larger whole, geometric lines or continuous rhythms that suggest a mathematical precision or a fluid time-space continuum. Such idealizations contradict the realities of high-speed production's aggravated rhythms and fragmented gestures. But they suggest an alternate underlying conception of the machine that dancing embodies.

In choreographies as diverse as those of Michio Ito and the Tiller Girls in the 1920s, in commentaries read earlier, dance's nonproductivity is viewed both as meaningful and meaningless in the face of the culture of the machine. The condensed gestures of Ito—like the "hieroglyphs" of the Balinese dancers—are viewed as deeply meaningful, whereas the fragmented, segmented gestures of the Tiller Girls are read as meaningless.

Valéry's insistence on dance's usefulness as a model for human action, because of its non-object-oriented, nonproductive nature, finds an unlikely echo in a contemporary text by Bertolt Brecht. *Les Sept Péchés capitaux* (*The Seven Deadly Sins*), his 1933 collaboration with Kurt Weill and George Balanchine, reads as a critique of Tiller-esque dance and Taylorist management methods. Brecht's play delves into the working conditions of the automated dancer and ends up revealing, underneath, the alienated laborer, the exhausted human motor. Brecht's allegory suggests that dancing can, in fact, be viewed as a productive labor, that the individual never disappears in automation, and that the smooth functioning of the machine depends on those who run it. And Brecht's main character, divided in two—the emotive dancer and the reasoning speaker/singer—belies the idealized "fusion" of dancer and dance.

Against the tradition in which dance is viewed as a purposeless, non-productive activity, and mocking the choreography of labor, Brecht's drama features a dancer whose work—and working body—are owned and controlled by her corrupt family. In their attempt to amass wealth, Anna's family sends her out into the world to make money, selling her through dancing, as poor families prostituted their ballet girls at the nineteenth-century Paris Opéra. The difference here is that while Anna toils body and soul for freedom of expression and simple civil liberties—freedom to love whom she chooses, to earn a living, to keep healthy—her labor is indentured to a family that grows fat as it drains the life out of her.

Along the way, Brecht's *ballet chanté* performs several ironic twists, starting with the premise that dancing is a money-making, sensible, productive activity; in a capitalist economy driven by desire, dancing can produce more desire, and thus more income. The dancer in Anna, however, invests her entire self in the work, paying for every gesture in sweat and pain, and reaping none of the profit. The "family values" espoused by her family back home in Louisiana are those that make for better capitalists: sleep with the rich man; don't overeat or you'll lose your job; don't be too proud or you'll never make good. In this case, making good means giving up all integrity to shore up the family fortune.

*Les Sept Péchés capitaux* premiered in Paris on June 7, 1933. With music by Kurt Weill and choreography by George Balanchine for Les Ballets 1933, and directed by Boris Kochno, the double role of Anna was created by singer Lotte Lenya (Anna I) and dancer Tilly Losch (Anna II). Weill had originally proposed Cocteau as librettist, and the piece might have followed in the wake of *Parade*, *Les Mariés de la Tour Eiffel*, and other Cocteau ballets. In this ballet, however, the dancer embodies Brecht's politics and aesthetics, embodying epic alienation. With this piece, Brecht experimented with a new combination of drama and dance, although the plays, both before and after this work, reveal an interest in and understanding of gesture and physicality onstage.[84] Just before formulating the "alienation effect" in a text inspired by a Chinese actor he had seen in Moscow, Brecht here uses the theme of dance and the body of the dancer to express alienated labor.

Balanchine's choreography combines classical ballet with defamiliarizing modern dance variations. Although restaged more than twenty years later by Balanchine with Allegra Kent and Lenya, who recorded the score, the archival record of the original production remains a libretto.[85] In the prologue, an opening, marked andante sostenuto, meanders into a lazy, strummed ballad, echoed in the singer's slurred evocation of "Louiz-yana." The mood is one of homesickness, as Anna, who has left her family to make her living out in the world, remembers the moon on the Mississippi. She dreams of a future homecoming: "We look forward to our homecoming and the sooner the better. It's a month already since we started for the great big cities where you go to make money. In seven years our fortune will be made and then we can go back."[86]

The seven sins are played out in vignettes charting the dancer's career on the road. In the first, "Sloth" (allegro vivace), the four male voices of the family chorus (with the role of the mother sung by the bass) burst in with the music racing behind them. Here the contradiction between what they say and what they do is clear: we know that it is Anna racing behind them, slave to the rhythm of the city, earning her bread by keeping to the beat, while they live their lazy Louisiana life. Amid the flutter, Anna II is described as a "lazy-bones"; the family hopes she will be able to pull herself together, out of the armchair, off of the mattress. The irony is apparent as they sing a hymn-inflected warning: to stay away from the devil, keep your nose to the grindstone. Their sustained advice is countered by a last flurry of fire and brimstone, and the music drops with Anna exhausted at the end.

The second sin, "Pride," is introduced in three-quarter time, which takes the song from an undignified carnivalesque folk tune to the grandiose, Strauss-like waltz of Anna II's idealism. Anna II has found a job as a cabaret dancer, but she does not like it; her dreams of a dance career are reduced to the sleazy reality of a cabaret job in Memphis. Anna I criticizes Anna II for her ideals: she "began talking about Art (of all things). About the Art (if you please) of Cabaret. In Memphis, the second big town we came to. It wasn't Art that sort of people came for. That sort of people came for something else."[87] But Anna II is found guilty of the sin of pride, for preferring to dance in serious self-expression rather than in commercial self-display. Her ideal is musicalized in the classical waltz Weill inserts into the song. But the dream-waltz gives way again to the family chorus, reminding her that when their morality is to be maintained, pride must not be allowed to get in the way. Anna's pride, a sign of her integrity in a world with none, is twisted into a sin. Her family urges her along the very path they insist must be avoided.

In "Anger" (molto agitato), the family rages that Anna is not sending them enough money. Their voices multiply in a frenzy of religious-sounding fervor. Anna I punctures this mock *Messiah* with the news that she and Anna II have arrived in Los Angeles, the "city of angels." Anna I chastises Anna II: "It took time to teach my sister that wrath would not do in Los Angeles, the third big town we came to, where her open disapproval of injustice was so widely disapproved."[88] Brecht's later Hollywood elegies echo Anna II's disgust.

Anna I preaches twisted biblical warnings in a brassy cabaret chant, with the instrumentation of shrill piccolos and snide clarinets: "If a curse or a blow can enrage you so, your usefulness here is ended. Then mind what the Good Book tells us when it says 'Resist not evil!' Unforgiving anger is from the Devil." As before, Anna II shows herself to be obedient to her "rational" irrational side; she is weary already and disillusioned by her struggle. "Right Anna?" her alter ego asks her for confirmation. "Yes, Anna," she replies in defeat.[89]

In "Gluttony," this sin is described as the sin of the dancer on a contract. Anna II must be thin; she must starve to keep her job. In a Philadelphia of mythic status, the capital city of the founding fathers' morality, Anna's gluttony is described in largo. To the mellifluous strains of strings, the family eulogizes the foods of Anna's home: "Crabmeat, pork chops, sweet corn, chicken." "Gluttons will be punished," they warn.[90] The family reminds Anna that there is hope if only she will offer herself up to serve them in a slavery that they call sinless.

In "Lust," Anna I narrates the tale of the fifth sin with a strident voice and rhythm that battles and overcomes a guitar-accompanied love song. This love song is the story of Anna II's preference for a man who has no money, a man whom she loves, over the rich man who keeps her. According to the family, there is no room for love in Anna's world; her arrangement with the rich man is "good" because it keeps the family alive; her love for the poor man destructive. Anna I tells the poor lover that if he tries to hold her, he'll bring her to destruction; but then she admits that she continues to see him: "Then I went to see her young friend and I said: 'If you're kind you won't hold her, for this love will be your sweetheart's bitter end.' . . . Then I'd meet him. . . . There was nothing going on. Naturally! Until Anna found out and worse luck, blamed the whole affair on me." Anna I continues: "Then the endless nights I heard my sister sobbing bitterly and repeating: 'It's right like this, Anna, but so hard!'"[91]

In "Avarice," the family chorus enters and stridently reports that the papers have said Anna is well set up in Baltimore. In a fast three-quarter allegro giusto, the family leaps to conclusions: "She must be doing all right and raking it in to get in the news like that"; "to be talked about helps a young girl up the ladder. But isn't she overdoing it?"[92] The family quartet parodies the polished sound of a barbershop quartet, covetous themselves of her "success."

In the final song, it is Anna's envy that they criticize as embracing all her other sins. To a tragic beat, Anna I characterizes Anna II as envious "of those who pass the time at their ease and in comfort, those too proud to be bought, of those whose wrath is kindled by injustice, those who act upon their impulses happily, lovers true to their loved ones, and those who take what they need without shame."[93] Anna's song turns into a triumphant, militaristic march as she shows Anna II the true path, and the family joins in with martial fanfare. Their triumph at the expense of Anna II's ideals leads directly into the epilogue, the same low-key, strummed ballad that opened the piece, doubled in its irony here because it is again presented as the comforting music of home. Anna II's final accession to her sister, "Yes, Anna," is dirgelike, wrung from a body that is tired to death by years of labor in the service of bourgeois—American—materialism.

Audiences were unenthusiastic at the ballet's opening. Serge Lifar's response was "C'est de la pourriture de ballet" (It's the spoiling of ballet).[94] Undaunted, the two husbands of the play's two stars pressed on to a London production. Losch's husband, Edward James, who had funded the original production, translated the libretto into English and retitled it *Anna-Anna*, a title perhaps less offensive to its potential British middle-class audience. The play opened at the Savoy in late June of the same year, and Weill was able to report, with some exaggeration, that it was "the great success of the season and furthermore Lenya is a great hit."[95] Brecht was not happy with either the audiences or the state of theater in

London or Paris. In a postcard to Helene Weigel he called London's theater "antediluvian," and in an interview he described the theater scene of both London and Paris as stuck in the year 1880.[96] Within three years, however, Brecht would be producing his work at the Unity Theatre in London and publishing in *The Left Review*,[97] and he tried to use *The Seven Deadly Sins* to get his career-in-exile off the ground.[98]

Brecht also used the piece to work out various elements of his epic theater; in *The Threepenny Opera* and in the essays he wrote following its production in 1928, Brecht developed his critique of conventional or "culinary" opera, as he called it, into a new genre with a new interplay of elements.[99] Central to epic theater are a set of production values and an acting style Brecht would later name the alienation effect. Based on reflections provoked by the Chinese actor Mei Lan-fang, whom Brecht saw perform in Russia in 1935, the term "alienation" describes the effect of a practice in which the actor indicates rather than personifies his character. "The actor must not only sing but show a man singing. His aim is not so much to bring out the emotional content of his song (has one the right to offer others a dish that one has already eaten oneself?) but to show gestures that are so to speak the habits and usage of the body."[100] The goal is to educate and provoke audiences to make conclusions (and act on them) rather than to bathe them in emotion. In Brecht's definition, "a defamiliarized illustration is one that, while allowing the object to be recognized, at the same time makes it appear unfamiliar."[101]

In the first essay that mentions *Verfremdungseffekt*, Brecht admires the skill of the actor; a later essay, "Short Description of a New Technique of Acting Which Produces an Alienation Effect," grew from his interest in this "masterly use of gesture," the actor's ability to achieve alienation "by being seen to observe his own movements." Just as epic acting reveals its choices and remains as close as possible to rehearsal style, the Chinese actor's mastery reveals the enormous amount of training and rehearsal he has had. Mei Lan-fang's style combines the physical labor of practice with the polish of performance: "The impression to be given is one of ease, which is at the same time one of difficulties overcome." The actor, in his portrayals of women or clouds, uses "his countenance as a blank sheet, to be inscribed by the gest of the body"; he "separates mime (showing observation), from gesture (showing a cloud)."[102]

The Chinese actor's aim, writes Brecht, "is to appear strange and even surprising to the audience. He achieves this by looking strangely at himself and his work." Throughout this essay, Brecht stresses the intensity of the art of the Chinese actor, whose movement has such power that he accomplishes his work with a "minimum of illusion." The Chinese actor is not pretending, says Brecht; he is not "in a trance."[103] He does not need to convince himself that he is the character he plays; he simply plays it.

Created before the formulation of *Verfremdungseffekt* and the recognition of its style in an Asian movement form, *The Seven Deadly Sins* uses dance as a model for alienated labor as well as the practice of epic alienation. By staging dance as labor that can be exploited for another's profit, Brecht critiques the Taylorist theory of productivity while ironically applying it to dance. By splitting his central character in two, Brecht exaggerates underlying differences between verbal and choreographic theater, but he also recruits dancing and dancer in the service of epic theater's detached illustration rather than embodied illusion. By revealing the dancer's fragmentation and fatigue rather than her disappearance into the anonymity of a group, or her submission to the smooth functioning of the whole or to geometric precision, *The Seven Deadly Sins* reminds its public of the "human motor" pumping away at the heart of mechanized industry.

Contemporary with Brecht's elaboration of an epic theater, Paris served as the dais for the rise to fame of another American dancer, Josephine Baker. Like the seemingly automatic performers of different Asian traditions considered in this chapter, and like Brecht's Anna, Baker's dancing both mimes and mocks the choreography of labor, reviving the model of the "human motor." But unlike the dancers subsumed into cosmic or capitalist superstructures, represented as anonymous or alienated, automatized or mechanized, Baker's dancing made her an icon, an internationally recognized star. She represented what looked like de-alienated labor, the pleasure of dancing "natural" or "primitive" dances unconnected to the machine age. Yet her image was constructed not only through live performance with a cult following but also through a particular, cinematic industry.

# 6.

## Submitting to the Machine

Le naturel que seuls les primitifs gardent devant l'objectif.

Henri Langlois

Vive le cinéma, vous comprenez la danse des images.

    Un film, c'est un ballet. Mais ce n'est pas la même chose qu'un ballet sur une scène de music-hall, d'où l'erreur qu'on a commise, il me semble, en tournant, sans rien y changer, des revues entières de music-hall. Et le rythme. Qu'a-t-on fait du rythme? (Ce n'est pas le même rythme au cinema.)

Josephine Baker, *Les Mémoires de Joséphine Baker*

Recalling Josephine Baker's dance revolution in Paris in the 1920s, poet, ethnographer, art collector, and critic Michel Leiris wrote in 1939, in his autobiographical *L'Age d'homme*, of the effect of her jazz on his postwar culture:

> In the period of great license that followed the hostilities, jazz was a sign of allegiance, an orgiastic tribute to the colors of the moment. It functioned magically, and its means of influence can be compared to a kind of possession. It was the element that gave these celebrations their true meaning, with communion by dance, latent or manifest exoticism, and drinks, the most effective means of bridging the gap that separates individuals from each other at any kind of gathering. Swept along by violent bars of tropical energy, jazz still had enough of a "dying civilization" about it, of humanity blindly submitting to The Machine, to express quite completely the state of mind of at least some of that generation:

a more or less conscious demoralization born of the war, a naïve fascination with the comfort and the latest inventions of progress, a predilection for a contemporary setting whose insanity we nonetheless vaguely anticipated, an abandonment to the animal joy of experiencing the influence of a modern rhythm, an underlying aspiration to a new life in which more room would be made for the impassioned frankness we inarticulately longed for.[1]

Leiris's characterization of his generation's comfort in Taylorist technical progress and abandonment to the animal joys of jazz aptly brings together the urbanity and "primitivism" of the U.S. imports, which were united in Josephine Baker's dancing.

Beginning with the debut of *La Revue nègre* at the Théâtre des Champs Elysées in 1925, Baker's dancing created images often described in France as natural, primitive, animal-like, even crazed.[2] Combining the liberatory spirit of Isadora with steps inspired by African-rooted rhythms and American jazz, Josephine's dancing brought to the French stage a remarkable combination of popular forms, including vaudeville, the Charleston, tap, and the swinging head and hip movements and staccato isolations from a pan-African dance vocabulary. Her early dancing in African American revues—captured on film—manifests the wide-eyed clowning that first got her noticed in the chorus line; her later more glamorous dancing, in film choreographies with elaborate Busby Berkeley–style staging, keeps her in the spotlight with exotic and elegant costumes and speaking and singing roles.

Although known for performances understood as interpreting eros or possession, Josephine Baker onstage and on film also gave expression to the machine age. Her clowning can be understood, like Charlie Chaplin's, as a parody of modern times: imitating the frenzy of the assembly line; mimicking the chorus-line engine; dancing the human motor that made these industry and entertainment teams run. Her dancing was a sensation that was described as new in 1925, yet it proposed an image of the human motor in the age of automation, reviving the thermodynamic model of the machine as a heat engine moving toward exhaustion. Josephine's dancing in the *Revue nègre* fit into a performance niche that had been created by acts such as the cakewalking Mr. and Mrs. Elks described by

Jean Cocteau as bringing to the old world the rhythm of the new, a rhythm that took over machines. It also can be seen as a complement to documentary or ethnographic films of African dance made prior to and contemporary with her own live and film performances.

Leiris's discussion of Josephine Baker sets up the terms within which her Africanness as well as her Americanness would be measured: the postwar technological fantasy speeding recovery from the technological trauma of the Great War; the pathology of the "dying civilization" in thrall to The Machine; the insanity of European war passing for order; the violence of that order imposed by the machines of war and work; and the submission to the violent rhythms both of work and leisure typified in jazz. Leiris's recollection makes clear that the popularity of *La Revue nègre* as well as its negative reception—as a "contagion" or sickness—were far from innocent, that French culture projected onto African American dance forms its own pent-up passions as well as anxieties, and that Baker's "primitivism" was also an effect of a "decaying," and technologically fascinated, industrialized society. Against the decay of Europe, Leiris would write later, Baker's dancing was a breath of fresh air, at once ancient and ultra-modern: "Along with sacred or profane [African American] music, tasted like a far-off breeze from Africa blowing into our industrialized culture, the image of a Josephine Baker letting loose in the Charleston brings together, under the sign of primitivism, the 'lesser Christs of obscure hopes' [les 'Christ inférieur des obscures espérances']."[3]

Josephine's performances in Paris have been read against the background of European taste "gone primitive" in the 1920s—to use Mariana Torgovnick's phrase; or the "Negrophilia" studied by James Clifford and Petrine Archer-Straw; or what was perceived as the contagion of the "tumulte noir" of African American jazz culture explored by Henry Louis Gates and Karen C. C. Dalton; or as what Ramsay Burt sees as the calculated expression of a "savage" Africanness choreographed impromptu by impresario Rolf de Maré.[4] Burt summarizes the reception of Baker's performance by the political left and right:

> Baker's supposedly African dancing—particularly when seen from a French utopian socialist point of view—also evoked an image of a mythical organic community, one that was in touch with

"primitive" natural essences with which over-civilised modern Westerners believed they had lost touch. From a more conservative point of view, contamination from contact with non-Western art was taken as a sign of the erosion and degeneracy of specifically national and racial identities.[5]

For Burt, Baker's performances were part of a constructed image as well as revelations of a natural talent. Yet Baker's work also manifests a negotiation with industry and technology—specifically with the apparatus of cinema in the 1930s—and develops the complexity hinted at by the image of her dancing with a skirt of bananas at her Paris debut.

To reduce Josephine Baker to the image of a "dancing machine" might seem to limit the many facets of her career that scholars in different disciplines have explored: her early stage career in African American variety shows; her stage stardom in France beginning with *La Revue nègre* in 1925; her return tours to the United States; her movie roles in France in the 1930s; her work for the French resistance during the Second World War; her family life with many adopted children; and her returns to the stage to revive her iconic image.[6] Yet Baker, in addition to performing a racially stereotyped "dancing machine," reinvented the concept in her career. Representing her native United States through modern dance and music forms, and given roles, on stage and screen, in which she figures an idealized and exoticized Africa, Josephine Baker in France stands as a hybrid image of modernity as well as of the pre-technological primitive.

Although a limited European colonial imagination casts Africa as a utopia removed from a too-mechanized society,[7] the broader imagination of French ethnographers read in this chapter, Baker's contemporaries, gains a different perspective studying African cultures that reconnect technology to ritual. From this perspective, Baker's performances enact a recontextualization of African material that allows Europeans to see their own—highly technological—savagery. A reading of Baker's performances in their French artistic and intellectual context may serve to emphasize her status as an object on exhibit. But it also allows an understanding of the way the components of her dancing—connecting her art to both African- and American-inflected modernisms—bring it into direct relation with technology understood through both ritual and work.

The intersections of dance and machines examined in previous chapters have shown that discourses of naturalness and of artifice, the human motor and the automata, were everywhere in play around dance performance in the early twentieth century. It is Baker's mix of nature and glamour, or the "primitive" and the technological, and what is at stake in such a merging in France in the 1920s and 1930s, that this chapter explores. Reading Baker's dancing in its French context requires exploring how other artists and artworks representing African culture came to the Parisian public's attention in these decades, and how the passion for what was called "primitive" art and culture—manifest in the borrowing of African art forms by European artists and the popularity of African American dances—interacted with museological concerns about how to display "primitive" artifacts as technological or sacred objects, and with the documentary or ethnographic ambitions of photography and cinema. Finally, it requires considering not only Baker's live performances—consumed "on the spot" as, Sartre famously said, cultural products, like bananas, should be—but also her creation of an exportable image, an international cinema star, who could use the medium to transcend restrictions imposed on live performers in her home country. The cinematic elaboration of her image, in movement and sound, allowed Baker some resistance to the kind of static representation that effectively made her an art object. Instead, she used cinema—or it used her—to regenerate the image of the human motor as both the engine driving the machine age and a critique of its mechanization.

PRIMITIVISM

In a lecture titled "La Sculpture nègre et l'art moderne," delivered on April 4, 1926, at the Fondation Barnes,[8] Paul Guillaume, who is often credited with organizing the first exhibition of African art in Paris in 1917, describes the influence of African motifs, especially African art's distortions of body parts, on the decorative arts at the Grande Exposition des Arts Déco in Paris in 1925. He pronounces on a European respect for "the negro soul as a source of vitality in a fatigued civilization,"[9] and he regrets the historical, economic, and social conditions that he blames for killing African art: Christian and Islamic conversion, which destroys belief in fetishes; agricultural changes that end the leisure for making art; and overseas markets that accorded high commercial values to African art, which created an industry of cheaply made or mass-produced objects. It remains to be seen, concludes Guillaume, whether this art will be resuscitated by "le Nègre civilisé d'aujourd'hui."[10]

In a special 1927 issue of *Cahiers d'Art* on *l'art nègre*, editor Christian Zervos outlines the journal's aim to present Negro art not as a curiosity but as part of "civilisation humaine," along with other great works of the past.[11] In an article in the issue, along with photographs of masks from Congo in the Terveuren collection, Louvre curator Georges Salles remarks that in spite of ethnographic, geographic, and philosophic studies, African art is rarely discussed in historical terms, and thus, ageless, it is submitted to the discourse of taste. "Primitivism" represents a late development, but, Salles wonders, is it understood as a permanent state or as a return to earlier forms? Salles emphasizes that although "scientifiques" are responsible for classifying African art in museums, it was the young generation of Paris painters who "discovered l'art nègre."[12]

Delight in the ahistorical "primitive" in post–World War I Paris goes hand in hand with fascination with the futuristic. The "primitive" is ancient and therefore, even as fashion, transcends fashion; it is timeless and therefore "modern." The fashion for primitivism in art and performance idealized the past in terms of a present marked by technology, mass culture, and cinema. In *Negrophilia: Avant-Garde Paris and Black Culture in the 1920s*, Petrine Archer-Straw has argued that the "African-American presence through jazz music and dance played its part in the development of both a modern art form and *l'ordre primitif*, as evident in Blaise Cendrars's ballet *The Creation of the World* in 1923."[13] She continues:

> Interest in blacks rested on two opposing perceptions . . . Europeans viewed black people as "primordial", with all the exotic notions that primitive innocence suggested. Alternatively, they saw blacks as being modern "new negroes", with a pace that matched an urban lifestyle. These two views were not contradictory, particularly for the avant-garde, which admired black people's "primitive" condition and believed that it provided a useful model for a postwar modern man. This dichotomy is seen

in the 1923 ballet *The Creation of the World*, a theatrical performance in which modern and primitivized forms blended easily together.[14]

The particular historical and artistic knot of issues surrounding Josephine Baker's work crosses separate strands that have until recently been held in place by the rhetorics of modernism. Archer-Straw summarizes: "Josephine Baker's performance in *La Revue Nègre* reinforced stereotypes of blacks at a time when Europe's blurred and limited image of them as Africans was changing to accommodate an increased awareness of urban African-American culture."[15] Baker's work addresses many modernist contradictions: primitivism, nationalism, and trans-nationalism in cinema (via dance); the image of the human motor—"savage" and machine age at the same time; African "primitiveness" manifest in the American jazz age; the "madness" surrounding technology as a kind of possession; and danced "authenticity" along with a cinematic artifice. Her example serves as a model of the "natural" produced through the artifice of the machine.

Although unique in Paris in 1925 because of their performer, Baker's early exotic dances followed a trend that had marked both European avant-garde performance art and the mainstream ballet companies discussed in previous chapters. In a wide range of what were referred to as "Negro," or sometimes "savage," dances, some with Cubist masks, some with puppets, and some even with banana costumes, artists staged performances of African-inspired dancing, often uniting themes of mechanization with shapes and steps characterized as primitive.

In her history of avant-garde performance art, RoseLee Goldberg includes several such examples from the annals of Dada in Zurich and Paris. Following the first Dada soirée in Zurich, in July 1916, Tristan Tzara summarized the evening's music, dances, theories, manifestos, poems, paintings, costumes, and masks under the rubrics: "Cubist dance," "Negro music," and "gymnastic poem." At the final Dada soirée in Zurich in April 1919, there were dances by Suzanne Perrottet and Käthe Wulff, with enormous "savage masks" for the dancers.[16] In Paris, Sophie Taeuber, who had worked with Laban and Mary Wigman, brought a new concentration on dance to Galerie Dada in 1917, and Hugo Ball choreo-

graphed an "African" dance: "I am rehearsing a new dance with five La-
ban-ladies as negresses in long black caftans and face masks. The movements are symmetrical, the rhythm is strongly emphasized, the mimicry is
of a studied deformed ugliness."[17] In one Futurist work, highly mechanized dancing was combined with "savage" dancing: the *Plastic Dances*
in 1918, conceived for less-than-life-sized marionettes by Gilbert Clavel
and Fortunato Depero, performed at a marionette theater, the Teatro dei
Piccoli, at Palazzo Odescalchi in Rome. Taller than the other puppets,
Depero's Great Savage had a stage drop from his belly, with tiny "savages" dancing on it.[18] In *Paris Noir*, Tyler Stovall sees the Dada "soirées
nègres" in a positive light as "public theatrical events that prominently
displayed blacks as comic figures in a critique of European racism and
Western civilization in general," like the Ballets Suédois's 1923 *La Création du monde*.[19]

Although associated with avant-garde innovations in the plastic arts,
primitivism can also be seen influencing dancing by the Ballets Suédois.
The impact of the current fashion for African art and African-style dancing on the company was apparent beginning with Börlin's *Sculpture nègre*,
presented in March 1920, followed in 1921 by the Brazil-inspired
*L'Homme et son desir* with a scenario by Paul Claudel, and *La Création
du monde*, both with choreography by Börlin and music by Milhaud, who
was inspired by jazz and other African-rooted forms. In these choreographies, the "primitive" dances function as an alternative to ballets that take
the machine age as their theme, and yet in their own way these "primitive" dances are intimately linked to the riddle of the dancing machine.

In these ballets as in others by Börlin, the dancers seem to disappear—
in these cases behind mask or blackface, or enormous constructed costumes—into an exotic otherness. In other ballets the performers had been
swallowed up, functioning, Léger imagined, as active parts of the set;
here, Léger writes, the "human material had the same spectacular value
as objects or décor."[20]

Subtitled *Ballet nègre*, *La Création du monde*, which premiered in October 1923, was inspired by Blaise Cendrars's 1921 *Anthologie nègre*.
While planning the ballet, Léger wrote: "It must be the only possible 'ballet nègre' in the entire world . . . a model of the genre."[21] Milhaud, a pro-
lific composer for ballet and cinema, had gone to hear jazz in New York

in the 1920s and was extremely interested in "jazz ballet" and "negro ballet." But the performance of *La Création du monde* used neither black musicians nor black dancers, and the performers were meant to become objects or décor—a rhythmic ensemble—by dancing Africanness, or dancing as Africans, which they were not. Following this imitation *ballet nègre*, Léger and de Maré would be instrumental in engaging and bringing to Paris the African American dancers and musicians who debuted as *La Revue nègre* in 1925.

African and African American dancing had been seen in Paris a generation before Josephine Baker arrived: live, at the Exposition Universelle, at the Nouveau Cirque, and on film. Baker's dancing is usually read in the context of a fascination with African art that includes, after Gauguin, the work of Picasso and other painters and the first exhibition of African sculpture in Paris—Paul Guillaume's Premiere Exposition d'Art Nègre et d'Art Océanien—which opened at the Galerie Devambez in May 1917.[22] But other significant antecedents included materials collected at the Royal Museum for Central Africa, in Tervuren, Belgium, founded by King Leopold II in 1897, and photographs from expeditions to Africa as well as early films.[23]

   Lumière films from the first few seasons presented, along with contemporary European stage dancing (such as Loie Fuller's) and popular European dances, African American performers such as the Elks praised by Cocteau, and various forms of Asian and African dance.[24] Thus cinematic images as well as photographs and avant-garde visual arts introduced African and African American dance forms to French audiences. Given the existence of this filmed record—albeit one of performances that had been staged for the camera—the *ballets nègres* by companies such as the Ballets Suédois would have functioned as a theatrical imitation of the "real" Africans the wider audience would have been able to see on film twenty years earlier.[25] White European dance staging black African dance in the 1920s works through a double reference to the artistic and ethnographic notions of an African original as well as to the photography and cinema that had given those images their widest diffusion in Europe. The "authentic" Africanness of dance was as much a cinematic construction as an effect of live performances.

JOSEPHINE BAKER'S USE VALUE

In Paris, Josephine Baker was described as a kind of exhibit, an art object whose iconic image was reproduced by many artists. But she was also, as a performer and sometime choreographer, a kind of ethnographer, piecing together dance steps from different sources. Baker's dance can be read, as part of the interest shown by French ethnographers, writers, and artists for African art and African American culture, alongside the contemporary review *Documents*, which brought together texts on contemporary African American performers with texts by ethnographers working on and in Africa.[26]

Like "Joséphine," *Documents* was a product featuring images of Africa and Africans, diasporic arts and transported art. The review, like Baker's career, was managed by Europeans, and like Baker's dance, it was a locus for the juxtaposition of African art forms and African American performance traditions. The most startling pages in *Documents* print photographs of African cultures along side film stills from early Hollywood musical talkies. In the first volume of *Documents*, the photo captioned "Bessie Love dans le film parlant 'Broadway Melody' qui passera incessament au Madeleine-Cinéma" appears above a photo of "Enfants de l'Ecole de Bacouya, Bourail," which was reprinted from an album dated 1869–71. Similarly, a photo titled "Canaques de Kroua, Oua-oua, côte est" appears over André Schaeffner's review of *Black Birds*.[27] This kind of merging was precisely what Baker's first "African" dances, performed with *La Revue nègre*, accomplished.

Baker should be counted among the artists who found more freedom to work in France, following in the tradition of American Creole musicians, artists, performers, and muses.[28] And as a woman of color in a France moving toward decolonization, Baker represented an image of "Africanness" as well as one of the Americanness defined by dances like the Charleston. Significantly, Baker herself described the intoxicating jolt of improvising Africanness in terms of the intoxication she experienced arriving in Paris: "Each time I leaped I seemed to touch the sky and when I regained earth it seemed to be mine alone. I felt as intoxicated as when, on the first day I arrived in Paris, Douglas had given me a glass of anisette."[29]

For Baker, dancing Africanness in France was as exotic as France itself;

this dancing performs a double displacement, bringing together different performance traditions in a juxtaposition that can be read in the context of both contemporary ethnographic museological and Surrealist artistic practices. France represented for Baker a closer contact with Africa, both the Africa on display in museums and that within geographical and cinematic reach.

In "On Ethnographic Surrealism," James Clifford sees the ethnographic practices of museums displaying African art in Paris in the 1920s and 1930s as intimately linked to the interests of Surrealist writers and artists in African and African American art.[30] In the convergence of events in 1925—the increasingly visible and political activity of the Surrealists (in the wake of the first Surrealist manifesto); the huge hit of *La Revue nègre* and its star; and the founding of the Institut d'Ethnologie (by Paul Rivet, Marcel Mauss, and Lucien Lévy-Bruhl)—Clifford finds the merging of ethnography and avant-garde art.

Reclaiming André Breton's insistence that surrealism was not a definable doctrine but an activity, Clifford attempts to recover a period between the wars when ethnography is "something unfamiliar" and surrealism "not yet a bounded province of modern art and literature"; he wants to study a "crucial modern orientation toward cultural order" more modernist than modern, that both exploits and explores the fragmentation and juxtaposition of cultural values.[31] To do this he links ethnography with the artistic avant-garde, viewing both as critical activities that parody, subvert, and transgress a contested reality. Without stabilizing either "surrealism" or "ethnography" as historical or disciplinary categories, Clifford proposes "ethnographic surrealism" as both a historical and actual tool for cultural analysis.[32]

Clifford traces, through well-known examples in literature, art, and essay, the (mostly French) foundations of the representations of a fractured modern reality—in the work of Baudelaire, Rimbaud, Cézanne and the cubists, Lautréamont, and in Walter Benjamin's writing on modernity. Clifford inserts into this tradition of what he calls "the ethnographic surreal" Apollinaire's *Calligrammes*, Fernand Léger's paintings, and the general surrealist interest in dreams, fetishes, and what Lévi-Bruhl called "mentalité primitive." Clifford draws a distinction between nineteenth-century Orientalism and what he understands as the more profound interest of twentieth-century metropolitan scholars and artists:

> Unlike the exoticism of the nineteenth century, which departed from a more-or-less confident cultural order in search of a temporary frisson, a circumscribed experience of the bizarre, modern surrealism and ethnography began with a reality deeply in question. . . . The "primitive" societies of the planet were increasingly available as aesthetic, cosmological, and scientific resources. These possibilities drew on something more than an older Orientalism; they required modern ethnography. The postwar context was structured by a basically ironic experience of culture. For every local custom or truth there was always an exotic alternative, a possible juxtaposition of incongruity. Below (psychologically) and beyond (geographically) ordinary reality there existed another reality. Surrealism shared this ironic situation with relativist ethnography.[33]

In the continuing play between the familiar and the strange that Clifford believes grounds "the modern cultural situation," ethnographers worked to make the unfamiliar comprehensible, whereas surrealists found in the familiar—for example, the Paris of *Paysan de Paris* or *Nadja*—a certain exoticism.

In *Documents*, Clifford finds a view of culture that "did not feature conceptions of organic structure, functional integration, wholeness, or historical continuity" but rather a conception of culture that "can be called, without undue anachronism, semiotic." The assemblage of images, artifacts, and ideas that makes both the journal *Documents* and later the Musée de l'Homme into "ethnographic museums" suggests that "cultural reality was composed of artificial codes, ideological identities, and objects susceptible to inventive recombination and juxtaposition: Lautréamont's umbrella and sewing machine, a violin and a pair of hands slapping the African dirt." *Documents* creates the order of an "unfinished collage rather than that of a unified organism."[34] Mauss and Rivet's humanism envisaged universals, including differences in bodily practices as well as belief systems, so that "no one time or culture could claim to incarnate the mankind on display at the Musée de l'Homme."[35]

For Clifford, the operative idea for what he calls "surrealist ethnography" is juxtaposition: "Ethnography combined with surrealism can no longer be seen as the empirical, descriptive dimension of anthropology, a general science of the human. Nor is it the interpretation of cultures, for the planet cannot be seen as divided into distinct, textualized ways of life. Ethnography cut with surrealism emerges as the theory and practice of juxtaposition."[36] The juxtaposition and collage integral to *Documents* for Clifford could arguably be found central to Baker's art, to the presentation and reconception of African and diasporic arts in Paris in the 1920s. For Clifford, *Documents* works like the museum, collaging articles such as found objects or works of art brought to the metropole from far away places or times. It might also be read as a "review"—a performance of the cultures that interested its eclectic team of writers. In this way, Baker too might be considered one of Clifford's "surrealist ethnographers," in the sense that she is re-creating or putting on display "African" dances, collaged or cited in a setting (at least) twice removed from their usual context.

Baker's work, especially into the 1930s, lends itself to another reading. Opposing the idea of the existence of such a "surrealist ethnography," Denis Hollier has argued that the concerns of French avant-garde writers and of museologists were very different. In the displacement of objects from Africa into French ethnographic museums, and in avant-garde interest in such objects, Hollier finds two very different passions. Against Clifford, he argues in "The Use Value of the Impossible" that the ethnographic museology of the 1930s was a reaction against French Surrealist formalist interest in African art in the 1920s.[37] Clifford's conclusion that ethnography and surrealism share an erasure of the difference between high and low in culture does not, in Hollier's view, take into account the shock provoked by *Documents*.

Hollier's history points out that *Documents* took its title from the spirit of inquiry of Georges Bataille's thesis at the École des Chartes and was founded in 1929 "a long way from the avant-garde";[38] its authors were dedicated to finding in objects a "documentary" value rooted in their exemplary everydayness. For Hollier, the review's subtitle (*Archeology/Fine Arts/Ethnography*) suggests that, although a "glossy" review,

*Documents* wanted to subvert the beaux-arts mandate. *Documents* contributors Georges-Henri Rivière, undertaking the rehabilitation of the Musée d'Ethnographie, and Paul Rivet, the museum's director since 1927, both declared themselves opposed to the primitivism "à la mode" of artists, poets, and musicians. Hollier disagrees with Clifford's reading of the review; for Hollier, what drove the organizers of *Documents* was a return to the "primitivism" of use value as opposed to exchange value in a resistance to 1920s formalism that marked the French 1930s. Hollier notes that "even in *Documents*, the ethnographers and the surrealists never actually had a common enterprise (or, to borrow James Clifford's all-too-seductive expression, there was never any such thing as 'surrealist ethnography'). There were merely 'encounters with ethnographers' to quote the title of Métraux's article on Bataille, and the ground for these encounters was a certain resistance to mercantile decontextualization."[39]

For the *Documents* collective, nostalgia for use value followed two inclinations, characterized by Hollier as "secular" and "sacred." Ethnographers' interest in use value takes them back to the technical, social, and economic utilization of objects; others, like Leiris, following Proust and Benjamin, are concerned with what Bataille calls the "unproductive use" of sacred objects.[40] The ethnographers undertake to rehabilitate the lowly, to "show everything" and "tell it all" in the museum. But for Bataille and Leiris, it is the unsayable that remains important. Attempting to reintroduce the "forbidden" into science, Bataille sets up an alternate system in which "everything has to be said . . . but on condition that everything may not be said."[41]

Without mentioning Marx, *Documents* "follows fairly closely the opposition between use value and exchange value that Marx puts in place in the opening of *Capital*, in his discussion of the analysis of merchandise."[42] *Documents* articles put into play Marx's notion of a use value that is inseparable from and intrinsic to the thing, and that is realized only in its use—and destruction. For Hollier, exchange value is, in Marx's definition, a common property of objects and not an exclusive or intrinsic quality; exchange value is a deferred use value, an object put on the market, rather than used, in order to be exchanged. The ethnographers of *Documents* wanted a museum that would not automatically reduce objects to their formal or aesthetic properties, in an exhibition space that would exclude objects' use value; rather they wanted to exhibit in such a formal space, at some remove from the culture of the object's actual use, what Hollier calls "a use value on vacation" or the Sunday side of workaday objects.[43]

*Documents* ethnographers tried to work out a new technique of collection and presentation of objects or "documents." Their resistance to exchange value and to exhibition leads both ethnographic and aesthetic thinking to what Hollier terms "the same exigency of the irreplaceable, the same nostalgia for a world subjected to the tyranny of use value."[44] Writing about fetishism, Georges Bataille praises it—nostalgically—and opposes it to merchandising; he does not, however, oppose fetishism to use value in Marxist tradition.[45]

The tyranny of the particular and that of use value are detailed as well in Benjamin's 1936 essay "The Work of Art in the Age of Mechanical Reproduction"; according to Benjamin, a work's uniqueness depends on its one use value and on its complete absence of exchange value. Its "authenticity" is founded in the ritual in which its use value resided initially. Thus the aura of a work of art is not to be found in a museum but in its "cult" value in a precise place and time. With Benjamin, Hollier argues that the use value of art in a pre-modern regime is not a matter of pure utilitarianism but of ritual and wholeness of place: "the thing only takes place on site. It cannot be transposed or transported."[46]

Jean-Paul Sartre's formula for cultural consumption, "Jazz is like bananas—it must be consumed on the spot,"[47] suggests another twist on the question of locale and use value. Baker's famous banana costume that put Paris in thrall was at once a mercantile gesture of her white promoters and a subtle commentary on colonialism and consumption. Capitalizing on Baker's color, her management and choreographer gave her a "savage" setting on a concert stage in which to perform both her natural talent and her artificial stardom. Transporting both her bananas and her audience, deferring the consumption of the first while offered for the consumption of the second, Baker, through her dancing, both mocks Parisian concerns about "authentic" African art and at the same time creates cultural capital.

It can be argued that through the 1920s and into the 1930s, her art was not simply one of juxtaposition, piecing together a step from Harlem with a Paris costume and an African drummer, but one of inclusivity that expressed the merging of forms from three continents. This was the operating procedure of *Documents* as Hollier describes it: the *Documents* collective was not so much engaging in the juxtaposition or collage of cultural artefacts but in a kind of classification that eluded restrictive and exclusive norms of classifying. The principle organizing the collection and exhibition of documents would be that of psychoanalysis, that every detail counts: "Nothing will be excluded, says Schaeffner. No object, no matter how formless."[48] Hollier identifies two tendencies at work for the *Documents* collective: to classify or to understand how certain objects or phenomena "declassify." He names these, respectively, the "absolute exception" and the "law of no-exception"; for Bataille, the concept of the "informe" (the "formless") declassifies.[49] Griaule, Rivet, and Schaeffner went after the rare, the beautiful, the monstrous; Bataille the reverse. For Bataille, beauty was not the exception but the statistical norm.[50]

Baker's merging of the beautiful and the comic, the exotic and the everyday, can be understood in these terms not as a simple collage of images but as the inclusion in her dancing of both choreographed form and elusive formlessness. While flouting European conventions about the body, Baker nevertheless respects the discipline and distance of the stage. Her dancing infuses life into form, undercutting the fixation of a glamorous or perfect image with the awkwardness and gags of physical comedy, and the imitation of possession. Ironically, dancing as if possessed permits Baker some ownership of her image, the possession of herself.

POSSESSION

Writing later about his experience of jazz in New York, Sartre emphasized the madness of jazz while trying to disconnect it from stereotypes of the machine age and African heritage: "It is not the century-old chant of Negro slaves. Nor the sad little dream of Yankees crushed by the machine. Nothing of the sort." Yet Sartre's text reinscribes jazz in both of these contexts: jazz is itself a machine of destruction, with musicians who "beat you" in a "hellish round" with a "deafening climax"; "Connecting rod, shaft, spinning top. They beat you, they turn, they crash, the rhythm grips you and shakes you." And it induces primal behavior: "you scream like a woman in childbirth. The trumpet player . . . transmits his hypnotic obsession." You leave in an "aftermath of nervous exhaustion."[51]

The popularity of African American forms of dance and music in France in the 1920s is embedded in a view of the trend called by dance critic André Levinson "a symptom of an epidemic contagion."[52] In his preface to Paul Colin's 1927 edition of lithographs, *Le Tumulte noir*, the satirist Georges Thenon (pseudonym "Rip") unabashedly describes the fashion for black dances as both a physical and mental illness: the "Charlestonesque epidemic" brought on by Josephine Baker and others is described as a "Charentonesque epidemic," that is, connected to the psychiatric hospital of Charenton. According to Rip, "Negropathy" and "Negromania" affecting the Parisian public will drive them, like the "ballerinas of the future," to a "special clinic."[53]

This dance—that both transports its participants and is imported from the exotic elsewhere—is at the heart of Paris; Rip explains that on Josephine's arrival, the Baedeker guide was replaced by the Baker guide. This dance is seen as a symptom of the general madness because it is African or African American—exotic, imported, bringing on "this period of national, secular, and obligatory lunacy." Yet in response to the pathologizing of her dance, Baker noted the similarities between this form and the possession experienced in religious ceremonies in African American churches: "One of the critics compared our movements to St. Vitus's Dance. 'What kind of dance is that?' I asked. 'It's a nervous disorder that makes you tremble all over.' 'That's not a sickness,' I retorted. 'It's the way we act in church back home.'"[54] As a response to the critical discourse applying the social pathologies of race and sex to jazz and jazz dance, the religious metaphor of possession applied to dancing marginalizes performers' work even as it attributes a ritual power to the dances. It connects black American forms to African source material that has the ring of authenticity and the weight of tradition.

Before going to Africa with the Mission Dakar-Djibouti, the study tour headed by Marcel Griaule in 1931, Leiris referred to Africa as a place of stories he had seen staged and read in his childhood, and to Europe as the locus of inventions he would describe with the term "primitive." He adds that "like many others, I came to ethnography via 'l'art nègre.'"[55] Many of the writers in the *Documents* collective admire the interpretation of African source material on French stages they otherwise find boring. Although the spectacles that interest the *Documents* writers never come from Africa—unlike the plastic arts imported from or influenced by Africa that interest them—frequently the spectacles feature African American performers and dance styles. Africa is the source of images and icons brought to life in American performances: Leiris's definition of the focus of *Documents*, viewed thirty years later, was that it concerned itself with "the irritating and the heteroclite, even the anxiety-provoking,"[56] but that going after objects was a way of bringing them to life.

As *Documents* displaces objects into its pages for study, it also has frequent recourse to theater as an image for its work of displacement (and staging); with the exception of the various "revues nègres" of the 1920s, it often devalues the contemporary theater's banality and shortcomings in favor of the global travel and witnessing of spectacles on site. Bataille remarks on the boredom provoked by a stage production of *80 Days Around the World* at the Châtelet, whose "young dancers' costumes stink of naphtaline."[57] In an article on Lew Leslie's *Black Birds* (1929–30), Leiris credits such spectacles with bringing to the "métropole" the possibility of magic (he also credits Roussel's *Impressions d'Afrique* with putting into his mind an imagined Africa that drives his interest in ethnography and the ethnographic mission).[58] He regrets that many shows are simply boring, and that even the best—for example, *Black Birds*—don't rouse the audience as the "real" African American possession could: "they don't completely vanquish our spinelessness or engender a hysteria as great as *Porgy*'s, a hysteria so intense that it must be capable of moving spectators to the immediate enacting of sordid acts or extravagant debaucheries"[59]—in this case, to raise the money necessary to bury the dead.

Leiris notes that there have been signs of the rebellion in literature and painting but few in the domain of the theater capable of giving the satisfaction represented in *Porgy*[60]:

> It would be wrong to characterize us as blasé, but the fact is that we have had enough of these plots that are always all the same, borrowed from our everyday lives, every day more worthless; it

isn't enough for us to act in the same way, for example, as these savages who consider that the best possible use of a telegraph pole is to transform it into a poison arrow (because isn't that just about what we are doing when we change a mask or statue created for complex, specific ritual purposes into a vulgar art object—an infinitely more bloody insult than the one made to European inventions by these above-mentioned savages, because it attacks a fatal and grave mystery, and not telegraphy, the fruit of a science that we can never scorn enough?).[61]

As a result, Leiris writes, "we would, by far, prefer to get closer to our savage ancestry."[62]

*Documents* manifests particular interest in getting closer to "savage ancestry" by reconstructing or reevaluating the body; for Leiris, it is the body that connects cultures and peoples, the modern and the primitive. In an article titled "Civilisation," in *Documents*, he argues that in the body's ornamentation and movements, in our everyday wear and behavior, there are signs of our "savagery": in a red nail pointed like a dagger, a fleeting gesture moving like the sudden swelling of a sail on a sea that begins to foam, "these are precious signs that make us understand better how close we are to savages."[63]

The presence of African Americans onstage fills a void in France created by theater devoid of ritual power. For Leiris, it is not a question of aestheticizing jazz, and the reviews and other arts deriving from it, as ("Great") Art but understanding how "shows like 'Black Birds'—the fruit of illegitimate love between magic and free play"—take us beyond art, to a point of human development where this bastard conception is not yet "hypertrophied": "This music and dancing, far from stopping at our skin, send deep, organic roots into us, penetrating with a thousand ramifications,—painful surgery—but giving us stronger blood."[64] Before the arrival of such spectacles, the closest thing to religion or ritual onstage in France, Rivière argues in "Religion et Folies-Bergères," was at the Moulin Rouge: "We have to go to the music-hall, among twenty pairs of legs, accompanied by an air by Christiné, in a conventional and magnificently ordered ballet of every object of our carnal desire, to find, finally reclaimed by eroticism, this spirit of religion."[65]

African dance's potential to represent madness plays a positive role for these French writers and artists. Against the madness of the de-ritualized and highly industrialized technological society Leiris sketches in this chapter's opening quotation, the madness of possession appeals to the *Documents* writers, who de-pathologize the gestures by interpreting them as culturally relative. It is ethnography that permits an understanding of the cultural relativity of gesture. In "La Mutilation sacrificielle et l'oreille coupée de Vincent Van Gogh," Bataille links contemporary behaviors recounted in pathological literature—such as automutilation—to ancient Greek mythology, and to sacrificial and ritual practices in a historical and cultural site he refers to as "autrefois."[66] Ethnography makes possible the interpretation of gesture in another system, for example, the logic of sacrifice, of "another time": "But how is it possible that gestures incontestably linked to madness [l'aliénation], even if they cannot, in any instance, be seen as symptoms of a determined mental illness, can be spontaneously designated as the expression [adéquation] of a veritable social function, of an institution as well defined, as universally human, as sacrifice?" In antiquity, Bataille points out, "madmen were able to describe their mutilations in this way."[67]

Such "primitivization" of gesture can be understood as allowing the French avant-garde to de-pathologize and revalue dance in the twentieth century.[68] Recombining ritual, religious, and erotic elements, Baker's dance brings alive a pre-modern "savagery" that makes the machine age livable. But their admiration for the ritual, "animal," or mystical qualities of dance does not ultimately set up a framework for the valuing of Baker's dancing as work. Because it resembles possession, and moves its audiences—even to the point of getting them to dance these dances[69]—it is not understood as work. Between the dance performer's work and the leisure of those watching or dancing with her, there is a significant gap. Baker's dance at once represents the labor of the working class and the potential of labor power to be capitalized on. Miming the motor force that makes labor "physiological expenditure" but also playing to and with the apparatus of cinematic stardom, Baker in her dancing walks the fine line between commodification and capital. This "symptom" found by some in her dancing might be understood, following a Lacanian reading of Marx's invention of the symptom, as the fissure between labor and value.[70] After building a career orchestrated by Europeans marketing "primitive" frenzy to a public tired of The Machine yet consuming its products, Baker moves on to dance that frenzy within the frame of cinema, as a dancing machine herself transcending the camera and simultaneously subject to it.

CINEMATIC TECHNO-TRANSCENDENCE

Dancing both the ritual and capital aspects of technology, and visually linked to the figures of African art and dance by her appearance, Josephine Baker was verbally linked to America in her accented French. Baker's starring roles in two French films, made a decade after her Paris debut, attempted to capitalize on her success as a dancer while filming her acting and singing. Following cinema into the realm of sound, Baker escapes certain stereotypes of the dancer and dancing machine while accumulating others.

Baker's film career has been considered in the context of the French colonial cinema of the 1930s and its influence on the development of a French national cinema[71]; both of the films explored in this section struggle to define her as a person of color in French colonial terms. In the 1934 *Zou Zou*, Baker, listed in the credits as Joséphine, plays the "twin" of Jean Gabin. In this film, Baker's dancing is a site of exclusion and isolation, representing Zou Zou's unclassifiable social-racial status and its sexual-erotic threat.

Described as a Creole and a Martiniquaise, Zou Zou is raised with her "brother" Jean by Papa Mélé (played by Pierre Larquey), a white circus performer who acts as father to them both. Introducing the "twins" to the circus crowd as a "miracle of nature," Papa Mélé describes their birth in Polynesia to a Chinese mother and Indian ("peau-rouge," that is, redskin) father, who renounced the two because their skin was not the same color as that of their parents. Mélé's banter with the circus crowd includes the observation that "freaks are not made like us" and "mysteries are not made to be understood." These observations reinforce moments from the opening scene, when two little boys, spying on Zou Zou in her trailer, remark, "elle a une drôle de tête" (she's funny-looking), and Zou Zou powders her face white.

Putting the children to bed after their performance that night, Papa Mélé answers Jean's complaint that Zou Zou doesn't believe they are twins. The same stork delivered them, on the same day, he explains, but dropped her down the chimney. When Jean asks if Zou Zou's father was also his, Papa Mélé explains that each had a different father, both of whom were beloved performers with the Cirque Romarin. But when asked to verify that he is their "papa," he explains that a father is, by definition for them, "a papa that one didn't know" ("un pere c'est un papa qu'on n'a pas connu"). Both fathers, he reports, communicated to him that they only fathered the children but could not be their "papa" the way Mélé would ("je n'ai pu etre que son père; tu seras son papa"). Jean concludes: "alors, on peut avoir deux pères?" (so it's possible to have two fathers?).

*Zou Zou* is full of unlikely plot lines that never quite meet; the story is based on a scenario by Carlo Rim, taken from a novella by Giuseppe Abatino, Baker's manager and partner. The narrative has Jean joining the navy and then going AWOL, moving with the family to Paris, and becoming an electrician at the music hall, where he is in his element surrounded by chorus girls. Zou Zou grows up with a sunny disposition, a love of animals, and a way with vegetables. When out with Jean, she clearly dotes on him, and he describes her as "my sister" to the friends who call her the pretty Creole.

To earn money, Zou Zou becomes a *blanchisseuse* (a laundress; literally, a "whitener"), working in a friendly laundry full of women doing ironing for the music hall cast. The significance of the *blanchisserie* is noteworthy: as the only person of color featured in the film, Baker is entirely at home in white society; yet the script finds her no man, and she remains attached to her brother. Too attached, according to her friend Claire, the daughter of the launderette's proprietor, who promptly falls in love with Jean when Zou Zou introduces them. Extending the metaphor of the *blanchisseuse*, Claire (her name means "light") is blond and genteel in spite of her working-class background. Confessing her love for Jean to her mother, Claire makes it clear that although Zou Zou is her friend, Zou Zou's attachment to Jean has something unnatural about it; it is both incestuous and threatening. When Zou Zou glimpses Jean in the arms of the platinum-haired music hall star one afternoon, she returns to work with a heavy heart. The laundry workers repeat the first line of the film: she has "une drôle de tête," and she declares herself "trompée" (betrayed).

One evening, at a dance hall, while Zou Zou watches Claire and Jean dancing together, she is approached by a lout who tells her she shouldn't be sitting alone. Dragged onto the dance floor, Zou Zou fights back; Jean joins the fray and punches the man out. Several nights later, Jean accidentally witnesses this man's murder on the street and is arrested for the crime. In need of money to bail Jean out of jail, Zou Zou throws herself at the music hall's director—having seen her dance a few steps, he wanted to "discover" her—and she becomes a star overnight. In Baker's trademark elegant, revealing costumes, Zou Zou performs several stage numbers, including the song "For me, there is only one man in Paris, and it is he" ("Pour moi, il n'y a qu'un homme dans Paris, et c'est lui"), clearly pointed at Jean. The musical number most praised, and most famous, from the film, puts Baker in feathers in a cage in which she sings of her longing for "home"—"Haiti."

After risking her career by leaving the opening night's performance during the show to testify on Jean's behalf at the police station, Zou Zou devotes herself to stardom. She gives up her unnatural desire for Jean, leaving him to Claire. And although Jean has distinguished himself only as a navy dropout and a Don Juan, he is wrongly accused and rightly freed from prison. Zou Zou, however, remains something of a freak. Under the guise of normalizing Frenchness, *Zou Zou* locates its heroine on the margins of society, as an orphaned circus performer; in the starched clean company of the "whitening" laundry; and finally on stage performing her confined exoticism ("Haiti"), her misdirected love ("Il n'y a qu'un homme dans Paris"), and the few, free dance steps that the script permits her.

In addition to the patent metaphors of the whitening and caging of Zou Zou's colorful personality, two cameos in this film reflect the stage persona of Josephine Baker: one, an uncredited dancer of color who appears briefly in an early scene, dancing at a port where Jean's ship has docked in Manila. To the tom-tom played by a dark-skinned drummer, this dancer performs a combination of African and Latin steps, hip rolls, legato arm movements, shimmies, pelvic thrusts, and isolations, while wearing a grass skirt and neckpiece. Watching her, Jean's female companion comments: "they are born dancing, for sure." The underlined naturalness of this performance is offset later in the film by the rehearsal scenes at the music hall, in which chorus girls and the American platinum star "Miss Barbara" (played by Illa Meery) go through their paces. These two figures represent Baker's double stage personality: the human motor of the first and the glamorous industry of the second.

Zou Zou is simultaneously "too natural" and shy, dancing her few kicks, tap steps, cakewalk, and Charleston moves onstage at the theater when she thinks the curtain is down behind her back. The resurgence of the exotic, performing Zou Zou is cast as a return of her childhood performance training and undoubtedly also her heritage—"born dancing." Yet Zou Zou hovers somewhere in between the natural native dancer and the fully financed star. Becoming a star in her case means giving the stage to her natural talent but not, in her dressing room, behaving with the prima donna's overwrought emotions. Significantly, both the "natural" Philippine dancer and the carefully choreographed American star appear topless (however briefly); Zou Zou does not, turning her back to the camera during a changing scene in her dressing room. Knocking at Zou Zou's door, the theater director and impresario are refused admittance. "Impossible, nous sommes toutes nues" (we're stark naked), says Madeleine Guitry as Josette, the star's dresser. Chuckling, the men look through the keyhole to find the two women fully dressed, deep in a session of strategic planning.

In the scene immediately following the dance in the Manila port, the action shifts to Zou Zou in France. As she clowns for a little French girl, the freedom of movement—although not the moves themselves—recalls that of the dark-skinned woman we have just seen dancing half-naked. Zou Zou jumps from the table, picks the child up in her arms, spins her around, and lands her on the ground. Then, during the ensuing dialogue, Zou Zou reaches to pull down her slit skirt, caught between her legs, and leaves her hand on the skirt. The gesture of modesty is extremely revealing: Baker has her back to the camera, and the back of her skirt, hitched up, remains where it is. The front panel of the skirt that she pulls down cannot be seen from the audience's perspective. Beyond the film scenario's story of the mainstreaming of the circus freak, or its attempts to contain Zou Zou and render her French, this gesture reads as one choreographed by Baker herself, acknowledging the constraints of proper femininity. In her tiny feathered costume, on her swing in her cage, such a gesture of modesty is unimaginable. But turning her back to the camera, Baker develops an interiority that is, perhaps ironically, one of the liberties of stardom.

Running along with and against this scenario is the history of Baker's own development as an actress, a film star, and a French citizen in the 1930s, after her early stage successes: acting and singing in a language she had learned "on the job" (with the help of diction lessons from Sacha Guitry);[72] creating a playful character with some depth, in Rim's script—a character who could negotiate the tastes of white French film audiences and represent Baker's dramatic breadth as well as her idealized visual image. Beyond Baker's reputation as a dancer, her status as a film star and as a "French" woman were significant elements in her return to the United States in 1935. Fayard Nicholas (of the Nicholas Brothers) reported seeing Baker in the audience at the Cotton Club in 1935, the first time he had seen an African American seated in the front row. "So when I saw Josephine Baker sittin' ringside, I said, 'Wow! it must be because she is a French citizen.'"[73] And like other "exotic" European dancers, she appeared in New York in a piece of Balanchine choreography titled *5AM*, made for her for the *Follies* at the Winter Garden.

In her second film, released the following year, Baker starred as Princesse Tam-Tam in the film of the same name (1935). Again based on a story by Abatino, and again struggling to define Baker's identity across cultures and genres, *Princesse Tam-Tam* has a more defined story line. While *Zou Zou* merged white themes with a hint of film noir, *Princesse Tam-Tam* unabashedly explores exotic people of color—some played by white actors—both abroad and at home, as well as toying with the idea of "interracial" romance, referred to as "des histoires de race" in the film. In *Princesse Tam-Tam*'s intertwined story lines, Baker's dancing serves as the key to her identity as an "uncivilized" colonial.

Like *Zou Zou*, *Princesse Tam-Tam* tells a story about the "civilizing" of the main character, the young Arab girl Alwina, as played by Baker.[74] Shot in Tunisia, the opening scenes show Alwina cavorting with lambs and stealing fruit in the market. Poorly dressed in a Bedouin-style robe, she dances for the children outdoors at a local ruin; although Alwina has none of the glamour of the star, she has the same joie de vivre as Zou Zou, and like Baker, she has a love of animals and children. In town, she meets up with an aristocratic French popular novelist, Max, played by Albert Préjean, who has come to Africa for inspiration, along with his co-writer, to escape a wife whose "barbarism"—that is, her scandalous liaisons and high-society nightlife—threatens his name and work. "We'll go to Africa," Max says to his assistant, "to the real savages."

The themes of savagery and civilization punctuate every scene with Alwina. Fascinated by the young woman, and sensing the potential for a titillating best-seller about her, Max undertakes a Pygmalion-like transformation. As part of the stratagem, he plans to make Alwina fall in love with him and then to chart her reactions to his advances. Alwina is brought to his villa and taught the rules of social conduct, whose senseless stupidity she constantly points out. In several pointed exchanges, Alwina underlines the "savagery" of the Europeans. When told that at the house the dinner bell will be rung to call her to dinner, and that she shall eat whenever she is hungry, she calculates what it might mean to eat all the time, and asks: "and what if I'm not hungry?" and is told: "Then you don't have to come to dinner." "Then why ring the bell?" she reasons. Later, to get back at the French tourists who have sneered at her and complained about the local food they have been given in the countryside, Alwina puts sand in the saltcellar. Max delights at the faces of the miserable sand-eaters and laughs as Alwina escapes.

Upset about rumors from France that his wife has been frequenting a maharajah, Max decides to finish the novel immediately and return home. At this point, the diegesis shifts to Max's novelistic rendering of what might happen if he were to take Alwina with him to Paris, introduce her to society as an exotic princess, and be revenged on his wife. Alwina is thus given piano and dancing lessons, taught how to dress and walk, and prepared for Parisian life. Presented as an uninterrupted continuation of the story line, this section of the film is not identified as Max's literary fantasy, a story within the story, until we return to the scene of its writing at the end of the film.

The early sequences of the film frame Alwina in racist and sexist stereotypes: she is portrayed as a child, as a monkey; she is called a savage, is at the point of being beaten by Max's servant Dar, and is kept under strict surveillance by him. But within Max's story, which at the end of the film we learn has been published as a novel, the "civilization" into which Alwina is introduced is just as bad: a hellish mix of backstabbing, scandal mongering, and racist insults conferred by Max's "savage" high society. She finds sympathetic partners in Dar, who warns her against eating out of the white man's hand, and the maharajah, who finally counsels her to leave Paris and return to her country. Presented to Paris society as the Princess of Parador, Alwina is admired for her beauty and style, but she is not quite princess enough to marry the maharajah, who says he saw through her from the first and urges her to return home. In a return to the first story line, after the novel ends, Max decides he will leave her his villa, and in the film's final scene, she cradles an infant while Dar makes pottery outside of the villa now taken over by animals, including a donkey browsing through Max's novel, *Civilization*.[75]

Both *Zou Zou* and *Princesse Tam-Tam* attempt to situate Baker's identity as an African American performer in Paris, both neutralizing or naturalizing her color by assimilating her to Frenchness as a performer or as a colonial "exotic." Although this assimilation to Frenchness via colonialism ignores her Americanness, her self-imposed exile from a country divided by segregation, and focuses instead on her Africanness (as a Tunisian or Martiniquaise), both film scenarios stop short at integrating her into French life. In *Zou Zou* she reaches stardom but remains single; in *Princesse Tam-Tam*, rather than losing her man and becoming a star, she remains the undiscovered Bedouin, happy at home with husband and child.

In both films, the making of the star echoes Baker's own rise to fame. After a stage career that cast the dancer from St. Louis as a primitive in Paris, the cinema is called into the service of civilizing her. Although Zou Zou labors in the laundry with other women to make France white and starched, her "natural" talent and beauty catapult her out of the working class to the top of the heap—out of the nineteenth-century novel and into twentieth-century cinema. Her labor is no longer hidden or undervalued but paid at a high price, although the film insists that it is her virtue, and not vice, that gets her there. In *Princesse Tam-Tam*, Alwina chooses the fulfilling life of poverty and domesticity in Tunisia over whatever stardom her patrons might have in mind for her, insisting again on her virtue, as opposed to the "savage" ambitions of Parisian society. In *Zou Zou*, the music hall stage becomes a huge film set when she becomes its star, enacting the very transformation that the film itself is accomplishing—making the stage star into a screen idol. In *Princesse Tam-Tam*, the maharajah's ballroom becomes her music hall stage, but it is already a fantasy Busby Berkeley set with coordinated chorus dancers in two-tone costumes. These big production numbers, like her stage shows, must be read as choreographies of an "industrialized" or "mechanized"—by the movie camera—naturalness.

Whether she is playing the role of simple colonial or glamorous star, what sings in Baker's performance in both *Zou Zou* and *Princesse Tam-Tam* is the simultaneous presence of opposites. Alternately playing the sequined glamour queen and the mocking (and self-mocking) comedienne, Baker accumulates stereotypes rather than destroying them. Commenting on a song performed at the Casino de Montmartre in 1919 characterizing jazz musicians as possessed ("These are musicians of whom one says / The poor guys have St. Vitus' dance"), Tyler Stovall argues in *Paris Noir* that such stereotypes of African Americans in Paris were overwhelmingly positive.[76] Successfully manipulating these stereotypes, allowing herself to be iconized and ironized, Baker used the typing for popular recognition and at the same time moved through it.

Summarizing Baker's career, Petrine Archer-Straw sees it as reproducing the story within the story of *Princesse Tam-Tam*: "Josephine's adoption by the mainstream suited the needs of colonialism. It reinforced notions of civilization that were constantly being questioned by the avant-garde. French audiences witnessed what they believed was her successful transformation from an African 'savage' to an urbane, sophisticated lady."[77] Archer-Straw's interpretation is based in part on the promotional materials prepared by Abatino, "Josephine Baker vue en 1925 et 1930" (Paris, 1930), including two photographs, one dated 1925 and the other 1926. In the first, Baker poses as "homegirl" buffoon; in the second, she poses in finery (with Abatino in a tuxedo), holding a stuffed Josephine doll. In such photographs, Archer-Straw argues, "allusions to puppetry are all too obvious."[78]

Even if only in a limited or contingent way, Baker's dancing reveals the capacity to transcend what Homi Bhaba characterizes as the "fixity" of the stereotype in colonial discourse: "Fixity, as the sign of cultural/historical/racial difference in the discourse of colonialism, is a paradoxical mode of representation: it connotes rigidity and an unchanging order as well as disorder, degeneracy and daemonic repetition. Likewise the stereotype, which is its major discursive strategy, is a form of knowledge and identification that vacillates between what is always 'in place', already known, and something that must be anxiously repeated."[79] Playing the roles imposed on her, Baker, in her performances, reflects both the "fixity" of clichés and the "daemonic" disorder crucial to the stereotype "as an ambivalent mode of knowledge and power."[80] Yet in another way, taken as a whole, Baker's career—moving across countries, languages, cultures, and media—allows her to reframe her dancing in different contexts that allow her to use "disorder, degeneracy and daemonic repetition" to play off of the fixation of her star image.

The snatches of dances she performs in these films serve as the stamp of authenticity that this is "la Baker" performing her trademark steps. Yet while her dancing brands the film with the mark of the star, it also has to be contained: Josephine dances in *Zou Zou* behind a closed curtain, for nobody—for herself; in *Princesse Tam-Tam* she dances for the local children—equally nobody—and when she dances in Paris it is only in the imagination of the author, first at a small café and later at a maharajah's ball, where enemies encourage her to dance, hoping it will disgrace her. When Zou Zou becomes a star, the dancing is minimized and formalized in the huge cinematic numbers that feature her, as if her dancing threatens to break out of the frame and the industry, society, and aesthetic it holds in place.

In her live performances, Baker's dancing could be seen as putting her at the mercy of the public she enthralled; in the cinema, her movement—in some ways, paradoxically—becomes the moment of resistance, in the nonverbal realm of the image, to the apparatus's construction of stereotypes. Cinema—the guarantor of twentieth-century "stardom"—continues to root her identity in her skin and in her (dancer's) body, but it makes Josephine more than a dancer, a dancing machine.

FIXITY

In spite of the control of her image and her career by its apparatus—represented within the films themselves by the impresario and the novelist who, in different ways, invent her stardom—cinema gives Baker the means to move out of the fixation of her image represented, for example, in Paul Colin's lithographs of her. Although both of these films manipulate her image for a white European audience, both gave her a performance arena beyond the frame, where her culture and color signified differently than they would have in the segregated United States. Despite its controlled production of her image, cinema made possible for Baker what dancing onstage alone could not. By collaborating with what Leiris called The Machine, the European mechanism for idealizing primitivism, by playing to the taste of a "dying civilization," Josephine complicated—if not entirely escaped—the simple commodification of her image.

In "Visual Pleasure and Narrative Cinema," Laura Mulvey argues that the representation of women in classic cinema—in particular, the glamorous star in the classic film—freezes narrative flow.[81] Meant to be looked at, the female star does not allow the spectator to identify with her but only to objectify her; the spectator is de facto constituted as male by aspects of film production and camera work that reinforce societal structures of sexual difference and unconscious structures organized around the castration and Oedipal complexes. Analyzed in Mulvey's feminist terms, Josephine Baker's two French films can be associated with the conservative Hollywood type of cinema, whose representations of women, Mulvey argues, can only be viewed as negative stereotypes whose waning should be welcomed. Thus the "machine" that Baker herself submits to in the production of these films is the cinematic apparatus that produces her as a star.

Yet this "machine" of film, in contradistinction to static portraits of Baker—which we see, for example, on screen in the film *Princesse Tam-Tam*—provides her with a vehicle that allows, however briefly, the transcendence of the dancer's submission to her audience and the co-opting of her image by visual artists who represent her. If her live dancing was subject to the demands of audiences and box office, her cinematic dancing, equally subject to those same markets, preserved something of the power of that liveness while harnessing it to the machine of the movie camera. Thus Josephine the human motor, the inexhaustible source of the jazz age, is mechanized through recordings that hold her image and becomes an example of the fantasy of "naturalism" facilitated by the machine.

Writing in 1930, the scenarist of *Zou Zou*, Carlo Rim, described most films as nothing more than a series of posed photos: "A film is a succession of snapshots more or less posed, and it only very rarely gives us the illusion of the unexpected and the rare. Ninety films out of a hundred are merely interminable poses. One doesn't premeditate a photograph like a murder or a work of art."[82] Although *Zou Zou* gives us snapshots of a dancer's career, Baker herself seems to be always breaking out of these framings on her way to stardom. And if stardom itself is the ultimate frame—the cage in one of her big musical numbers—Rim's scenario seems nevertheless to capitalize on Baker's larger-than-life energy to disrupt the static "posing" that he believes film too often falls into.

The question of the pose and the framed or frozen image in the dancer's representation has been especially important in recent discussions of Baker's work and life. In "Josephine Baker and Paul Colin: African-American Dance Seen through Parisian Eyes," Dalton and Gates consider Colin's images of Baker as if they were, in some way, equivalent to her work. Making an argument based on images as a substitute for performance, Dalton and Gates's article collapses the dancing body of Baker into the pictorial representation of her and then traces the elaboration of that dance, as seen through Parisian eyes, from the images.

Dalton and Gates describe this portfolio of images as a performance: "it is as though Colin has staged a spectacular, imaginary opening night." "The next image shifts the spotlight. The warm-up act is over. It is time for the vedette." "But the show must end, and with it the fantasy." "On a climactic double-page spread, the jazz musicians . . . play one last number. Then what happens? La Baker does one last, unforgettable, kaleidoscopic Charleston."[83]

The authors conclude that these pictures represent the "partial success that art can have in the grand combat against racism."[84] Despite the Parisian enthusiasm apparent in the prints, Colin is running the spotlight—as Zou Zou's brother, Jean Gabin, did in the film—and for Dalton and Gates, his representations ultimately belie a stereotyping of her image and a reduction of her achievement. But Dalton and Gates themselves are looking at Baker's dance through the "Parisian eyes" of its pictorial representation rather than live performance's simultaneous negotiation of the commodification of the performer by a paying audience and the performer's (sometimes limited) control of his or her representation.

Although transcending the sometimes participatory adulation of the live audience, Baker and her film image may not have successfully combated racism. Yet the cinema captured in time the movement that made her a popular performer, and it gave her another life. Josephine Baker, on film, dances not only for Paris but for posterity, for an audience that did not yet entirely exist.

### JOSEPHINE BAKER DANCES FOR POSTERITY

Although other forms of dancing, like the chorus line that Baker mocks and rises out of, suggest the mastery of machines, the successful streamlining of gesture and character accomplished by mechanization, Baker's so-called primitive dancing with its elements of hypnosis, or possession, suggested the malaise of the machine age. Baker's human motor staged the inescapability of the thermodynamic paradigm—the expenditure of energy in inevitable heat loss—and the exhaustion of the dancing machine.

Ramsay Burt has argued that "Baker's star image was a means through which concern about social and cultural instabilities, ambiguities and contradictions was ameliorated or defused. . . . By creating a positive image of personal enjoyment, Baker in effect supported the modernist myth of social, scientific and technological progress."[85] Yet her dancing ultimately parodied industry's production of meaningless fragmented gesture, and it resists the anonymity of modern streamlining. While the European science of work and American Taylorism "banished personality" and eliminated workers' desires,[86] Baker's talent overflowed stereotypes and categories; in the words of André Levinson, "her personality exceeded the genre."

Josephine Baker seems to transcend the imposition of the still frame and the pose, using cinema in a way Loie Fuller might have dreamed of, in spite of the co-opting of Baker's stage image for national, colonial, and commercial interests, Hollywood-ized dance, and global markets. While successfully negotiating the stardom constructed for her by the industry and by the apparatus, Baker maintains an aura of authenticity reserved for modern dance in the face of machine culture. That she does so while herself "submitting to the Machine" points to the complexity of a modernist formulation of naturalness held in place by artifice's massive machine.

# Conclusion

It is tempting to think of the "dancing machine" as a thing of the past, as an icon of a twentieth century obsessed with automobiles and airplanes, with machines of war and of space, with work and productivity, and with cinema. Present-day advertisements that continue to link dancers to cars or precision timepieces suggest an ongoing nostalgia for this twentieth century, and examples of both kinds of dancing machine can be found in contemporary concert dance. New York avant-garde dance, in the tradition of Merce Cunningham's early experiments, continues to explore the effect of new technologies on bodies and movement. Dancer-choreographers such as DanceKK's Koosil-ja Hwang rupture mainstream modern dance's typical effort-shape and bound-flow energy and, in tandem with experimental video, create a different kind of tension in movement, with a cyber hum.

At the same time, forms of dance inspired by technology and industrialized labor such as the dances grouped now under the rubric of "hip-hop" embody the drive and frenzy of automation, of robots, and the fragmented gestures of the assembly line and time clock (popping, locking), high-speed or slow motion effects of cinema and filmed martial arts, electricity (electric boogaloo), and strobe light effects (ticking).

From Josephine Baker to the forms of jazz, funk, and now—especially in France—hip-hop dance that have found their place on the concert dance stage over the last thirty years, there is, essentially, only a single step. Yet that step is a great stride, taken both within and against mainstream modern dance, and cultivating techno-culture while critiquing it.[1] We forget that in spite of the vibrancy of the live performances of these dances, and their neighborhood origins, they have, like the Jackson Five's performance of "Dancing Machine," been widely seen because they are themselves artifacts of recording and mass diffusion. We also forget that in spite of their uniqueness, which is rooted in the experience of African American and Latino youth in disadvantaged inner-city neighborhoods, their "authenticity" is also the product of a melting pot of images, cultures, and gestures, of images culled from mainstream media, film, and television. This live dancing imitates and stages mechanically reproduced forms.

The dissolution of boundaries between the human and the machine, life and its mechanical reproductions, has continued to occupy science fiction as well as science studies. Recent theorists of science and technology have challenged the distinctions between human and machine, and analyzed the confusion or converging of human and natural, technological inhuman or superhuman realms. In *Simians, Cyborgs, and Women*, Donna Haraway notes that the late twentieth century witnessed the breakdown of distinctions that a tradition of scientific thought had established: between human and animal (via language), between organism (human or animal) and machine, and between physical and metaphysical.[2] Theorizing their connections in scientific and cultural practices, Haraway concludes that the categories dividing human, animal, and machine have become, de facto, obsolete: "Late twentieth-century machines have made thoroughly ambiguous the difference between natural and artificial, mind and body, self-developing and externally designed, and many other distinctions that used to apply to organisms and machines. Our machines are disturbingly lively, and we ourselves frighteningly inert."[3] Haraway's analysis of the status of women in an age dominated by its machines extends the collapsing of categories of subject and object, human and animal, living system and machine system introduced into the critique of science and Western scientific thought in twentieth-century philosophy.

Gilles Deleuze and Felix Guattari, radical precursors in this direction of thought, ponder not the juncture of human bodies with machines but the body itself—its physical and psychic processes—functioning as many machines. Redefining the body physical and psychical in late capitalism, Deleuze and Guattari are not using the machine as a metaphor, describing the historical mechanization of bodies as "cyborgs" laboring both with machines and like machines in industry. Rather they cite machines as producing and structuring systems that aptly describe our bodies' operations, motions as well as emotions. In the opening lines of *Anti-Oedipus*'s critique of what they see as a psychoanalytic simplification of physio-organic systems and psycho-social fabric, Deleuze and Guattari speak of a multiple "ça" or "id" that is manifest in humans as "desiring machine": there is not one "ça" but many, and "It [id] is at work everywhere" ("ça fonctionne partout"); "Everywhere *it* is machines—real ones, not figurative ones; machines driving other machines, machines being driven by other machines, with all the necessary couplings and connections." Body parts are machines, as are the (cathexed) energies they emit or draw out: with the baby's mouth at the mother's breast, "an organ-machine is plugged into an energy-source-machine."[4]

Deleuze and Guattari shatter the distinctions held in place by classic analyses of capitalism—"the distinction of relatively autonomous spheres that are called production, distribution, consumption"—and insist instead that "everything is production," incorporating recording and consumption within production itself. Collapsed as well is the distinction between man and nature:

> We make no distinction between man and nature: the human
> essence of nature and the natural essence of man become one
> within nature in the form of production or industry, just as they
> do within the life of man as a species. Industry is then no longer
> considered from the extrinsic point of view of utility, but rather
> from the point of view of its fundamental identity with nature as
> production of man and by man.[5]

This "machinification" of the psychophysical might be seen as the inverse of the anthropomorphizing of machines; it is explicitly held up against the metaphor of machines and instead connects the machine to the "real" functioning of bodies and psyches in a philosophy of becoming not being. But it also echoes the paradox, studied in this book, of machines creating movement considered more natural, of machines disappearing into a mechanically produced "natural," of art—such as dance—internalizing machines' function rather than simply aestheticizing their form.

As twentieth-century conceptions of nature shifted from the principles of thermodynamics that permitted analogies with the human motor, the rise of the information machine, the descendent of Babbage's calculator, would affect the dancing machine in ways now being explored. A new field is developing that studies dance's interactions with the machines that dominated the second half of the twentieth century, reconceptions of the body based in information technologies as well as new technologies in medicine and physics.[6] It is important to consider these new technologies as not simply rupturing with earlier twentieth-century dancing machines but also continuing long-standing connections between dance and machines of different kinds.

In Isabelle Stengers's formulation, the twentieth century looked to irreversible processes for "a key to what it sought to understand in nature, to those phenomena to which it had to give a physical status."[7] This interest in irreversibility responds to cinematic or thermodynamic reversibility, legacies of the nineteenth century. Dance and cinema, as well as new imaging technologies, continue to experiment with reversals and repetitions, even if physics has gone a different route. The dancing machine stays with us in spite of theories of the erasure of all differences between human and machine, and of the cybernetic fantasy of the end of work.

In what Michèle Pridmore-Brown has summarized as a "cultural displacement from physical to informational systems," the new physics and information technology have emphasized information over energy, relation over event, reception over ontology,[8] and proposed a reconception of the entropy to which the thermodynamic machine was subject. "In the physical system [entropy] implies the running down and refrigeration of the universe . . . while in the informational system it offers the possibility for an increase of complexity leading to a richer order. In the informational system, randomness is not a threat; rather, it encourages the play of the intellect in making meaning."[9] In this understanding, Pridmore-Brown writes, "the entropic chill of the thermodynamic paradigm is offset by what can be thought of as the self-organization of the information paradigm."[10] Yet the modernist mandate for a "dance of the intellect" in meaning-making endures.

From the fascination with automata and their imitation in dance through the history of robotics, artificial intelligence, and artificial life, virtuality, and cybernetics, it remains to chart the intersection of dance and dancers with information machines in a world thought to have ended work and reconceived life in bodies. It remains also to consider how the more omnipresent network of technology, casting a wider net as it becomes ever more invisible, mechanizes bodies, ironically, even as it frees them.

*Reference Matter*

# Notes

INTRODUCTION

1. *New York Times*, October 23, 1972.

2. Mark Franko sees American dance in New York City in the 1930s as continuing to engage with and stage theories and practices of the left-wing labor movement; in particular he argues for its focus on expressivity as a form of resistance to machine culture. See Mark Franko, *The Work of Dance: Labor, Movement, and Identity in the 1930s* (Hanover, N.H.: Wesleyan University Press, 2002). For a more general view of links between dance and labor inspired by the "emotion aroused by prolonged movement in unison," see William H. McNeill, *Keeping Together in Time: Dance and Drill in Human History* (Cambridge: Harvard University Press, 1995); quote at 2.

3. Hillel Schwartz, "Torque: The New Kinaesthetic of the Twentieth Century," in *Incorporations*, ed. Jonathon Crary and Sanford Kwinter (New York: Zone Books, 1992).

4. Amy Koritz, *Gendering Bodies/Performing Art: Dance and Literature in Early Twentieth-Century British Culture* (Ann Arbor: University of Michigan Press, 1995), 2.

5. Walter Benjamin, "The Work of Art in the Age of Mechanical Reproduction," in *Illuminations*, ed. Hannah Arendt and trans. Harry Zohn (New York: Schocken Books, 1969), 223.

CHAPTER 1: ECONOMIES OF GESTURE

1. See Michel Serres, *Hermes IV: La distribution* (Paris: Editions de Minuit, 1977).

2. On the Jesuit ballets, see Rivka Feldhay, *Galileo and the Church* (Cambridge: Cambridge University Press, 1995), 151–57; on *Coppélia*, see Gwen Berger and Nicole Plett, "Uncanny Women and Anxious Masters: Reading *Coppélia* against Freud," in *Moving Words: Re-Writing Dance*, ed. Gay Morris (London and New York: Routledge, 1996), 159–82.

3. Jenny Uglow, introduction to *Cultural Babbage: Technology, Time, and*

*Invention*, ed. Francis Spufford and Jenny Uglow (London: Faber and Faber 1996), 2.

4. Simon Schaffer, "Babbage's Dancer and the Impresarios of Mechanism," in Spufford and Uglow, *Cultural Babbage*, 56.

5. Ibid., 71; text is from the poster for the exhibition, dated 1819.

6. Ibid., 55.            7. Ibid., 58.

8. Ibid., 63.            9. Ibid., 65.

10. Ibid., 76.

11. Ibid., 79–80. Schaffer also cites Brewster's *Natural Magic* (n.d.), which compared stage shows with Babbage's calculating engines: "Those mechanical wonders which in one century enriched only the conjurer who used them, contributed in another to augment the wealth of the nation. Those automatic toys . . . which once amused the vulgar, are now employed in extending the power and promoting the civilization of our species" (76).

12. Ibid., 80.

13. Ibid. Schaffer quotes Harry Collins's *Artificial Experts* (1990) here; we bring our abilities to the calculator, for example, while that work disappears and we see only the "magic" of calculation.

14. "Georges Vigarello, le corps et la danse," interview with Thilda Moubayed, *Dansons*, no. 7, n.d.

15. See Serres, *Hermes IV*, 42–63.

16. René Descartes, *Treatise of Man*, French text with translation and commentary by Thomas Steele Hall (Cambridge: Harvard University Press, 1972; first published in 1662). "The crux of Descartes' endeavor, in his *Man*, was the interpretation of physiological function in terms of matter in motion" (xxxv); Descartes writes: "And truly one can well compare the nerves of the machine that I am describing to the tubes of the mechanisms of these fountains [in the gardens of our kings], its muscles and tendons to divers other engines and springs which serve to move these mechanisms" (22).

17. Anson Rabinbach, *The Human Motor: Energy, Fatigue and the Origins of Modernity* (New York: Basic Books, 1990). In Rabinbach's account, it was the model of thermodynamics that facilitated Marx's formulation of the idea of labor power, which expands on the definition of individuals' labor as "physiological expenditure." In *Capital*, Marx cites Pelligrino Rossi's writings from the 1830s and 1840s on the "puissance du travail" used in hydraulics and mechanics, and borrows the concept of such force to describe first labor and then also labor power. According to Rabinbach, Marx's Helmholtzianism was a crucial component of his understanding of labor as physiological output and then, as labor power, as a universal force equal to that of nature: a "transcendental material-

ism" of the concept of "labor power," and as developed in European work-science, a materialism in the service of industrial modernity (49).

18. Ibid., 61.

19. Ibid., 55, 59, 60.

20. Jules Amar, *Le Moteur humain et les bases scientifiques du travail professionel*, 2d ed., with a preface by Henri Le Chatelier (Paris: H. Dunod and E. Pinat, 1923; first edition published in 1914). All translations are those of the author of this volume, unless stated otherwise.

21. Ibid., vi.

22. Ibid., ix.

23. Ibid., vii. Le Chatelier emphasizes that workers and owners alike must limit the *usure* of the human machine: "on ne peut refuser à cette dernière les soins que l'on accorde depuis longtemps à la machine à vapeur."

24. Ibid., 605. Amar writes:

Tant que l'industrie ne considère pas la durée du travail, l'homme est-il pour elle un outil précieux, utilisable sur place, se procurant partout où il vit le combustible qui l'alimentera, au besoin forçant la terre à le lui donner; nos moteurs thermiques n'ont pas toujours cette possibilité.

Son emploi doit être la préoccupation constante des chefs de l'industrie, des officiers qui commandent les troupes, des colons qui exploitent l'énergie considérable des milliers d'indigènes [fn] de tous ceux qui poursuivent la mise en valeur du travail humain dans les meilleurs conditions possibles. Car l'entretien de la machine vivante n'est pas moins délicat que celui des moteurs usuels.

25. Ibid., vii.

26. Ibid., 608.

27. Ibid. Amar writes: "Bien rares les moteurs qui approchent meme de loin de cette perfection mobile" (605).

28. Rabinbach, *Human Motor*, 2.

29. Ibid., 190. Rabinbach adds that Max Weber criticized Kraepelin's method but borrowed its emphasis on performance measured through productivity; the starting point for any investigation of large-scale industrial work should be physiological and psychological factors influencing "performance-ability" (197).

30. Ibid., 191.

31. Ibid., 191, 192. "The loss of energy is always lessened while the economic performance of work is constantly increasing" (192).

32. Ibid., 16. Rabinbach identifies three phases in European science of work: (1) theoretical study, 1867–1900; (2) growth of a laboratory science of

work and data collection from industry, 1900–1910; and (3) interventions in the workplace and efforts to influence state policy, including the first challenges from Taylor and U.S. industrial management (123). For Rabinbach, this European work-science aimed at "reducing suffering and exploitation" (17) while creating what Munsterberg called a "transformation of the psycho-physical capacity for performance." (192, quoting Munsterberg.)

33. Ibid., 117, quoting Marey.

34. On the importation of Taylorism into France, see in particular Charles S. Maier, "Entre le taylorisme et la technocratie: Idéologies et conceptions de la productivité industrielle dans l'Europe des annés 1920," 95–136; and Aimée Moutet, "Patrons de progrès ou patrons de combat? La politique de rationalisation de l'industrie française au lendemain de la Première Guerre mondiale," 449–92; in *Le Soldat du travail: Guerre, fascisme et taylorisme*, ed. Lion Murard and Patrick Zylberman, *Recherches*, nos. 32/33 (Paris: Recherches, 1978).

Rabinbach situates Taylor in a different trajectory from the physiologists concerned with fatigue: "As an engineer he considered the body as a 'machine,' which either operated efficiently or it did not. He did not consider, as did the physiologists concerned with the 'human motor' how energy and fatigue might be optimally calculated for long-term use, rather than productivity per se" (117).

35. Isabelle Stengers, *Power and Invention: Situating Science*, trans. Paul Bains (Minneapolis: University of Minnesota Press, 1997), 37.

36. Ibid.

37. Ibid., 38.

38. Rabinbach, *Human Motor*, 183.

39. In a footnote to the passage cited in n. 24, Amar briefly remarks: "A la suite d'une mission au nord de l'Afrique nous avons pu montrer que les indigènes du Maroc sont plus robustes que ceux d'autres regions" (*Moteur humain*, 605). Le Chatelier's preface shows less restraint. He writes that Amar, "voulant étudier d'une façon précise la fatigue produite chez l'homme par le transfert des fardeaux," set up an experiment requiring the same work every day and feeding the worker according to the work performed, to trace the daily changes in weight and fatigue, given that "la fatigue causée par un excès de travail étant accusée par une diminution de poids. N'ayant pu trouver en France des sujets d'experience qui consentissent à s'astreindre à la monotonie d'existence qui leur était imposée, il dut se transporter au nord de l'Afrique pour recruter des portefaix présentant sans doute, comme le dit Taylor, 'le temperament physique et moral du boeuf'" (x).

40. André Levinson, *1929, Danse d'aujourd'hui* (Paris: Actes Sud, 1990). Levinson remarks that Isadora in the 1920s showed the fatigue of the human mo-

tor (60). Her art "n'étant ni fondé en raison, ni basé sur un mécanisme etudié, ne se laissant ni conserver, ni transmettre, il dura ce que put durer la floraison de ce corps et l'épanouissement de cette extraordinaire nature" (73).

41. Martin Jay, *Downcast Eyes: The Denigration of Vision in Twentieth-Century French Thought* (Berkeley: University of California Press, 1993).

42. Jonathon Crary, *Suspensions of Perception: Attention, Spectacle and Modern Culture* (Cambridge and London: MIT Press, 1999), 358.

43. Etienne-Jules Marey, *Animal Mechanism: A Treatise on Terrestrial and Aerial Locomotion* (New York: D. Appleton and Co., 1874), 1; translation slightly modified. Marey goes on to argue that the comparison of animals—including the human animal—with machines is not only legitimate but useful. An understanding of certain mechanical phenomena, such as locomotion in bipeds and quadrupeds, and then, through a human "envy" of nature (for example, insects' and birds' ability to fly), a desire to imitate it lead us to build the machines that make progress possible: "by seeking inspiration from her we have the best chance of solving the problems which she has solved." In this way, Marey writes in his introduction to the book, the "impossibilities of the present . . . become realities" (4). Marey's study is comparative, applying mechanics to nature as well as deriving useful notions from the study of nature that show how the most complicated problems may be solved: "We may hope that a deeper knowledge of the different modes of animal locomotion will be a point of departure for fresh investigations, whence further progress will result" (2). In many studies, such mechanical phenomena are understood "by placing them beside the similar but less generally well known phenomena, which are evident in the action of ordinary machines" (1–2).

44. Etienne-Jules Marey, *Le Mouvement* (Paris, 1894); published in English as *Movement*, trans. Eric Pritchard (New York, 1895).

45. François Dagonet, *Passion for the Trace* (New York: Zone), 153. On the last page of *Mouvement*, Marey wrote of his projector (as translated by Pritchard): "We have therefore constructed a special apparatus, in which an unlimited length of film containing forty or sixty figures, or even more, is allowed to pass without cessation under the field of the objective." But Marey explains that the machine is noisy and that "the projected figures do not appear as absolutely motionless as one could wish." He concludes: "Having arrived at this point in our researches, we learned that our mechanic had discovered an immediate solution of this problem, and by quite a different method; we shall therefore desist from our present account pending further investigations" (*Movement*, 318).

46. Dagonet, *Passion for the Trace*, 157.

47. Ibid., 132.

48. Etienne-Jules Marey, "Fonctions et organes," *Revue Scientifique* 2, no. 1 (1903), as quoted in Virgilio Tosi, "Etienne-Jules Marey and the Origins of Cinema," in *Marey, Pionnier de la synthèse du mouvement* (Paris: Editions de la Réunion des Musées Nationaux, 1995).

49. Marta Braun, *Picturing Time: The Work of Etienne-Jules Marey, 1830–1904* (Chicago: University of Chicago Press, 1992), 174.

50. Dagonet, *Passion for the Trace*, 12.

51. Ibid., 23, 20, 20, 4.

52. Marey, "La Méthode graphique," as quoted in Rabinbach, *Human Motor*, 94.

53. Dagonet, *Passion for the Trace*, 30.

54. François Brunet, *Naissance de l'idée de photographie* (Paris: Presses Universitaires de France, 2000). Brunet considers the history of the conception of photography as an acheiro-poetic work. With its superhuman or theological resonance, this idealized "natural image" found expression in reflections on the photographic process as the development of an image from a negative, traced by light rays, such as Valéry's description of photography as a latent image coming to visibility. Such descriptions, Brunet notes, produced an idea of photography as "the negative of the poetic function, or more generally, the notion of photography as negativity" (335).

55. On the former, see Timothy Lenoir, "Models and Instruments in the Development of Electrophysiology, 1845–1912," *Historical Studies in the Physical Sciences* 17 (1986): 1–54; on the latter, see Brunet, *Naissance de photographie*.

56. Brunet, *Naissance de photographie*. Often applied to cinematography, C. S. Peirce's trio of possibilities for the sign—icon (a sign that bears a resemblance to what it represents); index (a sign with a physical connection to what it represents); and symbol (a sign whose relation to what it represents is a convention)—do not serve to describe photography, which he argues in various texts has partly an iconic (resemblance) and partly an indexical (physical) connection to what it represents. Considering that studies of the nature of the photographic image that apply C. S. Peirce's theory of the sign have, in the past, ignored Peirce's own experience with photography, Brunet notes, "we might well ask whether it isn't first of all as a source of errors that photography was progressively called upon in [Peirce's] semiotic theory" (310). For Brunet, the photograph serves, in Peirce's work, as a special case of icon, an "indexical" icon; more frequently it serves as a metaphor (322), but not simply as the "negative" one (324) more typical of the French history of imagining photography (335).

57. Ibid., 316–17, citing C. S. Peirce, *The Art of Reasoning* (ca. 1895).

58. Ibid., 317.

59. Benjamin, "Work of Art," 236–37.

60. Dagonet, *Passion for the Trace*, 15.

61. On Charles Fremont's studies of work at Marey's laboratory in 1894, as well as Marey and Demeny's work on endurance with soldiers, an early stage of a program for national physical education, see Marta Braun, "Movement and Modernism: The Work of Etienne-Jules Marey," in *Marey: Pionnier de la synthèse du mouvement*, 83–89.

62. Dagonet, *Passion for the Trace*, 59, 185.

63. See Rosalind Krauss, *The Optical Unconscious* (Cambridge: MIT Press, 1993).

64. See *Aura* 4, no. 1 (1998), edited by Cecilia Olssen. I also refer the reader to "Bodies of the Avant-Garde: Modern Dance and the Plastic Arts, 1890–1930," work in progress by Nell Andrew.

65. Martha Graham, quoted in Ramsay Burt, *Alien Bodies: Representations of Modernity, "Race" and Nation in Early Modern Dance* (New York: Routledge, 1998), 132.

66. Ibid. Discussing this passage, Burt writes that for Graham, "an assertion of the validity of modern American experience as a subject for choreography was a necessary counter to the superficially oriental, tribal, folk and other borrowed dance styles that typified the productions of Ted Shawn and Ruth St. Denis" (132–33).

67. See Franko, *Work of Dance*.

68. The Cinémathèque Française lists as the "very first cinematographic images filmed in Africa" *Les Rites des jeunes initiées dans les sociétés secrètes du Liberia* (The rites of young initiates in the secret societies of Liberia) by Hans Schomburgk, 1923. See "Rythmes et continents noirs," program for January 13–15, 1995, Cinémathèque de la Danse, Paris.

69. See William Rubin, *"Primitivism" in 20th-Century Art: Affinity of the Tribal and the Modern* (New York: Museum of Modern Art, 1984).

70. Levinson, *Danse d'aujourd'hui*, 17.

71. Ibid., 62.

72. Ibid., 18, introduced with the idea "Dis-moi comment tu danses, et je te dirai qui tu es!"

73. Ibid., 27. Levinson writes, "Le danseur qui n'est plus que l'esclave et le singe du rythme est réduit au néant" (105).

74. Ibid., 94. Levinson describes the messengers who "mettent en mouve-

ment le mécanisme" of *La Création du monde*; dancers in *Within the Quota* represent the "apotheosis of Americanism." See ibid., 98, 103, 100.

75. Mark Franko, *Dancing Modernism/Performing Politics* (Bloomington: Indiana University Press, 1995), ix.

76. Ibid.

77. Amy Koritz argues, in *Gendering Bodies/Performing Art*, that the aestheticization of dance performance in early-twentieth-century Europe both represented and permitted the separation of works of art from the bodies producing them. Allowing an increased valuation of dancers' work even as dancers themselves were "removed"—in all senses—from their work, modernism reestablished theater and ballet as elite art forms and female dancers as respected performers. In "Re/Moving Boundaries: From Dance History to Cultural Studies," in Morris, *Moving Words*, Koritz addresses the history of concert dance in its broader cultural context and puts forward a multidisciplinary approach to dance history that urges historians to "develop and capitalize on an ability to speak more than one disciplinary language in order to argue for the centrality of dance to any number of cultural formations. . . . Arguing against scholarship that speaks of the body abstractly, while grounding the body in the concrete, that is, in binary opposition to concept, language, abstraction, etc." (91). Koritz insists that cultural studies has to learn from dance scholarship just as dance historians have to learn to speak other disciplinary languages and proposes dancing as a ground for the study of the overlap of theory and practice, mind and body:

> The obvious distance codified dance interposes between the dancing body and the ordinary body-in-pain or body-in-pleasure makes it less useful to those who want to find in bodily life either those material conditions that, according to Marx, give rise to ideology, or, in a more utopian vein, a place free from the abstractions of ideology altogether. On the other hand, surely twenty years of poststructuralism ought to have taught us the impossibility of accessing unencoded experience of any sort. The obsession with the body to the exclusion of dance is perhaps symptomatic of a failure to think beyond the binary opposition between body and mind that seems to hold out the body as the realm where the problems of the mind take on a concrete form that removes from them the stigma of scholarly abstraction. (91)

78. Carol Martin, "High Critics/Low Art," in Morris, *Moving Words*, 325.

79. Ibid., 320.

80. Ibid., 325.

81. Andreas Huyssen, *After the Great Divide: Modernism, Mass Culture, Postmodernism* (Bloomington: Indiana University Press, 1986). For example, Huyssen writes that in Russia, a constructivist embrace of American technology and Taylorism was a rejection of conservative agrarian traditions in favor of a highly industrialized West (12). The historical avant-garde's attack on high culture, Huyssen believes, grew out of revolutionary politics (for example, in Russia and Germany after World War I) and in response to the modernization of big cities (for example, in Expressionism, Berlin Dada, Russian constructivism, Futurism, and proletcult, and in the earlier moments of French surrealism).

82. Ibid., viii–ix.               83. Ibid., viii.

84. Ibid., x.                    85. Ibid., 11.

86. Heidegger, "The Question concerning Technology," in *Basic Writings*, ed. David Farell Krell (San Francisco: Harper, 1993), 320.

87. Ibid., 328–29.              88. Ibid., 339.

89. Ibid., 318.                 90. Ibid., 324.

91. Ibid., 327.                 92. Ibid., 340–41.

93. Benjamin, "Work of Art," 236.

94. See, for example, Philippe Lacoue-Labarthe, *La Fiction du politique: Heidegger, l'art et la politique* (Paris: C. Bourgois, 1987).

95. Bruno Latour, *We Have Never Been Modern* (Cambridge: Harvard University Press), 66.

96. Latour, introduction to Stengers, *Power and Invention*, xiv and xx n. 14. Latour argues elsewhere that *things* resist science (his example is the irreversibility of time) but that humans are complacent. Against those tenants of hermeneutics versus science, who defend the subject versus the tyranny of the object, Latour argues on the side of Serres, Deleuze, and Stengers: "It is the object of science who does the job in the hermeneutic circle, not the human subject always ready to imitate a machine, or what he or she imagines the machine to be."

In a recent critique of Latour by Mary Louise Pratt, "On Tour with Latour: The Third World in *We Have Never Been Modern*" (a paper given at the MLA Conference, December 2001), Pratt suggests that Latour's hybrid might be given human shape as stereotyped "third world" peoples, which she suggests are invoked but not named in his text. Pratt qualifies Latour's discourse on the hybrid as alternately employing "innocent" and "paranoid" vocabulary, but by her own admission she does not take into account work in science studies—for example, Serres's and Stengers's, in addition to Latour's—that acknowledges the human element in the making of science and scientific objects, nor the merging of human subject and scientific object in the "quasi-objet" derived from Serres.

97. Serres, *Hermes IV*, 44–46.
98. Ibid., 46.
99. Maier, "Taylorisme et technocratie," 97.

CHAPTER 2: CHOREOCINEMA

1. Jean Cocteau, *Souvenir Portraits: Paris in the Belle Epoque*, trans. Jesse Browner (New York: Paragon House, 1990), 8.

2. Lynn Kirby, *Parallel Tracks: The Railroad and Silent Cinema* (Durham, N.C.: Duke University Press, 1997), 45–47. In one example, Kirby cites an anecdote of a cinema technician solving the problem of "flicker" with insight gained by observing fences from a moving train, creating the movie shutter inspired by the Pennsylvania Railroad's picket fence.

3. Cited ibid., 45–46. Kirby also quotes Anne Friedberg's description of the panorama and diorama as early foundations for a "mobilized virtual gaze" "designed to *transport*—rather than *confine*—the spectator-subject" (46).

4. Another pre-cinematic moment found in Auguste de Villiers de l'Isle-Adam's novel *L'Eve future* (Paris: Flammarion, 1992) is the train crash, anticipating a film by Edison, *Railroad Smashup* (Edison/Porter, 1904), as discussed in Kirby, *Parallel Tracks*, 60.

5. Villiers, *L'Eve future*, 193–95.
6. Ibid., 196–97.      7. Ibid., 269.
8. Ibid., 185.      9. Ibid., 251, 273.

10. Ibid., 240: "Vous avez un genre de positivisme à faire pâlir l'imaginaire des *Mille et Une Nuits!* s'écria Lord Ewald."

11. Ibid., 360. Electricity's seductive power is based on its "pas imperceptibles et tout-puissants qu'elle fait chaque jour." Electricity is the invisible, powerful barrier, the best guard, because it cannot be bribed: "Quels gardiens, quels suisses, quels veilleurs valent, en effet, l'électricité? Qu'on essaie de la corrompre!—alors surtout que l'on ignore même où elle est!"

12. Ibid., 325. When Edison asks Hadaly what she would think of a god who could neutralize the law of attraction and make the entire solar system fall into the abyss, she responds that it would register only as a small event in the "inevitable Infinite."

13. Although, in one tradition, cinema preserves or extends life by recording movement, Lisa Cartwright has also detailed another tradition beginning with Lumière's experiments in physiology that use film to document death. See Lisa Cartwright, *Screening the Body: Tracing Medicine's Visual Culture* (Minneapolis: University of Minnesota Press, 1995).

14. Among others, Vanessa Schwartz has argued, in *Spectacular Realities: Early Mass Culture in Fin-de-Siècle Paris* (Berkeley: University of California Press, 1998), that cinema capitalized on these earlier forms, including the public entertainments of panoramas and dioramas, museum exhibitions, and the popular press: "Cinema's success resided neither in its originality nor in its innovative technology, but rather in the way it materialized the inherently cinematic culture of the Parisian fin de siècle" (176).

15. Stéphane Mallarmé, *Oeuvres complètes* (1945; Paris: Pleiade, 1984), 878. "Je suis pour—aucune illustration, tout ce qu'évoque un livre devant se passer dans l'esprit du lecteur: mais, si vous remplacez la photographie, que n'allez-vous droit au cinématographe, dont le déroulement remplacera, images et texte, maint volume, avantageusement."

16. Jacqueline Rose, "The Cinematic Apparatus—Problems in Current Theory," in *Sexuality in the Field of Vision* (London: Verso, 1986), 212.

17. Emanuelle Toulet, *Cinématographe, invention du siècle* (Paris: Gallimard, Réunion des Musées Nationaux, 1993).

18. Stephen Kern, *The Culture of Time and Space, 1880–1918* (Cambridge: Harvard University Press, 1983), 117.

19. Tom Gunning, "An Aesthetic of Astonishment: Early Film and the (In)Credulous Spectator," in *Film Theory and Criticism*, ed. Leo Braudy and Marshall Cohen (Oxford: Oxford University Press, 1999), 819.

20. Ibid., 821. "The audience this theatre addressed was . . . sophisticated urban pleasure seekers, well aware that they were seeing the most modern techniques in stage craft. Méliès' theatre is inconceivable without a widespread decline in belief in the marvellous, providing a fundamental rationalist context."

21. Ibid., 825, 823.

22. Ibid., 822.

23. Ibid., 829. Following Kracauer and Benjamin, Gunning links the form of entertainment to the enterprise—industrialized labor—through their common mise-en-scène of lack: "The peculiar pleasure of screaming before the suddenly animated image of a locomotive indicates less an audience willing to take the image for reality than a spectator whose daily experience has lost the coherence and immediacy traditionally attributed to reality. This loss of experience creates a consumer hungry for thrills." According to Kracauer in "The Cult of Distraction," the masses experience "an essentially formal tension which fills their day without making it fulfilling. Such a lack demands to be compensated, but this need can only be articulated in terms of the same surface that imposed the lack in the first place. The form of entertainment necessarily corresponds to that of enterprise" (as quoted in Gunning, "Aesthetic of Astonishment," 831).

24. Gunning, "Aesthetic of Astonishment," 832.

25. Gilles Deleuze, *Cinema I: The Movement-Image*, trans. Hugh Tomlinson and Barbara Habberjam (Minneapolis: University of Minnesota Press, 1986), 4.

26. Ibid., 6–7.

27. Ibid., 6.

28. In this hesitation over the cinematograph, developed from his own camera, Marey was temporarily joined by Albert Londe, a photographer working at the Salpetrière clinic on the physiology and pathology of movement. See Denis Bernard and André Gunthert, *L'Instant rêvé: Albert Londe* (Nîmes: Jacqueline Chambon, 1993).

29. Dagonet sees the relationship between Marey and Bergson not as one of influence but of disagreement: "We may have had the idea that 'motion' was continuous and gradual, but our retinal apparatus was deceiving us. It is the latter that blends together or dissolves. The universe is made up in reality of surges and drops, ruptures that we synthesize and so diminish. It is we who construct a continuous, rounded scene. Mareyism would shatter an illusion that was being strengthened by the philosophy of Bergson" (*Passion for the Trace*, 11–12).

30. Braun, *Picturing Time*, 281. Braun points out that Bergson's first four years at the Collège de France overlapped with Marey's last (1900 until his death in 1904), and that the two knew each other and attended meetings of a scientific study-group on psychic phenomena (279–80).

31. Ibid., 279, 280.

32. Ibid., 280.

33. Henri Bergson, *Creative Evolution*, trans. Arthur Mitchell (New York: Modern Library, 1944), 328.

34. Ibid., 329.

35. Ibid., 331–32.

36. Ibid., 334, 335.

37. Henri Bergson, *Matière et mémoire: Essai sur la relation du corps a l'esprit* (Paris: Quadrige PUF, 1999), 139: "Les images ne seront jamais en effet que des choses, et la pensée est un mouvement."

38. Bergson, *Creative Evolution*, 332.

39. Ibid., 332.

40. Linda Williams, *Figures of Desire: A Theory and Analysis of Surrealist Film* (Urbana: University of Illinois Press, 1981), 18, citing Goudal.

41. Crary, *Suspensions of Perception*, 148.

42. Ibid., 147.          43. Ibid., 319–20.

44. Ibid., 13.           45. Ibid., 12–13.

46. Ibid., 138, 144. Bergson, for example, understood them as "auto-

matic": "*Matter and Memory* coincides historically with the construction of various forms of automatic perception in cinema, recorded sound, and other technological arrangements, in which premade images were consumed passively. Photography (though he does not explicitly mention it in *Matter and Memory*) seems to be his implicit model for the depreciation of experience when individual memory images 'are stiffened into ready-made things' [les choses toutes faites]" (*Suspensions of Perception*, 326).

47. Crary, *Suspensions of Perception*, 282. Crary gives as three examples Emile Javal, William James, and Bergson:

> Emile Javal (translator of Helmholtz' *Optics* into French) studied how vision occurs in short fast jumps, "saccadic" movements. This physiological schema of a disjunct field became part of new psychological models of the human subject. . . .
>
> As William James and others agreed, it was no longer a question of a succession of immobile states or views with a fixed relation between center and periphery, but rather of the primacy of *transitive* states in which the shifting fringes of perception were constitutive features of psychic "reality." . . .
>
> For Bergson, memory and perception interpenetrate each other. The "role of the body was thus to reproduce in action the life of the mind, to emphasize its motor articulations as the orchestra conductor does for a musical score." (Ibid., 291, 295, 317)

Crary notes that Bergson regretted the loss of individual memory; "*Matter and Memory* is one of the great affirmations of the amplitude and complexity of human life over against the intrusion of 'the mechanical' where this term designates not anything conventionally technological . . . but rather, as it did for his schoolmate Durkheim, an absence of complexity" (318).

48. Various performers from the French stage appear in Méliès's films, and modern dancers from Denishawn appear on screen as early as D. W. Griffith's 1917 *Intolerance*.

CHAPTER 3: ABSTRACTION

1. Kern, *Culture of Time and Space*, 130: "Taylorism and Futurism, the new technology, the new music, and the cinema had set the world rushing. But beneath there ran countercurrents. As quickly as people responded to the new technology, the pace of their former lives seemed like slow motion. The tension between a speeding reality and a slower past generated sentimental elegies about

the good old days before the gold rush. It was an age of speed but, like the cinema, not always uniformly accelerated."

2. Personal communication, Madeleine Lytton, Paris, 1986. Madeleine was a pupil of one of Isadora's adopted children, Lisa, in Paris. The source of the remark was her father, Neville Lytton, who saw Isadora perform and later arranged for his daughter to study with Lisa.

3. On this history, see, for example, Elizabeth Kendall, *Where She Danced: The Birth of American Art-Dance* (Berkeley: University of California Press, 1979).

4. Isadora Duncan, *My Life* (New York: Liveright, 1995), 28.

5. Ann Daly gives this date in *Done into Dance: Isadora Duncan in America* (Bloomington: Indiana University Press, 1995); 1878 is the date Isadora gives in her autobiography.

6. Duncan, *My Life*, 18.

7. Ibid., 58.

8. Ibid., 112, 113.

9. "Haeckel," by Georg Uschmann, in *Dictionary of Scientific Biography* (New York: Scribner's, 1970), 10.

10. Duncan, *My Life*, 62.            11. Ibid., 243.

12. Ibid., 243, 20.                   13. Ibid., 243.

14. Ibid.                            15. Ibid., 48.

16. John Dos Passos, *USA: The Big Money* (New York: Random House, 1937), 153–62.

> Isadora was at the height of glory and scandal and power and wealth, her school going, her millionaire was about to build her a theater in Paris, the Duncans were the priests of a cult, (Art was whatever Isadora did), when the car that was bringing her two children home from the other side of Paris stalled on a bridge across the Seine. Forgetting that he'd left the car in gear the chauffeur got out to crank the motor. The car started, knocked down the chauffeur, plunged off the bridge into the Seine. The children and their nurse were drowned.

17. In Dos Passos's version, it was Isadora's love of drink and fun that got her into the car that killed her, and it was her extravagant style, exaggerated by drink, that made her carelessness fatal:

> One day at a little restaurant at Golfe Juan she picked up a goodlooking young wop who kept a garage and drove a little Bugatti racer.
>
>     Saying that she might want to buy the car, she made him go to her studio to take her out for a ride;

her friends didn't want her to go, said he was nothing but a mechanic,
she insisted, she'd had a few drinks (there was nothing left she cared for
in the world but a few drinks and a goodlooking young man);
she got in beside him and
she threw her heavilyfringed scarf round her neck with a big sweep she
had and
turned back and said,
with the strong California accent her French never lost:
Adieu, mes amis, je vais à la gloire.
The mechanic put his car in gear and started.
The heavy trailing scarf caught in a wheel, wound tight. Her head was
wrenched against the side of the car. The car stopped instantly; her neck
was broken, her nose crushed, Isadora was dead. (Ibid., 161–62)

18. Ibid., 159, 156, 155.

19. Nijinsky's 1913 *Sacre du printemps* and Massine's 1914 *Joseph* (from
the *Legend of Joseph*; scenario by Harry Graf Kessler) could also be considered
"sandal" ballets, although *Sacre* stages a Greek- or Russian-inspired primitivism.

20. In *Gendering Bodies/Performing Art*, Amy Koritz reads Wilde's *Salomé*
and Maud Allen's *Salomé* dances within the framework of an opposition between
"elite" moralistic and erotic art held in place—at least publicly—in Victorian
Britain. This opposition, however, was constantly undermined both in France and
in the French-inspired private life of English elite, and its dissolution was of course
Wilde's goal with *Salomé*. Ken Russell rescues Wilde's French ideal of simultaneously elite and erotic upper-class entertainments in *Salome's Last Dance*, his film
version of the play, which represents the play being performed in a luxurious *mai-
son close*, with Wilde himself in attendance.

21. Oscar Wilde, *Letters*, ed. Rupert Hart-Davis (London: Rupert Hart-
Davis, Ltd., 1962), 589. Many attempts to stage the play failed during Wilde's
lifetime. "All the arts are free in England," Wilde wrote with frustration in July
1892, "except the actor's art; It is held by the Censor that the stage degrades and
that actors desecrate fine subjects, so the Censor prohibits not the publication of
*Salomé* but its production" (317). A first production, directed by Lugné-Poe at
the Théâtre de l'Oeuvre in Paris, premiered February 11, 1896. While in prison,
in 1897, Wilde hoped it would be performed by an Italian company, and he imagined that a successful run might affect public opinion and ultimately his imprisonment: "it would help me here greatly to have it done, as the papers have been
rather offensive, and I want to assert myself here as an artist" (656).

22. Ed Cohen, *Talk on the Wilde Side: Toward a Genealogy of a Discourse on Male Sexualities* (New York: Routledge, 1993).

23. Oscar Wilde, "The Harlot's House," in *Complete Poetry*, ed. Isobel Murray (Oxford: Oxford University Press, 1997), 134–35. Illustrations for "The Harlot's House" by Althea Gyles (1904) and Jean de Bosschère (1927) show silhouettes of nude female figures dancing in a burlesque, disorderly fashion with skeletons and puppets, and with a tuxedoed smoker in Gyles's version.

24. Edward Gordon Craig, *On the Art of the Theatre* (New York: Theatre Arts Books, 1956), 62.

25. Ibid., 67, 74.

26. Ezra Pound, "Dance Figure," in *Selected Poems* (London: Faber and Gwyer, 1928), 73.

27. Ezra Pound, "Ione, dead the long year," ibid., 92.

28. Carroll F. Terrell, *A Companion to the Cantos of Ezra Pound* (Berkeley and Los Angeles: University of California Press), 1:31. From the manuscript, Terrell concludes that Pound may also be referring to Landor's and Bulwer-Lytton's Iones. Terrell suggests that Ione is also the dancing woman of Canto VII, a society woman whose "gone cheeks" reveal her dissipation. The two figures are quite different, however, and Pound has noted the seven years that separate him from "Ione, dead the long year"; she is seven, not "ten years gone."

29. Ezra Pound, *Cantos* (New York: New Directions, 1970).

30. Ezra Pound, "In a Station of the Metro," in *Selected Poems*, 89.

31. Ezra Pound, *Gaudier-Brzeska* (New York: New Directions, 1970), 86–89.

32. Ibid., 83.

33. Terrell, *Companion to the Cantos*, 31.

34. Ezra Pound, *Antheil and the Treatise on Harmony* (New York: Da Capo Press, 1968), 37.

35. Ibid., 3.

36. R. Murray Schafer, ed., *Ezra Pound and Music: The Complete Criticism* (New York: New Directions, 1977), 255.

37. Ibid.

38. Ezra Pound, *ABC of Reading* (New York: New Directions, 1934), 63.

39. Ibid., 61.

40. Pound, *Antheil*, 37. "The Vorticist Manifestos of 1913–14 left a blank space for music" (37). The dance, except for Ito, does not even earn this comment; it was, for Pound, apparently still at the stage of "the usual, dull, theatrical"; "Effects of Music upon a Company of People," "Ripostes," in *Collected Early Poems of Ezra Pound* (New York: New Directions, 1965), 199–200.

41. Pound, *Gaudier-Brzeska*, 83.

42. David Antin, "Some Questions about Modernism," *Occident* 8 (spring 1974): 11.

43. Pound composed music himself, notably an opera, *Le Testament*, performed in 1926, which he admitted was an amateur work, and his *Treatise on Harmony* is typically bombastic; but all this, in addition to the music criticism he wrote under the pseudonym William Atheling, suggests that Pound's understanding of music was not simply impressionistic.

44. R. Murray Schafer, "Ezra Pound and Music," *Canadian Music Journal* 5, no. 4 (summer 1961): 28: "The *Cantos* though numerically incomplete have nevertheless always been structurally complete. Ideally a fugue has no point of termination. It could continue its contrapuntal involutions without ever coming to a logical point of rest." Pound wrote in 1928 that the *Cantos* would display a structure like that of a Bach fugue. See Ronald Bush, *The Genesis of Ezra Pound's Cantos* (Princeton: Princeton University Press, 1976), 3.

45. Antin, "Some Questions about Modernism," 11.

46. Ibid., 8.

47. In *The Notebooks of Martha Graham* (New York: Harcourt, Brace, Jovanovich, 1973), Graham carefully reconstructs the motivations and meanings of dances in a history that is clearly colored by time and concern for the reading public. Although Graham's rhetoric is powerful, statements such as the famous and frequently cited "the body cannot lie"—coined to explain her dance technique—should be read as neither broadly applicable to modern dance nor even indicative of the way the body signifies in her dances. As with Isadora Duncan's autobiography, Graham's explanation of her work needs to be read in conjunction with her choreography but not as *interchangeable with* or directly *explanatory of* that choreography. At times the rhetoric seems to stand in inverse relation to the dances. Her denial of bodies' figural or metaphoric potential in movement serves rather as a reminder—almost a warning—against misinterpreting her dance as anything other than pure movement, even though the dances are loaded with allegorical, symbolic, iconic, mythological, or historical meanings. In a dance such as the 1929 *Heretic*, it is difficult not to read Graham's role, the solitary figure in white destroyed by the judgment-bearing group, as an allegory she staged about her dancing—the dancing she says in her autobiography was so different that it put her outside the realm of women and dancers, with its flexed foot, use of the floor, and contractions. The soloist's choreography seems to say to the authorities onstage, "please don't interpret my dancing as heresy," even as it suggests to the audience, "please do see me as a visionary victim attempting to express myself against social constraints and religious injunctions."

48. Carl Van Vechten, introduction to "Susie Asado," in *Selected Writings of Gertrude Stein*, ed. Carl Van Vechten (New York: Vintage, 1972).

49. Robert Bartlett Haas, preface to Gertrude Stein, *How Writing Is Written: Volume II of the Previously Uncollected Writings of Gertrude Stein*, ed. Robert Bartlett Haas (Los Angeles: Black Sparrow Press, 1974), n.p.

50. Gertrude Stein, *Lectures in America*, cited in Van Vechten, ed., *Selected Writings*, 548.

51. Gertrude Stein, *The Autobiography of Alice B. Toklas*, ibid., 111–12. Toklas and Stein were part of a large following; La Argentina performed later in Paris to wide acclaim. For a study of Argentina's work and reception, see Ninotchka Bennahum, *Antonia Mercé, "La Argentina": Flamenco and the Spanish Avant-Garde* (Hanover, N.H.: Wesleyan University Press, 2000). Rebecca Mark has suggested that "Susie Asado" can be read as an erotic poem in which Stein's attraction to Argentina is coded in terms similar to those Stein used to refer to lesbian sexuality in her other works from the period, including her 1913 play *IIIIIIIII*. Mark, "Gertrude Stein's Portraits and Prayers," paper given at the conference "Hartley and the Cultural Force of Modernism," Tulane University, November 14, 1998.

52. *Transition* 14 (1923), quoted in *A Primer for the Gradual Understanding of Gertrude Stein*, ed. Robert Bartlett Haas (Los Angeles: Black Sparrow Press 1971), 63.

53. Gertrude Stein, "Susie Asado," in Van Vechten, ed., *Selected Writings*, 549.

54. Haas, preface to *How Writing Is Written*, n.p. (citing Hal Levy's notes from Stein's 1935 lecture).

55. The recording is Odeon disk no. 1935. Bennahum, *La Argentina*, 170. Bennahum adds: "The shattering power of those shoes and that footwork gave Argentina a momentum, a velocity, and a spirit altogether different from that of Duncan." In particular, she identifies a twist in the arched back between upper body (lifting) and lower body (driving down) (171).

56. Ulla Dydo, introduction to "Orta or One Dancing," in Gertrude Stein, *A Stein Reader*, ed. and with an introduction by Ulla Dydo (Evanston, Ill.: Northwestern University Press, 1993), 120.

57. Ibid., 121.

58. Ibid., 123, 128.

59. Ibid., 126.

60. Ibid., 127, 128, 129.

61. Ibid., 136.

62. See Stein, *How Writing Is Written*.

63. Ibid., 153.

64. Ibid.

65. Ibid., 152–53.

66. Ibid., 156, 157.

67. Ibid., 157.      68. Ibid., 160, 159.

69. Ibid., 159.

70. Ezra Pound, *Machine Art and Other Writings: The Lost Thought of the Italian Years*, ed. Maria Luisa Ardizzone (Durham, N.C.: Duke University Press, 1996), 103.

71. Ibid., 9–10.      72. Ibid., 88.

73. Ibid., 105.      74. Ibid., 89.

75. Ibid., 89–90.

76. Pound was influenced by the writing of Leo Frobenius.

77. Pound, *Machine Art*, 31, 108.

78. Ibid., 28, 28, 29 n. 34.

79. Ibid., 33.

80. My conclusion here offers an alternate view to the thesis of Amy Koritz in *Gendering Bodies/Performing Art*, which explores how a general acceptance of female dancers onstage coincided with a general devaluation of performers in terms of class. Here I am suggesting that an (idealizing) valuation of dance continues in Pound's high modernism because of dance's usefulness as a concept, despite a disregard for its (female) performers. Pound's interest in Michio Ito might be a counterexample. This question is taken up in chapter 5.

81. See Wendy Steiner, *Exact Resemblance to Exact Resemblance: The Literary Portraiture of Gertrude Stein* (New Haven: Yale University Press, 1978).

82. Daly, *Done into Dance*, 136.      83. Ibid., 137.

84. Duncan, *My Life*, 30.      85. Ibid., 51.

86. Daly, *Done into Dance*, 137.      87. Ibid., 137–38.

88. Koritz, *Gendering Bodies/Performing Art*, 70.

CHAPTER 4: BALLETS WITHOUT BODIES

1. F. T. E. Marinetti, "Manifesto of the Futurist Dance," in *Selected Writings*, ed. R. W. Flint and trans. R. W. Flint and Arthur A. Coppotelli (New York: Farrar, Strauss, and Giroux, 1972), 137. Jeffrey Schnapp, in *Staging Fascism: 18BL and the Theater of Masses for Masses* (Stanford: Stanford University Press, 1996), documents another configuration of theater, politics, and transport in Italian Fascism, the "thespian trucks" that promulgated Mussolini's political program by producing operas and plays locally across Italy in the 1930s.

2. Marinetti, "Manifesto," 138.

3. Ibid., 137. In Nijinsky's choreography, Marinetti fails to see Nijinsky's kinship with Isadora, celebrated by the sculptor Antoine Bourdelle among others.

4. Ibid., 116, 117.      5. Ibid., 116.

6. Ibid., 124.                    7. Ibid., 128.

8. Ibid., 123, 126.

9. These would include theories of acting inspired by William James's theory of emotion, Stanislavsky's method acting, and Meyerhold's biomechanics (sometimes referred to as a "Taylorism of the theater"), Foregger's mechanical dances, and Emile Jacques Dalcroze's eurythmy.

The director of the first production of Jarry's play, Aurélien Lugné-Poe, envisioned Ubu first as a tragic character, to be played as a somnambulist or hypnotized character (with tics); only during early rehearsals did the company of the Théâtre de l'Oeuvre realize that it was producing a farce that needed a comic actor, who took his cue for nasal voice, punctuated staccato delivery, and punchy gesture from Jarry's own personal style.

The conception of the actor as a machine follows in the long tradition of debate first about the fundamental nature of acting and second about the nature of actors. The first debate, organized around the question of the actor's involvement or detachment from his character, raises the question of the mechanism of emotion. The traditional argument counters that acting is a skill and an art, that the actor holds his passion in check even when deploying it in a psychological investment in his character.

The question of the emotions, control, and skill of the actor centers also on the debate, over centuries, about the morality of the actor pretending to be what he is not. This "anti-theatrical prejudice" is at the heart of anti-actor sentiment. See, on these debates about acting from ancient rhetorical strategies through Diderot's paradox of the actor, through classical schools of acting, Jonas Barish, *The Anti-Theatrical Prejudice* (Berkeley: University of California Press, 1981); and Joseph Roach, *The Player's Passion: Studies in the Science of Acting* (Ann Arbor: University of Michigan Press, 1993).

10. Under the charge of a mystical magician, the marionettes perform at the Shrovetide fair; each is a stereotype: Petrouchka, the pantomime Pierrot with a big heart and a tear in his eye, Columbine, and the Moor. When left alone, they come to life and act out a classic story of rivalry and lost love.

In love with Columbine and shunned by her, Petrouchka follows her to the Moor's room, where he finds her on the Moor's lap; fighting ensues, and in the next performance at the fair, the Moor kills Petrouchka before the public. In the crowd's ensuing frenzy, the dancer's body is replaced by a puppet onstage, and the live dancer reappears above the fairground proscenium, now as the soul of the maligned and unloved Petrouchka. The loose and staccato movements of Petrouchka are a tour de force for any dancer; in the fashion of other ballet automata such as Coppélia, Columbine retains a stiff upper body while tottering on her pointes; and the Moor uses a grounded second position with bent knees. But Petrouchka writhes as if at the end of a rope, or on strings that are pulled tight and then left slack, the ultimate puppet of a destiny beyond his control, the slave of his master and victim of jealous love. The gross stereotypes represented by the puppets are themselves telling about the traditional carnival life of Russia before the 1917 revolution. The Moor's room is decorated with the Islamic star, and the character wears modified blackface. The magician moves between the realms of Christian carnival and pagan mysticism, showmanship and black magic. In their pas de deux, the Moor and the ballerina mock ballet conventions, the Moor partnering crudely and belligerently, and the ballerina fully automated and expressionless. After the incomplete, interrupted manic solo of Petrouchka, performed facing his partner, the organized mock pas de deux suggests complicity between the puppets that eclipses Petrouchka's poor gifts. Modern dance, in the person of Petrouchka, fails the mating and partnering rituals upon which classical ballet's stories depend. Like the Faune, danced also by Vaslav Nijinsky, Petrouchka is a dreamer, a loner, an iconoclast, a remnant of "savage" life brought to the stage, but this time as failure, not as pleasurable fulfillment.

11. Marinetti, "Manifesto," 138–39.

12. Benjamin, "Work of Art."

13. Marinetti, "Manifesto," 139.   14. Ibid., 140.

15. Ibid., 140–41.                        16. Ibid., 141.

17. Giovanni Lista, *La Scène futuriste* (Paris: Editions du CNRS, 1989), 380.

18. For descriptions, see Giovanni Lista, *Théâtre futurist italien 2* (Lausanne: L'Age d'Homme, 1976).

19. Lista, *Scène futuriste*, 42.

20. Ibid., 375.

21. Ibid., 10.

22. Giovanni Lista, *Futurism and Photography* (London: Merrell Publishers, 2001), 22, 78.

23. Reprinted in Francis Steegmuller, *Cocteau: A Biography* (New York: Macmillan, 1970), 513–14. See also Carrie Noland, *Poetry at Stake* (Princeton: Princeton University Press, 1999).

24. *1909–1929: Les Ballets Russes à l'Opéra* (Paris: Bibliothèque-Musée de l'Opéra, n.d.), 38, 40.

25. Levinson, *Danse d'aujourd'hui*, 103.

26. Deborah Rothschild, *Picasso's Parade: From Street to Stage* (New York: Sotheby's Publications, 1991), 227.

27. RoseLee Goldberg, *Performance Art: From Futurism to the Present* (New York: Harry N. Abrams, 1988), 77.

28. Rothschild, *Picasso's Parade*, 171, 186.

29. Frank W. D. Ries, *The Dance Theatre of Jean Cocteau* (Ann Arbor: UMI Research Press, 1986), 187, quoting Cocteau in *Vanity Fair*, September 1917.

30. Ibid., 188, quoting Cocteau.

31. Ibid., quoting Apollinaire.

32. Rothschild, *Picasso's Parade*, has explored the elaboration of this character from Mary Pickford roles.

33. Cocteau, *Souvenir Portraits*, 45.

34. Ibid., 46.

35. Dated pre-1914, this image is reproduced in Rothschild, *Picasso's Parade*, 36.

36. Cocteau, *Souvenir Portraits*, 46–47.

37. Ibid., 47.

38. Ibid., 47–48.

39. In the collection of the Cinémathèque de la Danse, January 2001. I thank Nicolas Villodre for access to these films on video.

40. Nancy Van Norman Baer, "The Ballets Suédois: A Synthesis of Modernist Trends in Art," in *Paris Modern: The Swedish Ballet, 1920–25*, ed. Nancy Van Norman Baer (San Francisco: Fine Arts Museums of San Francisco, 1995), 31.

41. Erik Näslund, "Animating a Vision: Rolf de Maré, Jean Börlin, and the Founding of the Ballets Suédois," in Baer, *Paris Modern*, 45.

42. Lynn Garafola, "Rivals for the New: The Ballets Suédois and the Ballets Russes," in Baer, *Paris Modern*, 72. Garafola quotes Maurice Raynal: "Léger does away with the dancer as a representation of human elements. . . . The dancer, in his view, should become an integral part of the décor, a plastic element that will be a moving part of the décor's plastic element" (72).

43. Näslund, "Animating a Vision," 51, and Garafola, "Rivals for the New," 75, point out that de Maré never attended company class and never hired a ballet master for company class, which was taught by Börlin.

44. Quoted in Garafola, "Rivals for the New," 75.

45. Baer, "Ballets Suédois," 24, quoting Fernand Léger, "The Spectacle: Light, Color, Moving Image, Object-Spectacle"; see also Léger, "A Critical Essay on the Plastic Quality of Abel Gance's Film *The Wheel*," in *Functions of Painting*, ed. Edward F. Fry and trans. Alexandra Anderson (New York: Viking Press, 1965).

46. Interview published in *Scenario*, Mar. 1, 1921, quoted in Baer, "Ballets Suédois," 37.

47. Levinson, *Danse d'aujourd'hui*, 100, 94.

48. Ries, *Dance Theatre of Cocteau*, 191, quoting Cocteau's letter to Börlin.

49. Ibid., 190, quoting Cocteau's letter to Börlin.

50. Ibid., 191, quoting Cocteau's letter to Börlin.

51. Walter Benjamin, "Y (Photography)," in *The Arcades Project*, trans. Howard Eiland and Kevin McLaughlin (Cambridge: Harvard University Press, 1999), 692.

52. Jean Cocteau, "Les Mariés de la Tour Eiffel," in *Théâtre*, vol. 1 (Paris: Gallimard, 1948). See also Tirza True Latimer, "Ballets Suédois: Plot Summaries," in Baer, *Paris Modern*, 156.

53. Reis, *Dance Theatre of Cocteau*, 190; original text of "A Vol d'oiseau sur *Les Mariés de la Tour Eiffel*," published in *La Danse*, June 1921.

54. Reis, *Dance Theatre of Cocteau*, 190.

55. Judi Freeman, "Fernand Léger and the Ballets Suédois: The Convergence of Avant-Garde Ambitions and Collaborative Ideals," in Baer, *Paris Modern*, 88.

56. For a resumé of these arguments, see Burt, *Alien Bodies*, 35, 30.

57. Quoted in Garafola, "Rivals for the New," 80.

58. Ibid., 81.

59. Ibid.

60. Murphy, quoted by Gail Levin, "The Ballets Suédois and American Culture," in Baer, *Paris Modern*, 120–21.

61. Ibid., 121.

62. De Maré cited in Freeman, "Léger and the Ballets Suédois," 90.

63. Ibid., 95.

64. The first version is given in Baer, *Paris Modern*; the second in Burt, *Alien Bodies*.

65. Burt, *Alien Bodies*, 38.

66. Ibid., 37–38.

67. Ibid., 39.

68. Burt suggests the possibility that Börlin worked with Dalcroze in 1912 and in Geneva in 1919. Here he cites Bengt Håger, *Ballets Suédois* (New York: Abrams, 1990), as a source.

69. Burt, *Alien Bodies*, 41. *Skating Rink* is a modernist ballet, Burt concludes, because it features "Popular mass culture—skating, the dances of working-class dance halls, the silent cinema," evoking "the anonymous scale and monotony of city life" (38). Burt cites Léger's 1925 article "Popular Music Halls" as a source for choreography and Blaise Cendrars's praise for Börlin's work, like billboards and loudspeakers announcing "the beautiful rhythm of today" (38). But by Burt's own derivation, these spaces and this modernity are inherited from the nineteenth

century and are found in Baudelaire's texts by Benjamin (27–29). Burt names "circus, sport, and jazz" as omnipresent modern themes in 1920s ballets (30), three categories indicating wider interest in American modernity by artists in Europe. He quotes Andreas Huyssen: "In retrospect, it seems quite significant that major artists of the 1920s used precisely the then wide-spread 'Americanism' (associated with jazz, sport, cars, technology, movies, and photography) in order to overcome bourgeois aestheticism and its separateness from life" (*Alien Bodies*, 31–32).

70. Hebertot, to Rolf de Maré, July 13, 1921, quoted in Freeman, "Léger and the Ballets Suédois," 88.

71. Freeman, "Léger and the Ballets Suédois," 88.

72. Ibid., 104.

73. René Clair, *"A nous la liberté" and "Entr'acte": Films by René Clair*, English translation and description of the action by Richard Jacques and Nicola Hayden (New York: Simon and Schuster, 1970), 108–9.

74. Ibid., 109.                    75. Ibid., 110.

76. Ibid., 113.                    77. Ibid., 112.

78. Picabia, quoted in Garafola, "Rivals for the New," 73.

79. Rolf de Maré, "A propos de '*Relâche*,' ballet instantanéiste," *Commoedia*, Nov. 27, 1924, quoting Picabia, as quoted in Baer, "Ballets Suédois," 33.

80. Clair, *Films*, 121, shots 29–39.

81. Ibid., 121.                    82. Ibid.

83. Ibid.                          84. Ibid., 132.

85. Ibid., 133.

86. This is the version in the collection of the Museum of Modern Art, New York.

87. Clair, *Films*, 110.

88. Levinson, *Danse d'aujourd'hui*, 101.

89. Cocteau's cinematic dreamlike, dancelike sequences (such as those in *Sang d'un poète*, 1930) and choreographies such as *Le Jeune Homme et la mort* (a collaboration with Roland Petit, premiered June 25, 1946) would follow.

90. Ibid., 31, quoting Dudley Murphy, "Murphy by Murphy," autobiographical manuscript, January 1966.

91. Ibid., 28.

92. Cited and discussed in Matthew Affron, "Léger's Modernism: Subjects and Objects," in *Fernand Léger*, ed. Carolyn Lanchner (New York: Museum of Modern Art, 1998), 128.

93. Léger, "Critical Essay," 20–21. Cited in Judi Freeman, "Bridging Puritanism and Surrealism: The Origins and Production of Fernand Léger's *Ballet Mé-*

*canique,*" in *Dada and Surrealist Film,* ed. Rudolf E. Kuenzli (Cambridge: MIT Press, 1996), 29.

94. Léger, quoted ibid.

95. Freeman, "Bridging Puritanism," 29, quoting a letter from Léger to Gance, dated Nov. 11, 1922, from the Gance papers, Cinémathèque Française, Paris.

96. Léger, "Notes on the Mechanical Element" (1923), quoted in Affron, "Léger's Modernism," 123.

97. Léger, quoted ibid., 121.

98. Freeman, in "Bridging Puritanism," has carefully documented the contradictory writings, by those involved in the project, about how the project took shape and what the various collaborators contributed to it. Dudley Murphy had begun his film career at MGM in Hollywood but had made several independent poetic films, including one titled *Danse Macabre* to music by Saint-Saëns, in 1922. For other histories of *Ballet mécanique* in the context of avant-garde cinema, see Williams, *Figures of Desire.*

99. Freeman, "Bridging Puritanism," 41.

100. Ibid., 37–38.

101. Fernand Léger, *Ballet mécanique,* in Fry, *Functions of Painting,* 51. This text is cited and discussed in Freeman, "Bridging Puritanism," 45, where she notes that this text is "listed as c. 1924, but most certainly not written before 1926."

102. Freeman, "Bridging Puritanism," 39.

103. Ibid., 38–39, quoting Léger, "Film by Fernand Léger and Dudley Murphy, Musical Synchronism by George Antheil," *Little Review* (autumn–winter 1924–25): 42–44.

104. Jean Renoir, *My Life and My Films* (1974; reprint, New York: Da Capo, 2000), 91–92.

105. Blaise Cendrars, "Jean Börlin," single-page typescript, Dance Museum, Stockholm. On Cendrars see Marjorie Perloff, *The Futurist Moment: Avant-Garde, Avant Guerre, and the Language of Rupture* (Chicago: University of Chicago Press, 1986) and Noland, *Poetry at Stake.*

106. A typescript titled "Spectacles d'equipe," in Rolf de Maré's archive at the Dance Museum in Stockholm, that mentions plural signers but bears only de Maré's name, addresses "these publics, apparently so diverse, that cinema and sport bring together and have accustomed to merging in the brusque community of emotion" (typescript page numbered 3). Identifying, on the one hand, the flourishing theater that reaches a public that is "continually renewed" and, on the

other, the unique sports events that reach masses, the signers propose "to establish together the conditions for an art that would unite the resources of the theater with the resources of the stadium" (typescript page numbered 2). The text is not a manifesto but a program for performances that would combine music, song, speech, dance, and sports ensembles, pushing further than Gemier, Reinhardt, or Morax, and giving hungry stadium crowds more than competitive sports can give them. The collaborative work proposed in these pages is dedicated to bringing together "individual art and collective art" under the banner of the "esprit d'e-quipe," the collaborative spirit representative of "our era" and adopted as the symbol of these efforts (two different pages, each numbered 3, constituting the third and fourth pages of the typescript).

107. See Schnapp, *Staging Fascism*.

108. See, for example, Klaus Theweleit, *Male Fantasies*, trans. Stephen Conway in collaboration with Erica Carter and Chris Turner (Minneapolis: University of Minnesota Press, 1987).

109. Cendrars, "Jean Börlin."

110. Levinson, *Danse d'aujourd'hui*, 91, 105.

111. Ibid., 27: "Le danseur qui n'est plus que l'esclave et le singe du rythme est réduit au néant."

112. Ibid., 17.

113. Cendrars, "Jean Börlin."

CHAPTER 5: LABOR IS DANCING

1. Recounted in Bernard Dorey, *From Taylorism to Fordism: A Rational Madness*, trans. David Macey (London: Free Association Books, 1988), 185.

2. Frederick Winslow Taylor, *Principles of Scientific Management* (New York and London: Harper and Brothers, 1911), 12.

3. Ibid., 14: "each workman will work to his very best advantage and at his best speed."

4. Ibid., 25: "There is always one method and one implement which is quicker and better than any of the rest. And this one best method and best implement can only be discovered or developed through a scientific study and analysis of all of the methods and implements in use together with accurate, minute, motion and time study."

5. Andreas Huyssen, *After the Great Divide: Modernism, Mass Culture, Postmodernism* (Bloomington: Indiana University Press, 1986), 24.

6. Ibid., 183.

7. For a view of these questions read in the context of avant-garde dance in New York in the 1930s, see Franko, *Work of Dance.*

8. The three reasons Taylor gives for sluggish work are (1) the fallacy that an increase in output by man and/or machine would put others out of work; (2) defective management that allows workers to slack off or work slower; and (3) rule-of-thumb inefficiency (*Principles of Scientific Management,* 15–16).

9. Ibid., 26.

10. Ibid., 140.

11. Ibid., 141–42.

12. See Dorey, *Taylorism to Fordism,* 82–84: "Machines rather than human beings; robots rather than thinking beings . . . it is quite true that the Taylorist model of man excludes speech, desire, identity, sexuality and a number of other dimensions of the human personality. . . . In order to address the biological body and to elaborate a behavioural engineering, it is necessary to objectify the human subject, to reduce its complexity and to regard it not as something which speaks to another subjectivity, but as a concrete and desubjectivized manifestation of laws revealed by natural abstractions. . . . the black community was stereotyped in negative terms, as were unskilled labourers in general."

13. Pound, *Machine Art,* 79.      14. Ibid., 81.

15. Ibid., 82, 73.      16. Ibid., 81, 82.

17. Ibid., 89–90.      18. Ibid., 70–71.

19. Ibid., 71.      20. Ibid., 69.

21. See Paul de Man, "Yeats, Mallarmé and the Post-Romantic Predicament," Ph.D. dissertation, Harvard University, 1960, for a discussion of the exchange between Yeats and Symons, and Yeats's influence on Symons's book.

22. W. B. Yeats, *Essays and Introductions* (New York: Macmillan, 1961), 528.

23. Masaru Sekine and Christopher Murray, eds., *Yeats and the Noh: A Comparative Study* (Gerrard's Cross, U.K.: Smythe, 1990), 6.

24. Quoted in James W. Flannery, "W. B. Yeats, Gordon Craig and the Visual Arts of the Theatre," in *Yeats and the Theatre,* ed. Robert O'Driscol and Lorna Reynolds (London and Toronto: Macmillan, 1975), 97.

25. G. M. Pinciss, "A Dancer for Mr. Yeats," *Educational Theater Journal* 21 (1969): 386–91.

26. Yeats "greatly admired what he called Ito's 'genius of movement,' which is more significant than the fact that Ito was not actually a trained Noh performer and, apparently held no very high opinion of the Noh arts" (Sekine and Murray, *Yeats and the Noh,* 86). Sekine and Murray give as references Richard

Taylor, *The Drama of W. B. Yeats: Irish Myth and the Japanese Noh* (New Haven: Yale University Press, 1976), 112; and Helen Caldwell, *Michio Ito: The Dancer and His Dances* (Berkeley: University of California Press, 1977), 38–44.

27. Ito also developed an original set of coded movements, grouped into two ten-movement series—one designated "male" and one "female."

28. Yeats, "Introduction to *Certain Noble Plays of Japan*," in Yeats, *Essays and Introductions*, 224.

29. Ibid., 225.

30. Ibid., 235. Quoted and discussed in Koritz, *Gendering Bodies/Performing Art*, 89.

31. In the United States, Ito's dances have been restaged and performed by Satoru Shimazaki. My reconstruction of *Ladybug* here is based on his coaching for a 1982 performance at Harvard University's Agassiz Theater.

32. William Butler Yeats, "Among School Children," in *The Collected Poems of W. B. Yeats* (New York: Macmillan, 1956), 214.

33. Frank Kermode, *Romantic Image* (New York: Chilmark Press, 1957), 25.

34. Ivor Winters, "The Poetry of W. B. Yeats," in *W. B. Yeats*, ed. William H. Pritchard (Middlesex and Baltimore: Penguin Books, 1972), 273–75.

Paul de Man found in the difference between the grammatical and rhetorical meanings of the line a simultaneity of contradictory meanings that he used to argue for a deconstructive reading of the poem, in which "two entirely coherent but entirely incompatible readings can be made to hinge on one line." The first meaning, the one that criticism has considered almost exclusively, reads the poem as a rhetorical question: How can we separate dancer from dance? The two are inseparable. The second reading is literal: How can we, actually, separate them? And "since the dancer and the dance are not the same, it might be useful, perhaps even desperately necessary—for the question can be given a ring of urgency, 'Please tell me, how can I know the dancer from the dance'—to tell them apart." Paul de Man, *Allegories of Reading* (New Haven: Yale University Press, 1979), 12.

35. Told, in "Michael Robartes and the Dancer," that she is a figure for the embodiment of knowledge and for the "uncomposite blessedness" that beautiful women live in, the dancer sighs: "They say such different things at school" (Yeats, *Collected Poems*, 174).

The poet finds the "impassioned gravity" of the "beating breast" a better model for knowledge than the scholars with their "Bald heads forgetful of their sins." From the poet's point of view, the dancer takes us beyond thinking into the realm of experience; she has, in Yeats's words, "out-danced thought" (Kermode, *Romantic Image*, 59, quoting Yeats).

36. This translation was one of the books Yeats had brought with him to Thor Ballylee, the tower in the west of Ireland where he was living while writing "Among School Children" in spring 1926. I thank Professor James Miller for referring me to this passage.

37. Plotinus, *Ennead*, trans. Stephen MacKenna (1917–30; reprint, London: Faber and Faber, 1969), 294.

38. Ibid., 295, 316, 317.

39. Ibid., 317.

40. Yeats, "Introduction to *Certain Noble Plays*," 231.

41. Siegfried Kracauer, *The Mass Ornament: Weimar Essays*, trans. and ed. and with an introduction by Thomas Y. Levin (Cambridge: Harvard University Press, 1995), 71.

42. Ibid., 73, 70.
43. Ibid., 79.
44. Ibid., 84.
45. Ibid., 83.
46. Ibid., Levin introduction, 18.
47. Ibid., 77, 78.
48. Ibid.
49. Ibid., 69.
50. Burt, *Alien Bodies*, 88.
51. Ibid., 91–92.
52. Ibid., 92.

53. Nicola Savarese, "1931: Antonin Artaud Sees Balinese Theatre at the Paris Colonial Exposition," *TDR* 45, no. 3 (fall 2001), elaborates from a program of the performances the specific kinds of dances Artaud would have seen.

54. Antonin Artaud, "On the Balinese Theater," in *Selected Writings*, ed. Susan Sontag (Berkeley: University of California Press, 1976), 219. Sontag notes that between 1930 and 1935, Artaud on various trips to Germany had seen stagings by Appia, Meyerhold, Reinhardt, and Piscator as well as German Expressionist film. In 1924 he played in Jean Painlevé's filmed section for the Paris production of Yvan Goll's *Mathusalem* (Artaud, "Letters from 1931," in *Writings*, 616). The French text reads: "tout porte, tout rend l'effet maximum" (89).

55. Artaud, "Balinese Theater," 215–16.

56. Ibid., 225.
57. Ibid., 221.
58. Ibid., 222.
59. Ibid., 89.

60. Paul Valéry, *Degas, danse, dessin* (1934; reprint, Paris: Gallimard 1965).

61. Paul Valéry, "Théorie poétique et esthetique," in *Oeuvres* (Paris: Pleiade, 1957), 1:1390–1403.

62. Ibid., 1391: "épuisement total de ses forces, une sorte d'extase d'épuisement pouvait seule interrompre son délire, sa dépense motrice exasperée."

63. Ibid., 1396: "entretenu par la consommation intense d'une energie de qualité superieure."

64. Ibid., 1396, 1398.

65. Ibid., 1399: "procède toujours par la voie la plus économique, sinon toujours la plus courte: il recherche le rendement. La ligne droite, la moindre action, le temps le plus bref, semblent l'inspirer."

66. Ibid., 1402.

67. Ibid., 1394: "L'art comme la science . . . tendent à faire une sorte d'utile avec de l'inutile."

68. Ibid., 1396: "durée toute faite d'énergie actuelle, toute faite de rien qui puisse durer. Elle est l'instable, elle prodigue l'instable, passe par l'impossible, abuse de l'improbable; et, à force de nier par son effort l'etat ordinaire des choses, elle crée aux esprits l'idée d'un autre état, d'un état exceptionnel,—un état qui ne serait que d'action, une permanence qui se ferait et se consoliderait au moyen d'une production incessante de travail, comparable à la vibrante station d'un bourdon ou d'un sphinx devant le calice de fleurs qu'il explore, et qui demeure, chargé de puissance motrice, à peu pres immobile, et soutenu par le battement incroyablement rapide de ses ailes."

69. Valéry, *Degas, danse, dessin*, 27.

70. Ibid., 28.          71. Ibid.

72. Ibid., 31.          73. Ibid.

74. Ibid., 32. Valéry remarks that among the connections between the Universe of Dance and the Universe of Music, which are felt by all but understood by none, nothing is more mysterious than this perception of "the equivalence of duration [*durée*] or intervals of time. How can we judge that sounds succeed one another at equal intervals, hit equidistant beats? And what is the meaning of this *equation* affirmed by our senses?" (31–32).

75. Ibid., 32.

76. Ibid., 33.

77. Paul Valéry, *Cahiers*, in *Oeuvres* (Paris: Pleiade, 1957), 2:1122: "Dire qu'une chose signifie, c'est dire qu'elle conduit à une autre, non à un état où elle est inter[médiare]. Il y a inégalité fonctionelle entre le signe et la chose signifiée. C'est dire qu'en poésie—la distinction du signe et du sens change de nature— Comme dans la danse, les actes des membres ne sont plus définis par des choses extérieures. . . . En poésie, donc, changement de valeurs (du langage)."

78. Valéry, *Théorie poétique*, 1:1400: "Tout action qui ne tend pas à l'utile . . . se rattache à ce type simplifié de la danse."

79. Ibid., 1402: "Considérez un artiste dans son travail, éliminez les intervalles de repos ou d'abandon momentané; voyez-le agir, s'immobiliser, reprendre vivement son exercice . . . avec un rhythme; vous pouvez alors concevoir la réalisa-

tion d'une oeuvre d'art elle-même, dont l'objet matériel qui se façonne sous les doigts de l'artiste n'est plus que le prétexte, l'accessoire de scène, le sujet du ballet."

80. Ibid., 1403: "Qu'est-ce qu'une métaphore, si ce n'est une sorte de pirouette de l'idée dont on rapproche les diverses images ou les divers noms?"

81. Ibid.: "nous détachent du monde pratique pour nous former, nous aussi notre univers particulier, lieu privilegié de la danse spirituelle."

82. Ibid., 1400: "On ne peut le distinguer de sa forme de durée. Commencer de dire des vers, c'est entrer dans une danse verbale."

83. Ibid., 1402: "cet art, loin d'être un futile divertissement, loin d'être une specialité qui se borne à la production de quelques spectacles, à l'amusement des yeux qui se considèrent ou des corps qui s'y livrent, est tout simplement une poésie generale de l'action des êtres vivants."

84. Jenny's tango with Mac in *The Threepenny Opera*, during which she turns him over to the police while continually turning him away from seeing them at the door, and the comic-pathetic skating scene in *Der Hofmeister*, as it was performed by Hans Gaugler, are two examples. For the second, I thank Martin Esslin.

85. The Dance Collection of the New York Public Library has no record of the choreography of *The Seven Deadly Sins*, and Balanchine scholar Tim Scholl is unaware of the existence of any such notation or film record (personal communication, July 1998). In 1959, the New York City Ballet restaged the ballet, with Lotte Lenya as the singing Annie and Allegra Kent as the dancing Annie. Writing in the *New York Times* of Jan. 18, 1959, in "Dance: Those Deadly," John Martin comments: "the present production of the work is a better, a profounder and a generally more important one than the original. Time has passed and perspective grown; and on the evidence of reviews of the 1933 production and of an occasional eye witness with a good memory, it is safe to say that Balanchine has approached the task of revival with a creative comment that has stripped away irrelevancies and given us the essence of the piece straight."

86. Kurt Weill, *The Seven Deadly Sins*, German text by Bertolt Brecht and trans. by W. H. Auden and Chester Kallman (New York: Schott Music Corporation, 1956). Bertolt Brecht, *The Rise and Fall of the City of Mahagonny and the Seven Deadly Sins of the Petty Bourgeoisie*, ed. John Willett and Ralph Manheim and trans. W. H. Auden and Chester Kallman (New York: Arcade, 1996), 69. All quotations are from this volume.

87. Brecht, *Seven Deadly Sins*, 73.

88. Ibid., 75.

89. Ibid.

90. Ibid., 77.

91. Ibid., 78, 79.

92. Ibid., 80.

93. Ibid., 81.

94. Ronald Hayman, *Brecht* (London: Weidenfeld and Nicolson, 1983), 175.

95. Ibid., 175, quoting a letter from Weill to Hans and Rita Weill.

96. Ibid., 186.

97. Nicolas Jacobs and Prudence Ohlsen, eds., *Bertolt Brecht in Britain* (London: TQ Publications, 1977), 29.

98. A command performance at the Theater Royal in Copenhagen in 1936, however, was not a success: the king's response was "No, that is not what the famous Royal Ballet is there for." When the Nazi government asked the Danish ambassador to have the ballet closed after its second performance, the Danish government complied (Hayman, *Brecht*, 197–98).

99. Martin Esslin has noted that Brecht was undoubtedly influenced by new trends in theater: Meyerhold's stage "biomechanics"; Wedekind's view of dance as erotic education for women; Expressionist mime plays; Russian musical theater popular in traveling shows of the period; and staging innovations such as Piscator's 1928 production of *Good Soldier Schweik* on a moving belt (seminar, Stanford University, 1985).

100. Bertolt Brecht, "The Literarization of the Theatre," in *Brecht on Theater*, trans. John Willet (New York: Hill and Wang, 1964), 45; originally published in *Versuche* 3 (1931).

101. John Rouse, "Brecht and the Contradictory Actor," in *Theatre Journal* 36, 1 (March 1984): 32, quoting Brecht.

102. Bertolt Brecht, "Short Description of a New Technique of Acting," in *Brecht on Theater*, 139, 92.

103. Ibid., 92, 94, 95.

CHAPTER 6: SUBMITTING TO THE MACHINE

1. Michel Leiris, *L'Age d'homme*, as cited in James Clifford, "Negrophilia," in *A New History of French Literature*, ed. Denis Hollier (Cambridge: Harvard University Press, 1990), 902.

2. Tyler Stovall, *Paris Noir: African Americans in the City of Light* (New York: Houghton Mifflin, 1996), 70; T. Denean Sharpley-Whiting, *Black Venus: Sexualized Savages, Primal Fears, and Primitive Narratives in French* (Durham, N.C.: Duke University Press, 1999), 108, discusses André Levinson's "The Negro Dance." See Joan Acocella and Lynn Garafola, eds., *André Levinson on Dance: Writings from Paris in the Twenties* (Hanover, N.H.: Wesleyan University Press, 1991), 69–75.

3. Michel Leiris, *Afrique noire: La création plastique* (Paris: Gallimard, 1967), 30. Stovall, *Paris Noir*, 71, cites a short story, "Baton Rouge" from Paul Morand's *Magie noire*, about a dancer-singer named "Congo" who resembles Baker: "under modern names like the fox-trot or the camel walk, she imposed on them the old African totemic dances."

4. Mariana Torgovnick, *Gone Primitive: Savage Intellects, Modern Lives* (Chicago: University of Chicago Press, 1990); Petrine Archer-Straw, *Negrophilia: Avant-Garde Paris and Black Culture in the 1920s* (London: Thames and Hudson, 2000); Karen C. C. Dalton and Henry Louis Gates, Jr., "Josephine Baker and Paul Colin: African-American Dance Seen through Parisian Eyes," *Critical Inquiry* 24, no. 4 (summer 1998): 903–34; reprinted as the introduction to Dalton and Gates, eds., *Josephine Baker and La Revue Nègre: Paul Colin's Lithographs of "Le Tumulte Noir" in Paris, 1927* (New York: Harry N. Abrams, 1998), 4–12; Burt, *Alien Bodies*.

5. Burt, *Alien Bodies*, 63.

6. The scholarship on Baker has multiplied in the last decade. In addition to the biographies and autobiography, I have referred to different sources for the different aspects of Baker's career: on her dancing in the context of contemporary European modern dance, Burt, *Alien Bodies*; on her cinema, Sharpley-Whiting, *Black Venus*; and on her African American background and context in Paris, Stovall, *Paris Noir*. Here I am reading her stage and screen career in France along with French modernist texts on her reception and the reception of both African and African American art. See also Abdelkader Benali, *Le Cinéma colonial au maghreb: L'imaginaire en trompe-l'oeil* (Paris: Editions du Cerf, 1998), 109–13. Benali focuses on the construction of Baker's character in *Princesse Tam-Tam* as the Arabic counterpoint to "civilization" by considering the film's erasure of Tunisian history in its treatment of the footage of Roman ruins at Dougga.

7. Frantz Fanon, *Black Skin, White Masks*, is discussed and cited in Sharpley-Whiting, *Black Venus*, 118. See also Leiris, *Age d'homme*.

8. Paul Guillaume, *La Sculpture nègre et l'art moderne* (Paris: Toguna, 1999).

9. Ibid., 28: "l'âme nègre en tant que source de vitalité dans une civilisation fatiguée."

10. Ibid.

11. *Cahiers d'Art* (ed. Christian Zervos), nos. 7–8 (1927): 230.

12. Georges Salles, ibid., 247ff. In an article reproducing images from the film *Voyage au congo* made by Marc Allegret and André Gide, Gide speaks of the "beauty" more powerful than the "strangeness" of Massa villages. On the classi-

fication of African art in French museums, see Nélia Dias, *Le Musée d'Ethnographie du Trocadéro (1878–1908): Anthropologie et muséologie en France* (Paris: Editions du CNRS, 1991).

13. Archer-Straw, *Negrophilia*, 107.

14. Ibid., 109.

15. Ibid., 107.

16. Goldberg, *Performance Art*, 64, 74.

17. Ibid., 65, 66. No reference is given for the quote.

18. Ibid. A photograph represents the Great Savage as a black, wooden, primitivist or cubist construction, with a banana skirt (22). On the same page, Depero's drawings for costumes for *Macchina del 3000*, a mechanical ballet with music by Casavola (1924), include "I Costumi Delle Locomotive" (locomotive costumes). No credits are given for the photos.

19. Stovall, *Paris Noir*, 69.

20. Quoted in Garafola, "Rivals for the New," 73; translation modified.

21. Léger quoted in Baer, "Ballets Suédois," 27.

22. Garafola, "Rivals for the New," 72. The first exhibitions of African art in the United States are dated 1923 (Brooklyn) and 1935 (Metropolitan Museum). Walker Evans photographs of some of the artifacts from this 1935 exhibition were widely circulated.

23. See Dias, *Musée d'Ethnographie*.

24. A montage of films of dance credited to Louis Lumière, and dated 1895–1903, compiled by the Cinémathèque de la Danse, Paris, was accompanied with the following list: "Acteur Japonais (danse d'homme, 1897); Une scène au théâtre japonais (1897); Danseuses japonaises (1897); Les Ainos à Yeso (1897); Cynghalais: danses des couteaux (1896); Danseuses cambodgiennes (1902); Danse égyptienne (1896); Bal espagnol dans la rue (1897), Danse mexicaine (1897); Danse espagnole (1900); Danse du folklore français (1900); Nègres Ashantis: danse de femmes, danse du féticheur, danse du sabre 1 et 2 (1897); Danseuse de ballet (1896); Le Cake-Walk au Nouveau Cirque (1902); Danse Serpentine—Loie Fuller (1896)." I am grateful to Nicolas Villodre for providing this list, which he characterized as based on Henri Langlois's "cartons," elaborated from the Lumière catalogues, exact in the case of some films (those bearing a number) and not in others. Villodre also noted that the dancer filmed in *Danse Serpentine—Loie Fuller* (1896) is not Loie Fuller (conversation, Feb. 7, 2001).

25. Garafola, "Rivals for the New," 73, reports that de Maré himself financed documentary films of African dance, which Börlin used in preparing *La Creation du monde*. I was unable to see these de Maré films; Björn Ranung, senior curator of the African collections at the National Museum of Ethnography,

Stockholm, and archivist Thomas Skalm at the Rolf de Maré Study Center, Dans Museet, Stockholm, informed me that those films made by de Maré in Africa that are in the collection of the Rolf de Maré Study Center were travel films, not dance films, with negligible dance content (conversations, Stockholm, October 2000).

26. Leiris himself would become an ethnographer participating in the Mission Dakar-Djibouti (1931–33), claiming that jazz and spectacles such as Baker's led him to Africa and ethnography. See Leiris, *Age d'homme*, 109.

27. André Schaeffner, review of *Black Birds*, in *Documents* (1929; reprint, Paris: Jean-Michel Place, Collection "Gradhiva," 1992), 1:223.

28. See, for example, Michel Fabre, "New Orleans Creole Expatriates in France: Romance and Reality," in *Creole: The History and Legacy of Louisiana's Free People of Color*, ed. Sybil Kein (Baton Rouge: Louisiana State University Press, 2000), 71–100.

29. J. Baker and J. Bouillon, *Josephine* (London: W. H. Allen, 1978), 51–52, as quoted in Burt, *Alien Bodies*, 65.

30. James Clifford, "On Ethnographic Surrealism," in *The Predicament of Culture: Twentieth-Century Ethnography, Literature, and Art* (Cambridge: Harvard University Press, 1988), 117–51.

31. Ibid., 117.      32. Ibid, 119.

33. Ibid., 120–21.      34. Ibid., 131–33.

35. Ibid., 138–39.      36. Ibid., 147.

37. Denis Hollier, "La Valeur d'usage de l'impossible," introduction, in *Documents* 1:vii–xxiii. Published in English as "The Use Value of the Impossible," in *Absent without Leave: French Literature under the Threat of War*, trans. Catherine Porter (Cambridge: Harvard University Press, 1997), 125–44.

38. Hollier, "Use Value of the Impossible," 125.

39. Ibid., 217–18.

40. Ibid., 133.

41. Ibid., 136, 138.

42. Hollier, "Valeur d'usage," ix.

43. Ibid., xi.      44. Ibid., xiii.

45. Ibid., xxii      46. Ibid., xiii.

47. Jean-Paul Sartre, "Jazz in America," in *Reading Jazz*, ed. Robert Gottleib (New York: Vintage, 1996; first published in *Cahiers America*), 711.

48. Hollier, "Valeur d'usage," xvi: "Rien ne sera exclu, dit Schaeffner. Aucun objet, si informe soit-il."

49. Ibid., xviii.

50. Ibid., xix.

51. Sartre, "Jazz in America," 710, 711, 712.

52. Levinson, as quoted in Acocella and Garafola, *André Levinson on Dance*, 70.

53. Rip, preface to *Le Tumulte noir*, as trans. and cited in Dalton and Gates, "Josephine Baker and Paul Colin," 934.

54. Baker and Bouillon, *Baker*, 53, as quoted in Burt, *Alien Bodies*, 69.

55. Michel Leiris, "L'Oeil de l'ethnographe," in *Documents* 1:405–14.

56. Leiris, as quoted in Hollier, "Valeur d'usage," xvi.

57. Georges Bataille, review of *80 Days around the World*, in *Documents* 1:260.

58. See Leiris, "Oeil de l'ethnographe."

59. Michel Leiris, "Civilisation," in *Documents* 1:222.

60. "Nous sommes las des spectacles trop fades que ne boursoufle aucune insurrection, en puissance ou en act, contre la divine 'politesse' celle des arts qu'on appelle 'goût', celle du cerveau qu'on nomme 'intelligence' celle de la vie qu'on désigne par ce mot à l'odeur poussiéreuse de vieux fond de tiroir: 'moral'" (ibid., 221–22).

61. Ibid.

62. "Non pas que nous dansons ou nous tenons debout sur un volcan, mais que toute notre vie, notre respiration même est en liaison avec les laves, les cratères, les geysers et tout ce qui touche aux volcans" (ibid., 221). But in spite of the nearness of the magic, "quoique vivant en pleine magie, nous ne soyons tout de même plus assez ouvertement mystiques pour que, chaque jour, il nous soit loisible de signer un pacte avec le diable!" (222).

63. Ibid., 221. For an alternate view, see Archer-Straw, *Negrophilia*, 107: "Viewed from the distance of Europe's avant-garde circles, the genuine African artefact and black culture merged; admiration for blacks was bound up with general ignorance about racial distinctions, geography and a common desire for vitality and potency. Increased contact with 'real' African-Americans meant an intrusion on these dreams, as the imagined 'beatings of the jungle tam-tam' were replaced by 'le hot jazz.'" On the juxtaposition of photographs of Africans and African Americans with, for example, surrealist photographic images in the review, see also Archer-Straw, *Negrophilia*, 157: "The photographs' juxtapositions reveal a side to *Documents*' ethnography that focused on the abnormal. The journal used images of blacks, along with Jacques-André Boiffard's erotic and disturbing mouths, anuses and big toes, as part of a pictorial schema to depict altered states and a base low life. To situate blacks within this lower order did little to assist European society's understanding of black culture. *Documents* merely reinforced century-old fears of what blackness signified."

64. Leiris, "Civilisation," 222. Schaeffner describes the power of this re-

view's rhythmic orchestral frenzy of rhythm and orchestra, "sonorous and plastic rhythm"; in a merging of brass, tambourine and crazy movement: "music for the eye. Watercolor [eau-forte] for the ear" (review of *Black Birds*, 223).

65. Georges-Henri Rivière, "Religion et Folies-Bergères," in *Documents* 2:240.

66. Bataille, "La Mutilation sacrificielle et l'oreille coupée de Vincent Van Gogh," in *Documents* 2:455.

67. Ibid., 456.

68. This self-mutilation of the mentally ill is the modern remains of the concept of sacrifice which Bataille regrets has fallen into disuse ("pleine decadence"), although its expression in self-mutilation is "absurd" and "terrible." Self-mutilation is linked to the "spirit of sacrifice." For Bataille, modern madness allows the expression of the elementary drives, such as self-destruction; madness is primitive, it removes obstacles. This relativization of gesture and the suggestion of its different interpretations might also be understood as foundational for ethnopsychiatry.

69. Dalton and Gates ("Josephine Baker and Paul Colin") and Burt (*Alien Bodies*) have discussed this participation of the white audience in Colin's drawings and in a photograph of Chez Joséphine, respectively.

70. See Slavoj Žižek, "How Did Marx Invent the Symptom," in *The Sublime Object of Ideology* (London: Verso, 1989), 11–53.

71. In *Black Venus*, Sharpley-Whiting sketches the presence of a rising colonial cinema and its growing audience as a background to Baker's stardom; for a more complete theorization of this national cinema and its various sectors, see Dudley Andrew, *Mists of Regret: Culture and Sensibility in Classic French Film* (Princeton: Princeton University Press, 1995). For a more specific discussion of Maghrebin cinema, see Benali, *Cinéma colonial au maghreb*.

72. Reported in Jean-Claude Baker and Chris Chase, *Josephine: The Hungry Heart* (New York: Random House, 1993), 184.

73. Ibid., 195–96.

74. For the spelling of names from the film, I have relied on material from the commercially packaged video. Sharply-Whiting, in *Black Venus*, gives "Aouina" (meaning "spring"), and "Tahar" for her partner.

75. Baker and Chase elaborate on the mythology by reporting that Baker's manager "hired a real countess, a down-on-her-luck blueblood, to give Josephine lessons in how to speak, how to behave at table"; also, that the manager's sister said that when her brother took over Josephine's career, "she was a little savage. She did not know how to behave at table, she ate with her hands" (*Josephine*, 242).

In the 1940s, Josephine traveled frequently in Morocco, reportedly carrying messages for the Free French in her underwear. Although Jean-Claude Baker describes her comfortably naked at home, shocking the workers at her estate of Milandes, he explains that she was able to carry messages pinned to her underwear because, as she said, "who would dare search Josephine Baker?" (ibid., 240, 243). Tyler Stovall, however, argues that "a public figure like Josephine Baker could not operate effectively as a spy in wartime France" (*Paris Noir*, 128).

76. Stovall, *Paris Noir*, 72: "these stereotypes were overwhelmingly positive."

77. Archer-Straw, *Negrophilia*, 133.

78. Ibid., 97.

79. Homi K. Bhabha, "The Other Question: The Stereotype and Colonial Discourse," in *Visual Culture: The Reader*, ed. Jessica Evans and Stuart Hall (London: Sage Publications, 1999), 370.

80. Ibid.

81. Laura Mulvey, "Visual Pleasure and Narrative Cinema," in Evans and Hall, *Visual Culture*, 381–89.

82. Carlo Rim, "On the Snapshot," in *Photography in the Modern Era*, ed. Christopher Phillips (New York: Museum of Modern Art/Aperture, 1989), 39.

83. Dalton and Gates, "Josephine Baker and Paul Colin," 929, 928, 930, 931, 932.

84. Ibid., 933.

85. Burt, *Alien Bodies*, 81.

86. Rabinbach, *Human Motor*, 241, quoting French syndicalist Alphonse Merrheim (1913).

CONCLUSION

1. Following in the wake of Alvin Ailey, contemporary choreographers such as Ronald K. Brown have used African American dancers and dance idioms in concert dance. But such forms have also been adopted by "white" companies, including ballet companies such as the Joffrey (in Gerald Arpino's *Trinity*). Although such dancing contradicts much of mainstream modern dance practice and rhetoric (neoclassicism, purity, abstraction), it also benefited from the modern dancers researching popular and indigenous forms.

2. Donna J. Haraway, *Simians, Cyborgs, and Women: The Reinvention of Nature* (New York: Routledge, 1991), 151–53.

3. Ibid., 152.

4. Gilles Deleuze and Félix Guattari, *Anti-Oedipus: Capitalism and Schizophrenia* (Minneapolis, University of Minnesota Press, 1983), 1.

5. Ibid., 4. In Deleuze and Guattari's formulation, "man and nature are not like two opposite terms confronting each other—not even in the sense of bipolar opposites within a relationship of causation, ideation, or expression (cause and effect, subject and object, etc.); rather, they are one and the same essential reality, the producer-product" (4–5).

6. See, for example, *Danse et nouvelles technologies*, an issue of *Nouvelles de danse* 40–41 (fall–winter 1999).

7. Stengers, *Power and Invention*, 37.

8. Michèle Pridmore-Brown, "1939–40: Of Virginia Woolf, Gramophones, and Fascism," *PMLA* 113, no. 3 (May 1998): 408.

9. Ibid., 412.

10. Ibid., 418.

# Bibliography

Acocella, Joan, and Lynn Garafola, eds. *André Levinson on Dance: Writings from Paris in the Twenties*. Hanover, N.H., and London: Wesleyan University Press, 1991.

Amar, Jules. *Le Moteur humain et les bases scientifiques du travail professionel*. 2d ed. With a preface by Henri Le Chatelier. Paris: H. Dunod and E. Pinat, 1923. Originally published in 1914.

Antin, David. "Some Questions about Modernism." *Occident* 8 (spring 1974).

Archer-Straw, Petrine. *Negrophilia: Avant-Garde Paris and Black Culture in the 1920s*. London: Thames and Hudson, 2000.

Artaud, Antonin. "On the Balinese Theater." In *Selected Writings*, ed. Susan Sontag. Berkeley: University of California Press, 1976.

*Aura* 4, no. 1 (1998). Ed. Cecilia Olssen.

Baer, Nancy Van Norman, ed. *Paris Modern: The Swedish Ballet, 1920–25*. San Francisco: Fine Arts Museums of San Francisco, 1995.

Baker, Jean-Claude, and Chris Chase. *Josephine: The Hungry Heart*. New York: Random House, 1993.

Benali, Abdelkader. *Le Cinéma colonial au maghreb: L'Imaginaire en trompe-l'oeil*. Paris: Editions du Cerf, 1998.

Benjamin, Walter. "The Work of Art in the Age of Mechanical Reproduction." In *Illuminations*, ed. Hannah Arendt and trans. Harry Zohn. New York: Schocken Books, 1969.

———. "Y (Photography)." In *The Arcades Project*, trans. Howard Eiland and Kevin McLaughlin. Cambridge: Harvard University Press, 1999.

Bennahum, Ninotchka. *Antonia Mercé, "La Argentina": Flamenco and the Spanish Avant-Garde*. Hanover, N.H.: Wesleyan University Press, 2000.

Berger, Gwen, and Nicole Plett. "Uncanny Women and Anxious Masters: Reading *Coppélia* against Freud." In *Moving Words: Re-Writing Dance*, ed. Gay Morris. London and New York: Routledge, 1996.

Bergson, Henri. *Creative Evolution*. Trans. Arthur Mitchell. New York: Modern Library, 1944.

———. *Matière et mémoire: Essai sur la relation du corps à l'esprit*. Paris: Quadrige PUF, 1999.

Bernard, Denis, and André Gunthert. *L'Instant rêvé: Albert Londe*. Nîmes: Jacqueline Chambon, 1993.

Bhabha, Homi K. "The Other Question: The Stereotype and Colonial Discourse." In *Visual Culture: The Reader*, ed. Jessica Evans and Stuart Hall. London: Sage Publications, 1999.

Braun, Marta. *Picturing Time: The Work of Etienne-Jules Marey, 1830–1904*. Chicago: University of Chicago Press, 1992.

Brecht, Bertolt. *Brecht on Theater*. Trans. John Willet. New York: Hill and Wang, 1964.

———. *The Rise and Fall of the City of Mahagonny and The Seven Deadly Sins of the Petty Bourgeoisie*. Ed. John Willett and Ralph Manheim, and trans. W. H. Auden and Chester Kallman. New York: Arcade Publishing, 1996.

Brunet, François. *La Naissance de l'idée de photographie*. Paris: Presses Universitaires de France, 2000.

Burt, Ramsay. *Alien Bodies: Representations of Modernity, "Race" and Nation in Early Modern Dance*. New York: Routledge, 1998.

Bush, Ronald. *The Genesis of Ezra Pound's "Cantos."* Princeton: Princeton University Press, 1976.

*Cahiers d'Art*, nos. 7–8 (1927). Ed. Christian Zervos.

Caldwell, Helen. *Michio Ito: The Dancer and His Dances*. Berkeley: University of California Press, 1977.

Cartwright, Lisa. *Screening the Body: Tracing Medicine's Visual Culture*. Minneapolis: University of Minnesota Press, 1995.

Cendrars, Blaise. "Jean Börlin." Single-page typescript. Collection of the Rolf de Maré Study Center, Dance Museum, Stockholm.

Clair, René. *"A nous la liberté" and "Entr'acte": Films by René Clair*. English translation and description of the action by Richard Jacques and Nicola Hayden. New York: Simon and Schuster, 1970.

Clifford, James. "Negrophilia." In *A New History of French Literature*, ed. Denis Hollier. Cambridge: Harvard University Press, 1990.

———. "On Ethnographic Surrealism. "In *The Predicament of Culture: Twentieth-Century Ethnography, Literature, and Art*. Cambridge: Harvard University Press, 1988.

Cocteau, Jean. "Les Mariés de la Tour Eiffel." In *Théâtre*, vol. 1. Paris: Gallimard, 1948.

———. *Souvenir Portraits: Paris in the Belle Epoque*. Trans. Jesse Browner. New York: Paragon House, 1990.

Cohen, Ed. *Talk on the Wilde Side: Toward a Genealogy of a Discourse on Male Sexualities*. New York: Routledge, 1993.

Craig, Edward Gordon. *On the Art of the Theatre*. New York: Theatre Arts Books, 1956.

Crary, Jonathon. *Suspensions of Perception: Attention, Spectacle and Modern Culture*. Cambridge and London: MIT Press, 1999.

Dagonet, François. *Passion for the Trace*. New York: Zone, 1992.

Dalton, Karen C. C., and Henry Louis Gates, Jr. "Josephine Baker and Paul Colin: African-American Dance Seen through Parisian Eyes." *Critical Inquiry* 24, 4 (summer 1998).

————, eds. *Josephine Baker and La Revue Nègre: Paul Colin's Lithographs of "Le Tumulte Noir" in Paris, 1927*. New York: Harry N. Abrams, 1998.

Daly, Ann. *Done into Dance: Isadora Duncan in America*. Bloomington: Indiana University Press, 1995.

*Danse et nouvelles technologies: Nouvelles de danse* 40–41 (fall–winter 1999).

Deleuze, Gilles. *Cinema I: The Movement-Image*. Trans. Hugh Tomlinson and Barbara Habberjam. Minneapolis: University of Minnesota Press, 1986.

Deleuze, Gilles, and Félix Guattari. *Anti-Oedipus: Capitalism and Schizophrenia*. Minneapolis: University of Minnesota Press, 1983.

De Man, Paul. *Allegories of Reading*. New Haven: Yale University Press, 1979.

————. "Yeats, Mallarmé and the Post-Romantic Predicament." Ph.D. dissertation, Harvard University, 1960.

Descartes, René. *Treatise of Man*. French text with translation and commentary by Thomas Steele Hall. Cambridge: Harvard University Press, 1972.

Dias, Nélia. *Le Musée d'Ethnographie du Trocadéro (1878–1908): Anthropologie et Muséologie en France*. Paris: Editions du CNRS, 1991.

*Documents*. Vols. 1 and 2. 1929; reprint, Paris: Jean-Michel Place, Collection "Gradhiva," 1992.

Dorey, Bernard. *From Taylorism to Fordism: A Rational Madness*. Trans. David Macey. London: Free Association Books, 1988.

Dos Passos, John. *USA: The Big Money*. New York: Random House, 1937.

Duncan, Isadora. *My Life*. New York: Liveright, 1995.

Feldhay, Rivka. *Galileo and the Church*. Cambridge: Cambridge University Press, 1995.

Franko, Mark. *Dancing Modernism/Performing Politics*. Bloomington: Indiana University Press, 1995.

————. *The Work of Dance: Labor, Movement, and Identity in the 1930s*. Hanover, N.H.: Wesleyan University Press, 2002.

Freeman, Judi. "Bridging Puritanism and Surrealism: The Origins and Production of Fernand Léger's *Ballet Mécanique*." In *Dada and Surrealist Film*, ed. Rudolf E. Kuenzli. Cambridge: MIT Press, 1996.

Garafola, Lynn. "Rivals for the New: The Ballets Suédois and the Ballets Russes." In *Paris Modern: The Swedish Ballet 1920–25*, ed. Nancy Van Norman Baer. San Francisco: Fine Arts Museum of San Francisco, 1995.

Goldberg, RoseLee. *Performance Art: From Futurism to the Present*. New York: Harry N. Abrams, 1988.

Gordon, Rae Beth. *Why the French Love Jerry Lewis*. Stanford: Stanford University Press, 2001.

Graham, Martha. *The Notebooks of Martha Graham*. New York: Harcourt, Brace, Jovanovich, 1973.

Guillaume, Paul. *La sculpture nègre et l'art moderne*. Paris: Toguna, 1999.

Gunning, Tom. "An Aesthetic of Astonishment: Early Film and the (In)Credulous Spectator." In *Film Theory and Criticism*, ed. Leo Braudy and Marshall Cohen. New York: Oxford University Press, 1999.

Haas, Robert, ed. *A Primer for the Gradual Understanding of Gertrude Stein*. Los Angeles: Black Sparrow Press, 1971.

Haraway, Donna J. *Simians, Cyborgs, and Women: The Reinvention of Nature*. New York: Routledge, 1991.

Hayman, Ronald. *Brecht*. London: Weidenfeld and Nicolson, 1983.

Hollier, Denis. "La valeur d'usage de l'impossible." Introduction to *Documents* 1:vii–xxiii. 1929; reprint, Paris: Jean-Michel Place, Collection "Gradhiva," 1992. Published in English as "The Use Value of the Impossible." In *Absent without Leave: French Literature under the Threat of War*, trans. Catherine Porter. Cambridge: Harvard University Press, 1997.

Huyssen, Andreas. *After the Great Divide: Modernism, Mass Culture, Postmodernism*. Bloomington: Indiana University Press, 1986.

Jacobs, Nicolas, and Prudence Ohlsen, eds. *Bertolt Brecht in Britain*. London: TQ Publications, 1977.

Jay, Martin. *Downcast Eyes: The Denigration of Vision in Twentieth-Century French Thought*. Berkeley: University of California Press, 1993.

Kendall, Elizabeth. *Where She Danced: The Birth of American Art-Dance*. Berkeley: University of California Press, 1979.

Kermode, Frank. *Romantic Image*. New York: Chilmark Press, 1957.

Kern, Stephen. *The Culture of Time and Space, 1880–1918*. Cambridge: Harvard University Press, 1983.

Kirby, Lynn. *Parallel Tracks: The Railroad and Silent Cinema*. Durham, N.C.: Duke University Press, 1997.

Koritz, Amy. "Drama and the Rhythm of Work in the 1920s." *Theatre Journal* 53, 4 (2001): 551–67.

———. *Gendering Bodies/Performing Art: Dance and Literature in Early*

*Twentieth-Century British Culture.* Ann Arbor: University of Michigan Press, 1995.

———. "Re/Moving Boundaries: From Dance History to Cultural Studies." In *Moving Words: Re-Writing Dance*, ed. Gay Morris. London and New York: Routledge, 1996.

Kracauer, Siegfried. *The Mass Ornament: Weimar Essays.* Ed. and trans. and with an introduction by Thomas Y. Levin. Cambridge: Harvard University Press, 1995.

Krauss, Rosalind. *The Optical Unconscious.* Cambridge: MIT Press, 1993.

Lacoue-Labarthe, Philippe. *La fiction du politique: Heidegger, l'art et la politique.* Paris: C. Bourgois 1987.

Latour, Bruno. *We Have Never Been Modern.* Cambridge: Harvard University Press, 1993.

Léger, Fernand. "A Critical Essay on the Plastic Quality of Abel Gance's Film *The Wheel.*" In *Functions of Painting*, ed. Edward F. Fry and trans. Alexandra Anderson. New York: Viking Press, 1965. First published in *Comoedia* (1922).

Leiris, Michel. *Afrique noire: La creation plastique.* Paris: Gallimard, 1967.

Levinson, André. *1929, Danse d'aujourd'hui.* Paris: Actes Sud, 1990.

Lista, Giovanni. *Futurism and Photography.* London: Merrell Publishers, 2001.

———. *Loie Fuller: Danseuse de la Belle Epoque.* Paris: Stock, 1994.

———. *La Scène futuriste.* Paris: Editions du CNRS, 1989.

———. *Théâtre futurist italien 2.* Lausanne: L'Age d'Homme, 1976.

Maier, Charles S. "Entre le taylorisme et la technocratie: Ideologies et conceptions de la productivité industrielle dans l'Europe des annés 1920." In *Le Soldat du travail: Guerre, fascisme et taylorisme*, ed. Lion Murard and Patrick Zylberman, 95–136. *Recherches* nos. 32/33. Paris: Recherches, 1978.

Mallarmé, Stéphane. *Oeuvres complètes.* 1945; Paris: Pleiade, 1984.

Marey, Etienne-Jules. *Animal Mechanism: A Treatise on Terrestrial and Aerial Locomotion.* New York: D. Appleton and Co., 1874.

———. *Le Mouvement.* Paris, 1894. Published in English as *Movement.* Trans. Eric Pritchard. New York, 1895.

Marinetti, F. T. E. *Selected Writings.* Ed. R. W. Flint, and trans. R. W. Flint and Arthur A. Coppotelli. New York: Farrar, Strauss, and Giroux, 1972.

Martin, Carol. "High Critics/Low Art." In *Moving Words: Re-Writing Dance*, ed. Gay Morris. London and New York: Routledge, 1996.

Martin, John. "Dance: Those Deadly." *New York Times*, January 18, 1959.

Moutet, Aimée. "Patrons de progres ou patrons de combat? La politique de rationalisation de l'industrie française au lendemain de la Premiere Guerre mondiale." In *Le Soldat du travail: Guerre, fascisme et taylorisme*, ed. Lion Murard and Patrick Zylberman, 449–92. *Recherches* nos. 32/33. Paris: Recherches, 1978.

Mulvey, Laura. "Visual Pleasure and Narrative Cinema." In *Visual Culture: The Reader*, ed. Jessica Evans and Stuart Hall. London: Sage Publications, 1999.

*1909–1929: Les Ballets Russes à l'Opéra*. Paris: Bibliothèque-Musée de l'Opéra, n.d.

O'Driscol, Robert, and Lorna Reynolds, eds. *Yeats and the Theatre*. London and Toronto: Macmillan, 1975.

Phillips, Christopher, ed. *Photography in the Modern Era*. New York: Museum of Modern Art/Aperture, 1989.

Plotinus. *Ennead*. Trans. Stephen MacKenna. 1917–30; reprint, London: Faber and Faber, 1969.

Pound, Ezra. *ABC of Reading*. New York: New Directions, 1934.

———. *Antheil and the Treatise on Harmony*. New York: Da Capo Press, 1968.

———. *Collected Early Poems of Ezra Pound*. New York: New Directions, 1965.

———. *Gaudier-Brzeska*. New York: New Directions, 1970.

———. *Machine Art and Other Writings: The Lost Thought of the Italian Years*. Ed. Maria Luisa Ardizzone. Durham, N.C.: Duke University Press, 1996.

———. *Selected Poems*. London: Faber and Gwyer, 1928.

Pridmore-Brown, Michèle. "1939–40: Of Virginia Woolf, Gramophones, and Fascism." *PMLA* 113, no. 3 (May 1998).

Rabinbach, Anson. *The Human Motor: Energy, Fatigue and the Origins of Modernity*. New York: Basic Books, 1990.

Renoir, Jean. *My Life and My Films*. 1974; reprint, New York: Da Capo, 2000.

Ries, Frank W. D. *The Dance Theatre of Jean Cocteau*. Ann Arbor: UMI Research Press, 1986.

Rose, Jacqueline. "The Cinematic Apparatus—Problems in Current Theory." In *Sexuality in the Field of Vision*. London: Verso, 1986.

Rothschild, Deborah. *Picasso's Parade: From Street to Stage*. New York: Sotheby's Publications, 1991.

Rouse, John. "Brecht and the Contradictory Actor." *Theatre Journal* 36, 1 (1984): 25–41.

Rubin, William. *"Primitivism" in 20th-Century Art: Affinity of the Tribal and the Modern*. New York: Museum of Modern Art, 1984.

Sartre, Jean-Paul. "Jazz in America." In *Reading Jazz*, ed. Robert Gottlieb. New York: Vintage, 1996; first published in *Cahiers America*.

Savarese, Nicola. "1931: Antonin Artaud Sees Balinese Theatre at the Paris Colonial Exposition." *TDR* 45, no. 3 (fall 2001).

Schafer, R. Murray, ed. *Ezra Pound and Music: The Complete Criticism*. New York: New Directions, 1977.

Schaffer, Simon. "Babbage's Dancer and the Impresarios of Mechanism." In *Cultural Babbage: Technology, Time, and Invention*, ed. F. Spufford and J. Uglow. London: Faber and Faber, 1996.

Schnapp, Jeffrey. *Staging Fascism: 18BL and the Theater of Masses for Masses*. Stanford: Stanford University Press, 1996.

Schwartz, Hillel. "Torque: The New Kinaesthetic of the Twentieth Century." In *Incorporations*, ed. Jonathon Crary and Sanford Kwinter. New York: Zone Books, 1992.

Schwartz, Vanessa. *Spectacular Realities: Early Mass Culture in Fin-de-Siècle Paris*. Berkeley: University of California Press, 1998.

Sekine, Masaru, and Christopher Murray, eds. *Yeats and the Noh: A Comparative Study*. Gerrard's Cross, U.K.: Smythe, 1990.

Serres, Michel. *Hermes IV: La distribution*. Paris: Editions de Minuit, 1977.

Sharpley-Whiting, T. Denean. *Black Venus: Sexualized Savages, Primal Fears, and Primitive Narratives in French*. Durham, N.C.: Duke University Press, 1999.

Silver, Kenneth E. *Esprit de Corps: The Art of the Parisian Avant-Garde and the First World War, 1914–1925*. Princeton: Princeton University Press, 1989.

Spufford, Francis, and Jenny Uglow, eds. *Cultural Babbage: Technology, Time, and Invention*. London: Faber and Faber, 1996.

Steegmuller, Francis. *Cocteau: A Biography*. New York: Macmillan, 1970.

Stein, Gertrude. *How Writing Is Written: Volume II of the Previously Uncollected Writings of Gertrude Stein*. Ed. Robert Bartlett Haas. Los Angeles: Black Sparrow Press, 1974.

———. *A Stein Reader*. Ed. and with an introduction by Ulla Dydo. Evanston, Ill.: Northwestern University Press, 1993.

Steiner, Wendy. *Exact Resemblance to Exact Resemblance: The Literary Portraiture of Gertrude Stein*. New Haven: Yale University Press, 1978.

Stengers, Isabelle. *Power and Invention: Situating Science*. Trans. Paul Bains. Minneapolis: University of Minnesota Press, 1997.

Stovall, Tyler. *Paris Noir: African Americans in the City of Light*. New York: Houghton Mifflin, 1996.

Taylor, Frederick Winslow. *Principles of Scientific Management*. New York and London: Harper and Brothers, 1911.

Taylor, Richard. *The Drama of W. B. Yeats: Irish Myth and the Japanese Noh.* New Haven: Yale University Press, 1976.

Terrell, Carroll F. *A Companion to the Cantos of Ezra Pound.* Berkeley and Los Angeles: University of California Press, 1980.

Torgovnick, Mariana. *Gone Primitive: Savage Intellects, Modern Lives.* Chicago: University of Chicago Press, 1990.

Tosi, Virgilio. "Etienne-Jules Marey and the Origins of Cinema." In *Marey, Pionnier de la synthèse du mouvement.* Paris: Editions de la Réunion des Musées Nationaux, 1995.

Toulet, Emanuelle. *Cinématographe, invention du siècle.* Paris: Gallimard, Réunion des Musées Nationaux, 1993.

Valéry, Paul. *Cahiers.* Vol. 2. Paris: CNRS, 1957.

———. *Degas, danse, dessin.* 1934; reprint, Paris: Gallimard 1965.

———. "Théorie poétique et esthetique." In *Oeuvres.* Vol. 1. Paris: Editions de la Pléiade, 1957.

Van Vechten, Carl. Introduction to "Susie Asado." In *Selected Writings of Gertrude Stein.* New York: Vintage, 1972.

Vigarello, Georges. "Georges Vigarello, le corps et la danse." Interview with Thilda Moubayed. *Dansons,* no. 7, n.d.

Villiers de L'Isle-Adam, Auguste de. *L'Eve future.* Paris: Flammarion, 1992.

Weill, Kurt. *The Seven Deadly Sins.* German text by Bertolt Brecht. Trans. W. H. Auden and Chester Kallman. New York: Schott Music Corporation, 1956.

Wilde, Oscar. *Letters.* Ed. Rupert Hart-Davis. London: Rupert Hart-Davis, Ltd., 1962.

Williams, Linda. *Figures of Desire: A Theory and Analysis of Surrealist Film.* Urbana: University of Illinois Press, 1981.

Yang, Sandra Sedman. *The Composer and Dance Collaboration in the Twentieth Century: Darius Milhaud's Ballets, 1918–1958.* Ann Arbor: UMI, 1997.

Yeats, W. B. *Essays and Introductions.* New York: Macmillan, 1961.

Žižek, Slavoj. *The Sublime Object of Ideology.* London: Verso, 1989.

# Index

In this index an "f" after a number indicates a separate reference on the following page, and an "ff" indicates separate references on the following two pages. *Passim* is used for a cluster of references in close but not consecutive sequence.